T0326429

Science and Technology Policy
for Development

Advance Reviews

'Box and Engelhard pulled off a feat in their introduction in bringing the lessons of a very diverse set of papers written from very different standpoints into an unusually coherent intellectual framework. Along the way, individual papers look at experience of research in developing countries from Africa, Asia and Latin America. Several show the difficulties of trying to move from a "Mode 1" to a "Mode 2" structure, even with the support of a new government (South Africa) or of a conscientious donor (Sweden in Nicaragua). The Singapore experience of networking between policymakers and researchers stand out among the papers as particularly successful, but how easy is it to apply when the benefits of very high levels of education in a very compact society are not present?

The core dilemma from the point of view of the development community is how to give weight to the need, on the one hand, to help build the competent research institutions that any country or region needs, and at the same time encourage sufficient demand-led work on behalf of those with no market power to shape research agendas? At global level, the increasing interest in, for example, researching solutions to diseases of the poor, shows a better appreciation of the latter point. But there is surely far more to do, and this collection of papers should help focus minds on what approaches might have a chance of proving themselves sustainable.'

Richard Manning
(writing in a personal capacity)
Chair of the Development Assistance Committee of the OECD

'This book is a must for practitioners in science and technology policy in developing countries, with a rich array of case studies in the continuing search for demand driven policies which can well tap into globalized knowledge production.'

Jozef Ritzen
President of the Universiteit Maastricht and former
Vice President of the World Bank's Development Economics Department

Anthem Studies in Development and Globalization

Science and Technology Policy for Development

Dialogues at the Interface

Edited by

LOUK BOX & RUTGER ENGELHARD

ANTHEM PRESS
LONDON · NEW YORK · DELHI

Anthem Press

An imprint of Wimbledon Publishing Company

www.anthempress.com

This edition first published in UK and USA 2006
by ANTHEM PRESS
75-76 Blackfriars Road, London SE1 8HA, UK
or PO Box 9779, London SW19 7ZG, UK
and
244 Madison Ave. #116, New York, NY 10016, USA

British Library Cataloguing in Publication Data

A catalogue record for this book is available from the British Library.

Library of Congress Cataloging in Publication Data
A catalog record for this book has been requested.

1 3 5 7 9 10 8 6 4 2

ISBN 1 84331 227 1 (Hbk)

Printed in Singapore

THE EDITORS

Louk Box is professor of international cooperation and rector at the International Institute of Social Studies in The Hague. At the time of the workshop that brought the book's authors together, he was Professor of European International Cooperation at the University of Maastricht, and President of the European University Association for the Study of Science, Society and Technology (ESST).

Rutger Engelhard is managing partner of Contactivity bv, Leiden, the Netherlands, and a Programme Associate of the European Centre for Development Policy Management (ECDPM, Maastricht, the Netherlands).

CONTENTS

ACKNOWLEDGEMENTS

This book is based on the rewarding exchanges that took place in a workshop entitled 'Providing Demand', held in Leiden in 2004. The workshop brought together researchers from a variety of backgrounds, social scientists and practitioners from the global South and the North, with very differing views on development policies and especially science and technology for development. They were invited by the editors to their share their views and experiences so that common learning could take place.

There was no agenda – there was no paradigm. This meant that a benevolent confusion prevailed during the sessions. Yet there was one exciting realization: rapid changes are taking place at the researcher–policy maker interface, and new models are emerging. From the researchers' point of view, the work on the two modes of knowledge production was criticized and amended. The policy makers present acknowledged that traditional modes of top-down technology planning need at least to be critically reviewed, making place for notions like the varying composition of epistemic communities, and the influence of public interest groups.

The organizers are grateful to the Netherlands government (Directorate General for Development Cooperation, Department of Research) and the University of Maastricht Faculty of Arts and Culture for their support, both for organizing the workshop and for the publication of this book. Without their encouragement this volume would not have seen the light of day.

Thanks are also due to Ms Willie Pronk for her gentle and effective logistical arrangements, and to Hanne Johnsrud and Irene Norlund for their assistance in building a diverse group of workshop participants into a small intellectual community that produced this book.

Valerie Jones did the impossible as our editor. She transformed our papers into readable English. Language editing is a job that often goes unmentioned. As authors we owe her our thanks for making our work accessible.

All participants were saddened to hear that one of their colleagues, Moussa Kola Cissé, passed away in September 2004. It is therefore appropriate that we dedicate this volume to the memory of a man who incorporated the many worlds that meet in this book: the worlds of civil society advocacy, government policy making and intellectual freedom. He was unable to contribute a chapter to this volume, but we hope that his spirit will live on through the discussions he inspired and which are reflected here.

ACRONYMS

ACP	African, Caribbean and Pacific countries
ACTS	African Centre for Technology Studies
ADB	Asian Development Bank
ALC	African Laser Centre
AMU	Arab Maghreb Union
ANC	African National Congress
APEC	Asia Pacific Economic Cooperation
ASARECA	Association for Strengthening Agricultural Research in Eastern and Central Africa
ATPS	African Technology Policy Studies Network
AU	African Union
AZEF	Arid Zone Ecology Forum (South Africa)
BECA	Biosciences East and Central Africa initiative
CBO	community-based organization
CERN	l'Organisation Européenne pour la Recherche Nucléaire
CGIAR	Consultative Group on International Agricultural Research
CHEPS	Center for Higher Education Policy Studies, University of Twente (the Netherlands)
CIDA	Canadian International Development Agency
CIMMYT	Centro Internacional de Mejoramiento de Maíz y Trigo (International Maize and Wheat Improvement Center)
Cirad	Centre de coopération internationale en recherche agronomique pour le développement
COMESA	Common Market for Eastern and Southern Africa
CREST	Centre for Research on Science and Technology, Stellenbosch (South Africa)
Danida	Danish International Development Agency
DfID	Department for International Development (UK)
DGIS	Directorate General for Development Cooperation (DGIS), Netherlands Ministry of Foreign Affairs
EAC	East African Community

ECA   Economic Commission for Africa
ECOWAS   Economic Community of West African States
ENDA-TM   Environnement et Développement du Tiers Monde
ETC   Action Group on Erosion, Technology and Concentration
EU   European Union
FAO   UN Food and Agriculture Organization
FDI   foreign direct investment
GDN   Global Development Network
GEF   Global Environment Facility
GMO   genetically modified organism
HSRC   Human Sciences Research Council (South Africa)
IAC   InterAcademy Council
IAEA   International Atomic Energy Agency
ICST   international collaboration in science and technology
ICSU   International Council for Science
ICTs   information and communication technologies
IDPAD   Indo-Dutch Programme on Alternatives in Development
IDRC   International Development Research Center
IFPRI   International Food Policy Research Institute
IFS   International Foundation for Science
IIASA   International Institute for Applied Systems Analysis
IIED   International Institute for Environment and Development
INRA   Institut National de la Recherche Agronomique
IMF   International Monetary Fund
IPM   integrated pest management
IRRI   International Rice Research Center
LDCs   least developed countries
MDGs   Millennium Development Goals
MMRPs   Multi-annual, Multidisciplinary Research Programmes
NACI   National Advisory Council on Innovation (South Africa)
NARI   national agricultural research institute
NATO   North Atlantic Treaty Organisation
NCHE   National Commission on Higher Education (South Africa)
NEPAD   New Partnership for Africa's Development
NGO   non-governmental organization
NPT   Non-Proliferation of Nuclear Weapons Treaty

NRF	National Research Foundation (South Africa)
NRI	Natural Resources Institute (UK)
NSTB	National Science and Technology Board, Ministry of Industry and Trade, Singapore
OAS	Organization of American States
OAU	Organization of African Unity
ODI	Overseas Development Institute (UK)
OECD	Organisation for Economic Cooperation and Development
PATTEC	Pan-African Tsetse and Trypanosomiasis Campaign
PPP	public–private partnership
PRSP	Poverty Reduction Strategy Paper
R&D	research and development
RAPID	Research and Policy in Development programme (ODI)
RAWOO	Netherlands Development Assistance Research Council
RECs	regional economic communities
RTD	research and technology for development
S&T	science and technology
SADC	Southern African Development Community
SADCC	Southern African Development Coordinating Conference
SANPAD	South Africa-Netherlands Research Programme on Alternatives in Development
SAREC	Sida Department for Research Cooperation (Sweden)
SDC	Swiss Agency for Development and Cooperation
Sida	Swedish International Development Agency
SIT	sterile insect technique (IAEA)
SMEs	small and medium enterprises
SPAAR	Special Programme for African Agricultural Research
STS	science and technology studies
THRIP	Technology and Human Resources for Industry Programme (South Africa)
TRIPS	WTO Agreement on Trade-related Intellectual Property Rights
UDEAC	Customs and Economic Union of Central Africa
UNA	Universidad Nacional Agraria / National University of Agriculture (Nicaragua)
UNAN-León	Universidad Autónoma de Nicaragua-León (Nicaragua)
UNAM-Managua	Universidad Autónoma de Nicaragua-Managua (Nicaragua)
UNCTAD	United Nations Conference on Trade and Development

UNDP	United Nations Development Programme
UNECA	United Nations Economic Commission for Africa
UNESCO	United Nations Educational, Scientific and Cultural Organization
UNFCCC	United Nations Framework Convention on Climate Change
UNI	Universidad Nacional de Ingeniería (Nicaragua)
UNIDO	United Nations Industrial Development Organization
UNU-INTECH	United Nations University – Institute for New Technologies
USAID	United States Agency for International Development
USDA	United States Department of Agriculture
WOTRO	Stichting Wetenschappelijk Onderzoek in de Tropen (Netherlands Foundation for the Advancement of Tropical Research)
WTO	World Trade Organization

PREFACE

Scholars who wish to use their knowledge to change the world sometimes approach policy makers. At times, practitioners cooperate with policy makers to increase the effectiveness of their work. Policy makers occasionally get together with both scholars and practitioners to improve their policies. And practitioners may involve scholars in to broaden their understanding of practical realities. In each case, cooperation can improve the quality and the effectiveness of their work. Such cooperation does indeed occur, but by no means always.

At the Netherlands Ministry of Foreign Affairs many policy makers are fully cognizant with the realities of development cooperation. There are also those who have continued to learn as researchers, in their own free time or otherwise. Yet within the Ministry the relations between practice, policy and research are not always self-evident. This is immediately apparent when policy makers and researchers meet. Their experiences are often quite different, as are their quality standards. The languages they use may also differ, even though formally they are speaking the same tongue. There are preconceived ideas – about ivory tower scholars or rule-loving bureaucrats, for example – on both sides. Even when scholars seek cooperation, they fear that their independence or scientific excellence may be meddled with, while policy makers fear they may not receive timely replies or have enough time to read the relevant literature.

This book can help to put such anxieties to rest, in a certain sense. The fact that so many wise things can be said about the interfaces between policy, practice and science already points out that things do not move by themselves, even though knowledge is being exchanged in international cooperation, through the internet, among communities of practice, at conferences, in the field, and during seminars, workshops and lectures.

International cooperation does require such exchanges – not just through dialogue between science, policy and practice, but also between the poor and the rich, North and South, and East and West. A more diverse and more complicated interaction is hardly possible. Those who wish to engage in lifelong learning will enjoy such exchanges. Those who do not would better opt for another career.

Caroline Wiedenhof
Head, Research & Communications Division
Netherlands Ministry of Foreign Affairs

FOREWORD

CALESTOUS JUMA[1]

This is a book about optimism. It builds on the convergence of evidence that three factors have contributed to rapid economic transformation in emerging economies: investment in infrastructure, the development of small and medium enterprises, and public support for knowledge-based institutions. Such public support and the accompanying policies can take very different forms. They include public investment in higher education, but equally important, the creation of professional associations and public interest groups that focus on competence building. But they also require leadership and courage to explore new economic avenues.

Major changes have taken place in the so-called developing countries in the last decade. Some countries, including Brazil, India and South Africa, have become regional hubs for technology development. Others have lagged behind, partly because of the failure of their governments to invest in knowledge-based institutions or to adopt supportive policies.

This volume captures the essential elements of these developments and stresses the critical role of public policy in technological innovation. In other words, public policy plays a much greater role in technological innovation than is generally acknowledged. In Singapore's unique set-up, a powerful 'epistemic community' has directed the country along the path to biotechnological prowess in a relatively short period. Sunil Mani painstakingly analyzes the judicious policy mix that underlies Singapore's success.

Mani makes a strong argument that public policies matter, provided they are based in effective knowledge networks. Osita Ogbu shows the operation of such a network at the African level, providing a case study for policy makers elsewhere. The fascinating work by Carolyn Wagner indicates that not only did regional science and technology hubs develop quickly throughout the 1990s, but they also became integrated at the global level. The pessimists who argue that the centre of global innovation marginalizes the technological periphery need to study Wagner's findings. They may also wish to read Bert Uijtewaal's chapter on agri-technological innovation, in which a transnational pharmaceutical company proposes to hand over its intellectual property rights to a national government, provided it takes care of the legal implications.

The chapters in this book demonstrate that new alliances are emerging between the various actors involved in development. UN Secretary-General Kofi Annan has called for new global compacts between industry, civil society and government to spur equitable development. The contributors to this volume indicate that there is hope. A global learning process is occurring, linked through knowledge networks, spurred by epistemic communities that are driving new science and technology policies – as in the case of the International Atomic Energy Agency analyzed by Jacques Gaillard *et al.* Such learning can only take place if there is effective dialogue and interactions can occur at the interface between public and private institutions.

This book is testimony to the importance of such dialogue and interactions. It will help to inspire new thinking and action on the role of technological innovation in development. It is an excellent antidote for pessimism.

Note

1. Calestous Juma is Professor of the Practice of International Development, and Director of the Science Technology and Globalization Project at the Belfer Center for Science and International Affairs, Kennedy School of Government, Harvard University. He is editor of *Going for Growth: Science, Technology and Innovation in Africa.* London: Smith Institute, 2005.

DIALOGUES AT THE INTERFACE:
AN INTRODUCTION

LOUK BOX[1]

It is trite to state that science and technology (S&T) are a necessary condition for economic development. It would be more relevant to ask the question: how are S&T policies linked with development policies? What have we learned from the many lessons, so that effective policy experimentation can take place?

This is one of the key issues in current debates around science and technology for development. As argued in the report of the UN Millennium Project Task Force on Science, Technology and Innovation,[2] there is an urgent need for policy experimentation to stimulate learning in developing countries. The international community set itself the Millennium Development Goal (8, target 18) to 'make available the benefits of new technologies'. If it is serious about achieving this target, the report argues, new avenues of policy learning will need to be opened up and changes in traditional social relationships will need to be made.

This book is about those changing social relationships. The authors focus on the question of what social relations make for successful science and technology policies. In particular, the various chapters illustrate what happens at different social interfaces, such as between policy makers and researchers, and between the users and producers of knowledge. In other words, they are interested in the knowledge networks that are emerging between the many different actors involved in the development of science and technology.

This book is the outcome of a workshop that brought together scholars and policy makers from the global South and the North, from private and public organizations, to review their experiences. A plant geneticist working with a multinational company was able to share views with a civil society leader; an African policy maker argued with an Asian technology researcher. This made for a great diversity of views stemming from neo-classical economics to constructivism. The ensuing papers therefore do not share one theoretical background. What did unite the authors was a common concern for research–policy linkages. In this context, research was taken to mean any systematic effort to increase the stock of knowledge, and 'policy' as any purposive course of action followed by an actor or set of actors.[3] Linkages are seen as the communication and patterns of interaction among the actors involved. Such patterns may consolidate into knowledge networks in which information is evaluated or prioritized. A number of authors stress the communication aspect of such patterns, especially in the form of dialogue between actors or, through them, between institutions like ministries, universities or companies. The subtitle of this book reflects this orientation: *Dialogues at the Interface* refers to communication between these different institutions.

The Netherlands Directorate General for Development Cooperation (DGIS) co-sponsored the workshop because it wished to learn from experiences in science and technology for development. Policy learning[4] has become an increasingly important issue within DGIS and the Netherlands Ministry of Foreign Affairs. After the path-breaking study of its Swedish sister agency, *Does SIDA Learn?*,[5] DGIS tackled this question by proposing new approaches to policy learning, especially in the area of development-oriented research, or science and technology for development. Theo van de Sande gives a review of the relevant Dutch policies in the 1990s. The Netherlands is interesting in this respect because it used to be one of the larger donors,[6] it initiated demand-led development research, and supports a development research advisory council with a balanced representation from the global South and North.

In *Priority setting in research for development: a donor's perspective*, Van de Sande elaborates on what came to be known as the 'Ganuza dilemma'. Essentially this comes down to the question 'who will formulate whose demand', or, who is to choose the priorities if no consensus exists among the scientific, economic and political communities in a developing country. In the past, Northern researchers often did so, but this led to fragmented or policy-irrelevant research. DGIS therefore adopted a three-step approach: 'First, identify the groups in the developing country whose interests should be served by a specific research programme, on the basis of development criteria. Second, identify local researchers who are closely affiliated with that group. Third, accept priorities that are the result of a conditioned demand orientation in a dialogue with the research and policy-making part-ners'. Van de Sande's contribution provides good reading for those who wish to learn from that approach: there are no short cuts to demand-led re-search priority setting. What is needed is the availability of trusted commu-nication channels at the interface between the groups one wishes to serve, and the researchers who are interested in doing so. In many cases, too few stakeholders were involved, the research was spread too thinly, and the re-sulting impact was therefore limited.

Networks of intellectual freedom fighters in Africa

In the first essay, *Knowledge dependence and its discontents: the demand for policy research in Africa in the era of globalization*, Osita Ogbu pin-points the need to use existing knowledge networks, or generate new ones. He argues that new intellectual freedom fighters are emerging. After inde-pendence 'there was a congruency between the intellectual ideology of the time and the development policy focus', which led to strong research–policy linkages. Subsequently, globalization 'fostered knowledge dependence, through un-negotiated policy options that tied development aid to the accep-tance of 'external' knowledge'. Yet the emergence of policy networks like the African Technology Policy Studies Network (ATPS) allow for new linkages between research and policy.

Such platforms provide a market for the contestation of policy ideas and for policy entrepreneurship that is critical in bridging the research–policy gap. Ogbu argues that policy research priority setting involves many players and can be demand or supply driven, depending on coalitions for policy change and institutional arrangements on the ground. In Africa, he con-cludes, all of these conditions have been either weak or absent: 'few re-searchers and policy makers understand the importance of generating tech-nology from technology, the wider implications of technological innovation for Africa's economic renewal, or the need to re-engineer existing institu-tions to supply knowledge to the productive sectors'. Given 'little capacity in this field, it has been difficult to generate any demand for research or for senior scholars to assume the role of S&T policy entrepreneurs or champi-ons'.

Ogbu stresses the need for policy platforms that will allow policy entre-preneurs to articulate supply and demand. New institutions like the New Partnership for Africa's Development (NEPAD)[7] can do this, since they work at the continental level, to bring together expertise in research and policy. Through innovative approaches like ATPS and NEPAD, a demand for science and technology policy research is being created. They can sensitize policy makers to the relevance of such research in the policy process and integrate technology planning in economic and social plans. They can provide for the necessary training and organization of researchers so that they are capable of influencing policy. Last, but not least, such institutions can generate the entrepreneurial skills that are needed to translate ideas into action.

John Mugabe, however, wonders why regional agreements have performed so poorly in Africa. In his contribution, *Regionalism and science and technology development in Africa*, he shows that Africa currently boasts some 20 regional agreements. Although most of them refer to science and technology (S&T), very few have 'collectively harnessed and applied S&T to solve common development problems'. Why is this so?

Mugabe argues that institutional conditions need to be satisfied before technology policies can be made effective. He shows that regionalism 'remained elusive' after independence, partly due to problems in individual countries that could not be solved collectively. He sees globalization as one of the reasons for the renewed interest in regionalism, particularly in relation to developments in S&T, including information and communication technologies (ICTs). Regionalization is fostered by cheaper communication, allowing for greater transboundary movements of people, goods and finance. His analysis of regional (COMESA, SADC) or continental cooperation agreements (AU) reflects this rekindling of interest in S&T. In addition, African governments are increasingly subscribing to international or global agreements with implications for S&T development (like the Convention on Biological Diversity, the UN Framework Convention on Climate Change, and the Montreal Protocol on Substances that Deplete the Ozone Layer). It is these agreements that allow for institutional development and for policy learning in an African context on the basis of greater international cooperation.

Seven factors determine Africa's limited capacity to harness S&T for development:

- the links between scientific and political institutions are weak;
- S&T policies focus on organizational rather than on programmatic issues;
- too little, and in many cases declining, funding for R&D;
- the quality of science and engineering education is declining at all levels;

- the loss of scientific and technical expertise to other regions of the world;
- R&D institutions in many countries are getting weaker; and
- the links between public R&D institutions and private industry are weak.

Through NEPAD, Mugabe argues, innovations in regional cooperation are being made. An African Ministerial Council for Science and Technology now exists. Networks and centres of excellence in science and technological innovation are being established, such as the African Laser Centre, the Biosciences Initiative and the Biosciences East and Central Africa (BECA). In addition, 'an advisory panel on biotechnology' exists, 'a working group to design common African indicators or benchmarks for assessing the status of S&T, and a task force to encourage more African women to engage or participate in science and engineering. Each country has also committed itself to increasing national annual public expenditures on R&D to at least 1% of GDP'. NEPAD has mustered political support for such initiatives and maintains the political will to put S&T on the agenda of individual countries, regional arrangements and continental institutions like the African Union. By strengthening the ties between scientific and political institutions and concentrating on particular areas (like biotechnology), funding for S&T policies could be acquired. Yet the most important element of all is that African scientists are speaking to African policy makers. Through the NEPAD network African priorities can be translated into relevant research programmes and, ultimately, policy measures that involve both public and private actors.

Towards a critical mass of researchers in Latin America

How can developing countries create and maintain a critical mass of researchers able to consistently and systematically contribute to a knowledge base? This is the focus of Léa Velho's contribution, *Building a critical mass of researchers in the least developed countries: new challenges*. Using a case study of capacity building in Nicaragua, she analyzes the material on the basis of a model of knowledge production first proposed by Gibbons *et al.*[8] The latter note that a new mode of knowledge production is emerging that is more in tune with the demands of poor people in poor countries. The existing mode of knowledge production is characterized by hierarchical relations within disciplines, allowing for little transdisciplinary exploration, through strict peer-review standards; the model is rather closed to influence from outsiders. Juxtaposed with this so-called mode 1, Gibbons *et al.* develop a mode 2, which is characterized by horizontal relations involving different disciplines, allowing review and influence from 'outsiders' or users, because knowledge is generated in the context of its application. Velho takes this distinction one step further, and wonders what its implications are for creating a critical mass of indigenous researchers who can respond to local realities.

She notes that mode 1 resulted in 'one type fits all' recommendations to train researchers according to standards set in Northern universities. Policy makers would copy these and training programmes would be developed accordingly. In both the North and in the South, however, the limits of the model have become clear. Mode 1 capacity building will not work in developing countries since 'it takes too long, it requires resources not available in those countries, and it does not attend to criteria of social relevance which are currently required of public universities'. Alternative paths were developed in mode 2 fashion. 'In policy terms, research training is being "decoupled" from its strong association with academic careers and the reproduction of the academic profession'. Velho therefore wonders 'how does this debate on the changing nature of knowledge production and use affect research training in the least developed countries (LDCs), which have not yet been able to develop a critical mass of researchers, nor have the educational structures to train them.'

To answer this question Velho studied a research capacity building programme in Nicaragua. Funded by the Swedish SAREC, it aimed 'to strengthen research capacity and support research which can contribute to the solution of important development problems of Nicaragua'. In other words, problem-oriented research capacities were to be generated. It meant that the mode 2 discourse was adopted, and participatory approaches or demand orientation were stressed. In practice, however, Velho notes that a mode 1 logic was followed, dictated by the very structure of SAREC's interventions. Even though SAREC wished to follow a participatory and demand-oriented approach it was forced to impose a rather top-down mode 1 logic. This limited the effectiveness of its programme as Velho demonstrates.

What is the general relevance of this argument? Velho notes that the Nicaraguan case is not unique. Graduate training in developing countries can be singularly ineffective in creating a critical mass of research capacity. Doctoral training often leads to dissertations or articles, which may be read by no one in the country concerned and are therefore ineffective. The production of such articles or books does not correlate with technological development for Velho's native Brazil, which boasts significant graduate training, yet 'Brazil's potential in the global knowledge economy remains largely unrealized'. New links with private enterprise and other actors are needed to generate significant innovations.

The inefficiency of the prevalent model needs to be corrected. Graduate students often work for years individually, whereas we know that effective links are made through teamwork. The selection of research topics is, moreover, based on mode 1 criteria in the sense of the contribution to a disciplinary stock of knowledge, which may preclude local relevance. Nicaraguan students would study in Sweden, requiring time for adaptation, and weakening their links in the national research context. Most importantly, the SAREC model makes for a fundamental asymmetry in relations, due to the funding arrangement and a lack of awareness of Nicaragua's contributions to the programme.

Velho therefore concludes 'that it is very unlikely that LDCs will be able to build research capacity simply by adopting the research training schemes developed in the advanced countries and offered by development cooperation agencies. Such schemes are based on a mode 1 knowledge production and utilization'. She calls for a mode 2 approach, which 'would mean that capacity building would focus not only on graduate education, but also on creating opportunities for interactions among researchers and between them and other social actors, bringing together different types of knowledge that are necessary to address a particular problem'. New *'dialogues at the interface'* are required for significant capacity development.

An epistemic community at work in Asia

Sunil Mani takes us to Singapore, where everything seems to work. In the unique environment of this technological city-state an S&T innovation system has been developed that is the envy of many countries. Singapore first developed a critical mass of research scientists and engineers, and then put in place a set of research grants to encourage both local and foreign enterprises to invest in R&D. In other words, it did what Velho calls for in her contribution to this book. How did this work – did Singapore follow a mode 2 approach? What measures were taken or policies enacted, and how did they come about?

In *Epistemic communities and informed policy making for promoting innovations,* Mani argues that a largely informal yet highly effective local network of scholars and policy makers provided guidance – an epistemic community. According to Haas, this is 'a network of professionals with recognized expertise and competence in a particular domain and an authoritative claim to policy-relevant knowledge within the same domain or issue area'.[9] In other countries without such communities to aid government policy making, most policy instruments fail to achieve the desired results. In the absence of informal professional networks, innovation policy making tends to be *ad hoc* and subject to political compulsion. The genius of the Singapore model appears to lie in a specific arrangement at the interface: a remarkably effective linkage among top politicians and scientists.

Singapore was chosen as a case study because of the dramatic improvements it has made in its innovation system, without the bureaucracy of a Ministry of Science and Technology. Moreover, it has successfully made the transition from electronics manufacturing to research in the life sciences and biotechnology. How?

Mani begins by asking how expertise can be mustered to guide effective S&T policy making. Countries with much expertise can use the elaborate process of green papers and white papers to involve different actors and stakeholders. National advisory councils may be utilized as rather formal or structured assemblies of certain actors. 'Epistemic communities need to be distinguished from bureaucratic bodies. The latter operate largely to preserve their missions and budgets, whereas epistemic communities apply their knowledge to a policy undertaking, subject to their normative objectives. Thus, members of an epistemic community are not policy entrepreneurs'. However, 'the existence of epistemic communities within otherwise bureaucratic bodies has allowed some developing countries to graduate within a short time from being mere assemblers to designers, manufacturers and exporters of high-technology products'. This arrangement allows for flexible linkages on the one hand, yet it also permits rapid decision making and implementation of policies, especially if the political leadership is involved.

Singapore started its biotechnology venture in the 1980s with the creation of a molecular biology research centre, in much the same way NEPAD is doing in Africa, as described by Mugabe. It dramatically increased funding for the sector, especially for capacity development in the form of training programmes for life-sciences researchers. At the same time it attracted foreign investment and companies, where the graduates could be employed. Gradually an indigenous research capacity developed and local patents could be registered. Mani notes that 'with high-tech products now accounting for more than 50 per cent of manufactured exports, Singapore has the rare distinction of being a major competitor on world markets'.

In the case of Singapore, a few trends stand out:

- the high levels of public expenditures in education, with sustained growth;
- the absolute priority given to the natural sciences and engineering;
- partnerships with top universities abroad;
- the creation of public research centres, linked to industrial (private) needs; and
- a wide variety of incentive schemes to attract capital.

It is this carefully managed mix of institutional development (through government) and informal priority setting (through the epistemic community) that appears to underlie Singapore's success. It was the very creation of a critical mass of researchers, at the outset, which allowed the effective distribution of incentives in a later phase. Mani therefore concludes that policy sequencing is one key to success. From another perspective it appears that such sequencing allowed policy learning in the epistemic community, which could so maintain its influence on policy making. Such learning results in 'informed policy making [which, in turn,] leads to better and more relevant policies demanded by the users – firms and research establishments'.

Singapore may well be exceptional in its capacity for policy learning. Yet other countries could learn from the peculiar mix of carefully orchestrated formal instruments and informal priority setting at the interface between the worlds of science and policy. One question that remains is the extent to which the Singapore model can be characterized as a mode 2 approach to capacity building in Velho's analysis. Surely, a user orientation dominates and knowledge production in the context of application; and surely outsiders (like politicians) are involved in the process of priority setting (as in the epistemic community). Yet just as surely, the approach does not rhyme with a democratic or participatory logic allowing the balancing of *different* research agendas, or necessarily with transdisciplinary dialogue.

Linking research agendas in South Africa

How do *different* research agendas reflect and represent the research interests of constituencies? That is the question that Johann Mouton raises in his chapter, *Science for transformation: research agendas and priorities in South Africa*. If Mani argued in favour of one coherent agenda, Mouton faces the co-existence of different research agendas, which were (or could be) in conflict with each other. The case of South Africa is special in that under apartheid, it reflected a situation analogous to that in Singapore, but driven by an all-white epistemic community. The African National Congress (ANC) developed a counter-agenda, through probably an equally coherent epistemic community, which, however was more inclined to follow a mode 2 approach. What happened after the ANC took over to promote science for social transformation?

The ANC found the apartheid research agenda to be fragmented, uncoordinated and not serving the interests of all South Africans. It therefore proposed a drastic reversal of priorities that was in line with national socio-economic imperatives, thus serving the entire nation. The agenda could follow some of the lessons learned by the NGOs that had confronted the apartheid regime, which were based on university campuses. In this way, it linked up with local community priorities, in line with mode 2 prescriptions. The ANC government then followed the course outlined by Mani – it issued a green paper, and then a white paper that was based on the notion of a national system of innovation. The final aim was to serve the needs of the entire nation rather than any particular interests.

A special place was given to the interests of marginal groups like the rural poor, or women. These do not have a voice in most agenda-setting forums, but through the mentioned NGOs they were, however, heard. In the past such NGOs had not received government funding, but had obtained support from donor agencies such as SAREC, or indeed, DGIS. Given their activist stance, they were trusted by the respective constituencies. In Van de Sande's terms, the Ganuza dilemma had been resolved ... for the time being. Mouton notes that with the arrival of formal research funding schemes under the ANC government, these NGOs were starved of support. Donor support had to be channelled through the formal research institutions and so could no longer reach the activist NGOs, and, it could be added, a mode 2 type of knowledge production reverted to mode 1.

How then, are the interests of different constituencies represented in the current setup in South Africa? Mouton reports survey data of 2002 in which intended beneficiaries are cross-tabulated with the type of research organization. He concludes that most research was 'carried out for specific contracting agencies, industry, government and specific interest groups'. The poor had disappeared.

Mouton goes one step further and distinguishes between the *directionality* of the research agenda ('who are the main actors driving the process?') versus the *degree of interventionism* in agenda setting (the 'steering versus shaping of research priorities'). He argues that government and business are the main actors. There is little space for 'alternative' agenda setting, as happened through the South Africa–Netherlands Partnership for Alternatives in Development Programme (SANPAD)[10] in the case of HIV/AIDS research. This programme continued to function outside the government, and could thus maintain its poverty orientation. The poor reappeared.

On the whole, however, the production of scientific knowledge in South Africa is strongly tied to 'white, male and ageing scientists' who produce 90 per cent of all articles. In this sense the ANC government has not succeeded in its ambition to transform South African research. Even though the government formally indicated that it would go for mode 2 type knowledge production, the reality has turned out to be 'somewhat different', according to Mouton.

In fact, a 'homogenization of demand' has occurred instead of a heterogenization or confrontation of different research agendas. With 'steering from the top', there has been an 'increasing blurring of institutional boundaries'. Paradoxically, the result achieved has been the opposite of what was intended; whereas the government intended to follow a mode 2 type of knowledge production leading to diversity, a mode 1 dominated process emerged that left the poor and the marginalized aside. The question then becomes: 'how can a developing country such as South Africa create/generate demand for research that is *heterogeneous* in terms of the range of interests it serves, *representative* of who is involved in the research, and *critical* in terms of the nature of the research to be conducted?'

Mouton analyzes a case in which research demand is articulated through a diversity of actors. He shows that the 'articulation of research demand occurs in self-organizing systems which in turn are embedded in other related networks'. This brings us back to the main focus of this book; if 'dialogues at the interface' of different institutions are promoted, diversity can be realized in S&T policy for development. The question then becomes: are there tools for promoting such dialogue which are not location specific?

A toolbox for policy dialogue

How do we make a trustworthy description of the research, technology and development situation in a country that allows for dialogues at the interface? Wiebe Bijker outlines the main ingredients of a methodology. He warns that no methodology can serve as a recipe, yet it may contribute to the creation of a new cooperation strategy between different actors or stakeholders.[11]

Bijker follows a constructivist approach. 'Scientific knowledge is constructed in laboratories, on the land of small farmers, in the offices of funding agencies, at international conferences, and in editorial offices. It is not a matter of asking clever questions of nature, who then shouts back a clear 'yes' or 'no'. He argues that such an approach allows for '*the very possibility* of a policy dialogue on the contents of an S&T policy agenda', since 'technology is not constructed merely by engineers, but also by marketing departments, managers, anti-technology action groups and users'.

The author proposes 'an extended conception of policy dialogue that, in addition, recognizes the socially constructed character of science and technology and therefore stresses the need to encompass a variety of other aspects as part of a successful research and technology for development policy'. In this way he solves the Ganuza dilemma referred to above, and allows for an approach as argued by Mouton. More actors can become involved, and more institutions like firms, universities, NGOs or indeed government departments.

He distinguishes various levels of dialogue that can usefully be applied to the cases examined in this book. *Intra-national* dialogues involve national organizations and local stakeholders (as in the contributions by de Lattre-Gasquet, Mouton, Uijtewaal, Velho). *Intra-regional* dialogues involve actors from several countries (as in the studies by Mugabe and Ogbu). *International* dialogues involve actors from different regions or at the global level (as in the chapters by Dufour, Gaillard *et al.* and, to a certain extent, Wagner).

Bijker stresses that 'to be a true *dialogue*, the policy dialogue must be interpreted as an ongoing, *open learning process*'. He provides specific indicators for the process to be open and learning-oriented. Policy dialogue and policy learning are thus operationalized and can be tested in practice – they are no longer blurred concepts, but have 'come of age'. Bijker shows how S&T policy dialogues need to be embedded in broader development policies, especially those dealing with the effects of globalization. He specifies the types of actors and issues to be raised, and the landscape in which they function.

Gradually, Bijker develops his toolbox which includes a 'checklist for designing and evaluating diagnostic studies, a workshop for training researchers, and advice to the relevant government agency to prepare the policy-making infrastructure'. The workshop is conceived as a 'learning laboratory' for all; the diagnostic study allows for dialogue along institutional interfaces. The question that still needs to be answered, however, is what has been the practical experience with these types of policy dialogue.

Bridging the research–policy divide

How can policy makers best use research for evidence-based policy? How can researchers promote their findings in order to influence policy? How can interactions between researchers and policy makers be improved? Julius Court and John Young address these questions in *From development research to pro-poor policy: evidence and the change process*, on the basis of the ODI's Research and Policy in Development (RAPID) programme. The programme examined a large number of case studies, in an attempt to pinpoint what happens at the researcher–policy maker interface.

Conceptually, the programme distinguishes between three spheres or clusters of issues embedded in an environment of external influences:

- context issues, pertaining to politics and institutions
- evidence issues, highlighting approaches and credibility
- links issues, concerning influence and legitimacy.

The issues derived from 50 case studies and a literature review of relevant material regarding civil society influence on policy making. The programme commissioned detailed case studies and evaluations and invited experts from very different backgrounds to review the findings. Through a process of 'triangulation' and peer review, they then assessed the impacts of research on policy.

According to Court and Young the main factors that affect research uptake into policy are as follows:

1. *political and institutional context,* including variables such as 'power relations, political contestation, institutional pressures and vested interests';
2. *policy maker demand*, including the need for 'consensus on the nature of the solution';
3. *the influence of street-level bureaucrats* on implementation;
4. *topical relevance* for policy issues of the day;
5. *the perceived credibility* of key researchers and their approaches;
6. *operational usefulness* or problem-solving capacity;
7. *presentation or packaging* of results in appropriate language;
8. *interactivity* between researchers and policy makers and the emergence of formal or informal networks;
9. *epistemic communities* that allowing for the exchange of perspectives; and

10. *the legitimacy of researchers' links* to relevant local communities.

Again, these factors can be tied to the studies presented in this book. Mugabe analyzes the political and institutional context and the relative effectiveness of regional groupings in Africa. Policy maker demand comes back in Ogbu's provocative analysis; the influence of street-level bureaucrats appears in Velho's analysis of SAREC, and in Van de Sande's discussion of the Dutch agency DGIS. Mugabe clearly illustrates topical relevance (biotechnology, ICTs), which also figure prominently in the studies by de Lattre-Gasquet and Mani. Researcher credibility is an issue addressed by Uijtewaal, and the study by Gaillard *et al.* of the IAEA exemplifies operational usefulness. Mani's analysis clearly shows interactivity in the close formal and informal ties in Singapore's epistemic community. Bijker and Mouton insist on the relevance of researcher–community linkages.

Court and Young raise a number of unanswered questions concerning, for example, the effects of democratic governance, the role of civil society institutions and access to international research and policy networks. We now know that networks matter, but how do they work, and why?

Emerging global knowledge networks

The networks created by international collaborations in science and technology (ICST) offer opportunities for developing countries to acquire knowledge for local development. Such collaboration represents a growing share of scientific activities, Caroline Wagner argues in her contribution *International collaboration in science and technology: promises and pitfalls*. What are the dynamics of such networks and how can they be put to use by policy makers and researchers?

Wagner bases her analysis on a remarkable set of data on the authorship, including co-authorship, of scientific publications in 1990 and 2000. She wished to know if scientists from developing countries participated in co-authoring, thus indicating a virtual network between authors in the global South and North. She found that a significant change had occurred over the decade – 'at the regional level, researchers from more countries joined in collaborative research, as evidenced by co-authorships in internationally recognized peer-reviewed journals'. She confirms the findings of Mugabe and Ogbu that in this period the African network became much better integrated and centred on a few hubs, or centres of excellence. For both Africa and elsewhere she indicates that countries that were peripheral in 1990 became 'more closely tied to the regional level in 2000'. Regional hubs, in other words, take their place in a global system that cannot be simply characterized by a flat centre–periphery model under US–UK dominance.

Nevertheless, there is still a clear hierarchy in the networks, with the most scientifically advanced countries as core members. The relevance of the regionalization that Wagner proves from her data is that new strategies at local, national, regional and global levels can be considered. At the local level, research institutions link with local communities, as Mouton has shown. The national level is the level at which funding and fiscal or other incentives are organized, as shown so clearly by Mani in the case of Singapore. The regional level allows knowledge sharing among states with common problems, like the Southern African region analyzed by Mugabe. The global level is for megascience projects in fields such as nuclear physics. Wagner brings these and other considerations together in a framework for evaluating special considerations for stakeholders in ICST decision making at the different levels.

Through her painstaking analysis of co-authorship networks, Wagner opens a window onto the global organization of science and technology. Through a judicious capacity development at the local or national level, contributions to and from the regional or global level are realized.

Going global: cooperation in knowledge-based development

Most of the essays in this volume deal with the local, national or regional levels of policy making. But what happens at the global level of S&T demand-led policy and practice? In their chapter on *Priority setting in technical cooperation: expanding the demand for knowledge-based development*, Jacques Gaillard, Royal Karstens and Ana María Cetto describe how the Technical Cooperation Programme of the International Atomic Energy Agency (IAEA) evolved from a technology-driven to a demand-based approach. They deal with the question: what conceptual and organizational changes were made to foster demand-led research at the national level?

IAEA's roots go back to the 1950s, when US President Eisenhower stressed the need to control the spread of nuclear materials while ensuring their benefits for all of mankind. From the start, technical assistance was a major activity, leading to the creation of a technical cooperation programme in the 1960s. In 1997 a new approach saw the light and the orientation to nuclear technology changed into one stressing national capacity development and institutional self-reliance. The IAEA changed from a technology transfer approach to one aiming at sustainability and local ownership through country programme frameworks based on thematic planning. This change, by the way, was not unique to the IAEA, but also happened at other international organizations like UNDP and the World Bank.

The change meant that IAEA gradually became involved in a wide variety of activities, prioritized by its member states, like human health, agricultural productivity, water resources management and the environment. As noted by Mugabe, Ogbu and Wagner, regional cooperation agreements became ever more important, through regional resource units that provide both research and training facilities, and centres of excellence. Current technical cooperation priorities therefore include human health (24%), nuclear safety (24%) and agriculture (12%).

Gaillard *et al.* argue in favour of continuing the trend towards regional and national institutional development through capacity building or knowledge transfer. In answer to the questions 'how can development strategies become more knowledge based?' and 'how can research strategies be more demand based?' the authors propose that greater use be made of knowledge brokers working at the intersection of different institutions. Such individuals could periodically assess programme effectiveness in terms of local development constraints. In line with other authors in this volume, they argue that 'science and development partnerships work best in proximity to the problem where collective efforts can harness the labours of those most seriously affected with those capable of effecting the necessary scientific and technological advancements'.

Harnessing foresight: exploring the future

What S&T development options are available, and how can we best harness their potential? Marie de Lattre-Gasquet, in her contribution, *The use of foresight in setting agricultural research priorities*, shows how foresight activities can be useful tools in public decision-making processes. Research organizations can use foresight activities to assist in the definition of research priorities, which in turn can help in meeting future challenges.

Foresight is 'the process involved in systematically attempting to look into the longer-term future of science, technology, the economy, the environment and society with the aim of identifying the areas of strategic research and the emerging generic technologies likely to yield the greatest economic and social benefits'. It allows preparation for different futures, by identifying current trends, and by proposing different courses of action. It allows 'collective learning […] with a view to long-term strategic decision making'.

Through problem definition, system parameter setting, scenario development and strategic choice formulation, possible futures are explored. This
process allows for communication among stakeholders or actors and a focus
on the longer term. Coordination of actor strategies thus becomes possible
and a shared world vision or consensus may come about, leading to commitment among key actors. In essence, this is quite close to the notion of the
epistemic community in the Singapore case described by Mani.

De Lattre-Gasquet concludes that 'S&T foresight looks at science in progress ('*la science qui se fait*') and fulfils a number of functions. It provides
a means for making choices in relation to science and technology and identifying priorities. It also offers a mechanism for integrating research opportunities with economic and social needs, and thereby linking science and
technology more closely with innovation, wealth creation and enhanced
quality of life. It can help to stimulate communication and partnerships
among researchers, research users and research funders'.

In order to be effective in evaluation and planning, such foresight activities need to be embedded in research organizations. The author presents
three case studies to show how this can be done, at the level of a commodity
(cocoa), a country (the Netherlands) and the world (futures for food, agriculture and the environment). In each case, she shows how interactions between researchers and stakeholders took place, allowing for dialogue and, in
the end, for consensus and commitment. Foresight can therefore be considered as another toolkit for dialogue, alongside the one proposed by Bijker.

Public–private partnerships

Much reference is made to public–private partnerships in S&T, but precious
little empirical material is available on specific examples in developing
countries. The UN Millennium Project report[12] attaches great importance to
the role of the private sector, yet the question can be asked: why do we have
so few good case studies? In preparing for this workshop, the same problem
arose. Few private firms were willing or able to contribute to our common
understanding of what they do, what problems they face, and what strategies
they have chosen. In terms of de Lattre-Gasquet's analysis, it proved to be
hard to involve private sector actors in our foresight activity.

It was therefore very fortunate that Bert Uijtewaal did take part. The title
of his contribution, *Development of sustainable control of diamondback
moth in cabbage and cauliflower by public–private partnership*, may sound
technical, but the reality of the case is remarkably practical. How can a

partnership be made between a public and a private actor in solving an insect problem through genetically modified (GM) crops? The technical problem, he points out, is relatively simple in comparison with the legal and social issues that emerge when advanced S&T innovations such as genetic modification are involved.

Crop losses due to the diamondback moth cost the global agricultural sector US$ 1 billion each year. Natural enemies are 'rarely sufficiently effective, and so must be supplemented with other control tactics', and plant breeders have not succeeded in developing resistant varieties. Uijtewaal's company therefore developed sustainable resistance through the introduction of two genes from a soil bacterium *Bacillus thuringiensis* (Bt) with which there is wide experience in other crops like cotton and corn. Although no significant environmental or health problems have emerged, this genetic modification has been the subject of NGO lobbying and advocacy worldwide.

Aside from the possible ecological consequences (genetic pollution), the use of GM plant material has important legal consequences. The 'project concept' therefore started from the premise that the private partner would invest in 'making the product', and the public partner in 'releasing the product'. The latter included field testing, human and environmental safety assessment and socio-economic impact assessment.

The company would transfer its intellectual property (IP) rights free of charge to a public organization, which in turn would make it available to local farmers and breeders. This meant that the public partner would become the IP holder, with the associated rights and duties, but the company reserved the right to 'develop its own hybrids that may be released in parallel with the public varieties'.

Uijtewaal concludes that the main challenges are not technical but organizational. Who will own the intellectual property of the plant material and the regulatory dossier that goes with it? Who will pay for product release? Who will manage the partnership and guard the public interest to 'ensure the safe and sustainable use of the material' or its reproduction? These are only some of the questions that the partnership faces and show how delicate public–private cooperation arrangements can become.

This case also shows the diverse range of interests that need to be brought together, at local, national and even global scales. Public interest groups in the North (such as Greenpeace) have serious reservations about GM; governments in the South may not know how to find a balance between national interests and global concerns; and Northern donor agencies might find themselves right in the middle (as Dufour argues). Individual researchers in multinational companies (like Uijtewaal) may see the public and private benefits of a new technology, yet the boards of these companies will also be concerned about their public image. The IAEA case shows that only through timely investments in both regional and national institutional capacity development can the problems for complex technologies like biotechnology be reduced.

'Joining up' knowledge for development

Paul Dufour provides a fitting 'coda' or final chord for this volume. In his essay *The emerging contextual space for priority setting in development research,* Dufour reflects on his long experience in the field as a staff member of the Canadian International Development Research Centre (IDRC). He argues in favour of policy learning and suggests that more 'joined up decision making' is required. This will require, among other things, taking a hard look at science advisory bodies, science communication and public engagement. His chapter brings together many of the issues raised elsewhere in this volume, and broadly outlines the future we face in the realm of S&T for development.

Based on an analysis of case studies undertaken by IDRC in India, the Maldives, South Africa and Vietnam, Dufour concludes that in these countries 'good governance, strong economic development and well developed social and environmental practices are all dependent to some extent on a sound knowledge strategy'. Such strategies need 'to be embedded in decision structures that are both independent of states, but also linked to some form of accountability'. They need to be independent to allow for legitimacy, as argued by Mouton; they need linkages to provide policy coherence, as argued by Mani. Dufour points out that the mushrooming of new actors (like advocacy groups) is not necessarily for the better of society. Yet governments, NGOs and researchers are all actors in a new form of knowledge production, leading to complex and multiple knowledge networks.

The question then becomes: how do the different actors take their responsibility for 'socially inclusive innovation' at the global level, and what role do knowledge networks play? A global science advisory board does not exist, even though certain institutions provide clues about its possible emergence. Dufour mentions the InterAcademy Council, which brings together a worldwide group of national academies. At the outset of this introduction, reference was made to the UN Millennium Project Task Force on Science, Technology and Innovation. These developments indicate that knowledge networks are increasingly becoming integrated and provide a research–policy nexus (as argued by Court and Young).

Yet, Dufour argues, we first need to face a number of challenges. 'Knowledge networks of the future, especially those affecting the South, will be challenged by at least three key facts – that knowledge does not substitute for ethics, that new technologies require social and institutional innovation, and that geopolitical developments may hamper rather than strengthen international knowledge networks'.

This requires a 'renaissance of development research' at the level of international organizations and the donor agencies that support them.

Wrapping up

Networks involving producers, brokers and users of knowledge play an increasingly important role in bridging gaps to promote 'socially inclusive innovation'. The authors in this volume concentrated on the place where these actors meet, at the research–policy nexus.

The volume shows that we may move beyond the traditional dichotomies, like the one between mode 1 and mode 2 knowledge production. Maybe it is time to argue, as some have done,[13] in favour of a mode 3 of knowledge production that is highly diverse in nature, yet carries elements of disciplinary knowledge production, which is user context sensitive and involves knowledge networks composed of different actors. Possibly, mode 1 is increasingly becoming a caricature given the changes in the world of science and technology, as Dufour argues. And, just as possible, the mode 2 type of knowledge production was an ideal that even in the case of South Africa was hard to achieve, according to Mouton.

What remains is the need for dialogue among the relevant actors. This is easier said than done, as Uijtewaal describes, even if the good will is there among most actors. Yet, as the contributors to this volume conclude, the need for dialogue at globally emerging interfaces is clearly evident.

Notes

1. Louk Box (box@iss.nl) is Professor of International Cooperation and Rector at the International Institute of Social Studies, The Hague, the Netherlands.
2. UN Millennium Project (2005: 1).
3. See the chapter by Court and Young.
4. Kan (2005:1).
5. Swedish Court of Auditors (1988).
6. Box and Boer (1994).

7. See the chapter by Mugabe.
8. Gibbons *et al.* (1994).
9. Haas (1992: 3).
10. See the chapter by Van de Sande.
11. See Wieberdink (2004).
12. UN Millennium Project (2005).
13. Box (2001).

References

Box, L. (2001) *To and Fro: International Cooperation in Research and Research on International Cooperation*, Inaugural Lecture, University of Maastricht. Maastricht University Press.

Box, L. and Boer, L. (1994) The tenuous interface: Policymakers, researchers and user-publics: The case of the Netherlands development cooperation. *Knowledge and Policy*, 6(3/4): 158–175.

Gibbons, M., Limoges, C., Nowotny, H., Schwartzman, S., Scott, P. and Trow, M. (Eds.) (1994) *The New Production of Knowledge: The Dynamics of Science and Research in Contemporary Societies*. London: Sage.

Haas, P.M. (1992) Introduction: epistemic communities and international policy coordination, *International Organization*, 46: 1–35.

Kan, H. (2005) *Opening the Black Box: Developing a Framework to Analyse Processes of Cross-national Learning*. Young Researchers Workshop of ESPAnet, Bath, University of Bath. www.bath.ac.uk/eri/events/EVENT05-ESPANET/ESPAnet%20school/Bath% 20YRW%20Kan.pdf

Swedish Court of Auditors (1988) *Lär sig SIDA? En granskning av SIDAs förmåga att lära sig av erfarenheterna (Does SIDA Learn? An Analysis of SIDA's Ability to Learn from Experience)*. Stockholm: RRV.

UN Millennium Project (2005) *Innovation: Applying Knowledge in Development*. Final report of the Task Force on Science, Technology and Innovation, lead authors Call estous Juma and Lee Yee-Cheong. New York: Earthscan. www.unmillenniumproject.org/reports/tf_science.htm

Wieberdink, A. (2004) *Troubled Waters: The Ambivalence of South–North Partnerships in Research for Development* – A Case Study. Utrecht: International Books.

VISIONS FROM THE SOUTH

KNOWLEDGE DEPENDENCE AND ITS DISCONTENTS: THE DEMAND FOR POLICY RESEARCH IN AFRICA IN THE ERA OF GLOBALIZATION

OSITA OGBU[1]

In the early days of independence there was a congruency between the intellectual ideology of the time and the development policy focus of many African states, with strong demand for domestic policy research. In contrast, the era of structural adjustment and current globalization fostered knowledge dependence, through unnegotiated policy options that tied development aid to the acceptance of 'external' knowledge. Today, there are new opportunities due to new leadership in the continent and the various new economic development plans that could provide the basis for a stronger domestic research–policy interface. The development of the continent will require a political leadership that appreciates the intellectual capacity of Africans, a core of confident, liberated intellectual freedom fighters who are ready to use their knowledge to liberate the continent from poverty, and the emergence of new institutions such as the African Technology Policy Studies Network (ATPS) that would provide the platform.

1. Introduction

There is a great deal of interest in understanding policy-making processes in Africa, and the role of research in informing policy decisions and actions. Ideally, equal emphasis should be placed on both. It is only when we understand the political economy of decision making that can construct the form and content of policy advice based on new knowledge, and direct such advice to appropriate decision centres.

In spite of the urgency of the need to understand the role of research in informing policy decisions and actions, very little intellectual capital has been spent on such inquiries. Yet, donor agencies and some African governments continue to spend a great deal of resources on policy research. The research-policy nexus is not linear, even in advanced countries, and even when governments of those countries are funding the research. Carol Weiss noted the haphazard connection between social science research and policy making in the United States, and the misguided belief by many social scientists involved in policy research that the results of their work would be used by the government. Weiss observed that they 'tend to believe that if officials ignore relevant research, they are either ignorant, uncaring, or overtly "political" in the pejorative sense of the word'.[2] This means that in assessing the research-policy interface, a fair amount of value must be assigned to serendipity and knowledge externalities that may not be readily captured and quantified.

In Africa the situation is even more complicated. The policy terrain is murkier, due largely to domestic pressures and the heavy external influence from decision centres located outside the official bureaucracies. Borrowing from work on the politics of trade policy making in Africa, it has been noted that '... the underlying forces behind policy epochs and episodes vary from country to country and from regime to regime weaved around ethnic, military or other ruling and bureaucratic interests in a manner that suggests a forced consensus ... the loss of policy autonomy in most countries and the absence of the organized private sector as key players in the policy process compound the picture'.[3]

In addition, a tradition of contesting ideas has not been firmly established in Africa, due to the lack of a home-grown vision by the leadership, inadequate knowledge-generating infrastructures and weak intellectual censorship, especially in the 1980s and 1990s. Such contests would have forced the competing constituencies to rely on research to support and advance their positions on how to attain a given vision. In the United States in the 1930s, such contests were sometimes played out in the arena of science and technology (S&T) policy making. Between 1933 and 1935, for instance, Karl Compton, then President of MIT, proposed that greater funding be directed to university-based scientific research in order to generate innovation that firms could use to create new industries that would in turn create jobs. Unemployment was a major issue at that time, and Compton lobbied President Roosevelt and the public with a campaign, 'science makes jobs', stating that 'federal funding could make jobs by making science'. His views were hotly contested by those who held that technological innovation caused unemployment by raising productivity without providing other avenues for taking care of the resulting redundancies. They therefore urged the President not to heed the Compton campaign but rather to regulate the pace of technological change in order not to exacerbate the unemployment problem.[4]

Three important points emerge from this example with respect to the research-policy interface. First, it is useful to have a market for contestation of policy ideas. Second, policy entrepreneurship is critical in bridging the research–policy gap. Third, policy research priority setting involves many players and can be demand or supply driven, depending on the coalition for policy change and the institutional arrangements on the ground. In Africa, all of these conditions have, for the most part, been either weak or absent.

2. The legacy of dependence

Without labouring the point, colonialism was anti-indigenous knowledge and technology. It created a legacy of knowledge and technology dependency that is still very much in evidence. The cultural emasculation of the colonial era denied Africa both the capacity to generate, disseminate and adapt knowledge in an orderly and progressive manner, and the establishment of a knowledge order that would have evolved systematically as societal requirements became more complex.

Africa is perpetually going through forced technological transitions, first by colonialism, second, by post-colonial ties, and most recently by globalization. Unfortunately, this last transition is embedded in consumerism without a corresponding interest in building indigenous production technology capacities and capabilities. As Ali Mazrui put it, 'the West's consumption patterns have arrived, but not necessarily the West's technique of production'.[5] In the same vein, Kabiru Kinyanjui noted that 'the cultural dynamism of any society enables its members to discard old ideas and techniques and to be receptive and accommodating to new knowledge, skills, technologies and patterns of life … A central obstacle to this process in Africa has been the separation of African culture from the culture that guided major economic, technological and political changes in society'.[6] Apart from the material reality of this dependence, both the psychological dimension and the phenomenon of self-doubt it engendered have been profound, and have enormous implications for research agenda setting, research–policy links and technological renaissance.

3. The convergence of national vision and intellectual ideology

On coming to power after independence, African leaders and their economic advisers had a common focus and strategy. The focus was industrialization and the strategy was import substitution. The spirit of *Uhuru* (freedom), *Ujamaa* (self-help), and the indigenization polices of the many newly independent countries were used to rally society, policy advisers and the research community to a common cause. While this is not the place to debate the efficacy of these policies and programmes, what is important is that there was a convergence of national vision and intellectual ideology. There was agreement on the vision, and on the path to take to attain it. It was therefore easy to agree on a set of research priorities and on the research infrastructure that would feed into the development policy process. In the pursuit of this agreed strategy, it was easy to mobilize intellectual capital both from Africa itself and from other countries pursuing similar strategies.

The point here is that the ownership of a development strategy and the goals of a society are critical to influencing the direction of research and its practical application, and hence, to bridging the research–policy gap. Policy advisers must be chosen by the policy makers themselves and their nationality should really not matter. In the demand for research, the centrality of this point cannot be overemphasized. Part of the reason for the economic success of Botswana was its independence in choosing its key advisers, some of whom were non-nationals. These were not fly-by-night advisers but resident experts who took time to understand the policy environment and to explain their positions in open seminars, including one-to-one meetings with cabinet ministers and parliamentarians.[7]

In the field of S&T policy, the convergence was both subterranean and explicit in the early days of independence. In pursuit of an industrialization strategy, it was clear that an independent technological trajectory was being charted. The import policy was in favour of capital goods, and there was robust research that supported this policy and emphasized indigenous technological capability building, learning and knowledge spillovers.

4. Knowledge dependence, policy autonomy and demand for research

Policy making in Africa in the 1980s and 1990s was dominated by what is widely known as the 'Washington consensus'. By implication, two institutions in Washington, the International Monetary Fund (IMF) and the World Bank, agreed on both the diagnosis for the lack of economic progress in

Africa and the preferred solutions. Needless to say, African leaders and peoples were not consulted; they disagreed significantly with both the analysis of the problems and the solutions that the two institutions forced them to adopt. Interestingly, at this time African leaders met under the auspices of the Organization of Africa Unity (OAU) and produced their own blueprint for Africa's economic renewal, the Lagos Plan of Action.[8] This platform had a clear roadmap specifying how to lay solid scientific and technological foundations for sustainable social and economic development in Africa, but it was completely subverted by the Washington consensus.

The neoclassical thinking and the market fundamentalism so central to the Washington consensus did not allow for any alternative view. African governments, by then heavily indebted and reliant on the IMF and the World Bank to bail them out of their economic quagmires, capitulated and reluctantly adopted their policies. The ideas and knowledge from Washington were backed by financial resources, and the role of the IMF as the global arbiter of good policies precluded access to other external sources of finance if a country's rating, in their judgement, was unsatisfactory. Many in civil society and the international community did not fully appreciate the dangers inherent in this strategy of bundling together economic ideology and aid.

These predatory tactics stimulated a game plan on the part of African policy makers, who adopted 'stop and go' tactics as far as the implementation of the agreed policies was concerned. Not fully convinced about the policies in the first place, they took a piecemeal approach to their implementation and used delaying tactics to extract further monetary concessions from the Bank and IMF, almost on a *quid pro quo* basis. The two Washington institutions, anxious to show quick and positive results, coupled with other political considerations, often obliged. Rather than improve economic performance, this cat and mouse game created more development problems. It did not occur to African governments that mobilizing the intellectual capital of their own citizens and other disparate but friendly views from the international community to challenge the Washington consensus would have been a better strategy.

However, with its growing financial muscle and influence in Washington, the government of Japan sought to encourage an alternative view. It sought to promote economic policies that emphasized the role of the state, drawing lessons from the public policies that had produced the East Asian economic miracle. Unfortunately, it gave resources to the World Bank to conduct the research and to document how these policies worked. Evidently, the Bank was not prepared to contradict itself, exposing by implication that their policy prescriptions for Africa were ideological and that the only alternative view was still its own.

The outcome of this exercise was a book, *The East Asian Miracle: Economic Growth and Public Policy*.[9] In a critique of the book, and more importantly of the process of writing the book, Robert Wade indicated that the 'final document reflects an attempt at compromise between the well-established World Bank view and the newly powerful Japanese view. The result is heavily weighted towards the Bank's established position, and legitimizes the bank's continuing advice to low-income countries to follow the "market-friendly" policies apparently vindicated by East Asia's success'.[10] This experience is important because even though the World Bank's paradigm emerged intact, it conceded some intellectual grounds to another powerful donor. There was no such concession to poor African countries. It therefore became extremely difficult to view the Bank as an honest broker that was willing to draw from certain intellectual traditions and cultures but not from others.

The loss of sovereignty and policy autonomy in most of Africa was aptly captured by Joseph Stiglitz in an account of Ethiopian experience with the IMF.[11] The Ethiopian government, after due analysis, decided that it made better economic sense to pay off a loan owed to an American bank, at a huge interest rate, by drawing from its foreign reserves that were attracting very low interest. Rather than applaud this sensible domestic initiative, the IMF officials were upset, and threatened to cut Ethiopia from its programme. At issue was not the economic sense of the action itself, but that the action was not authorized by the IMF. As Stiglitz put it 'to Ethiopia such intrusiveness smacked of a new form of colonialism; to the IMF, it was just standard operating procedure'.

There is virtually no country in Africa that has not experiences such policy emasculation. In the late 1990s, for example, the Ugandan Ministry of Trade and Industry wanted to initiate a process to recreate and support its research unit that was virtually non-existent. The minister was asked how his ministry generated the knowledge and facts with which his officials negotiated with the World Bank and the IMF on trade policies. Looking baffled, he calmly explained, in a fatherly but resigned voice, that they did not negotiate. In a nutshell, he said 'they have the money, they have the ideas and we need the money. What is there to negotiate?'

What this minister did not realize was that, as George Soros noted in a discussion of reality, fallibility and reflexivity, 'the shortcomings of dominant ideas and institutional arrangements become apparent only with passage of time, and the concept of reflexivity justifies only the claim that all human constructs are potentially flawed ... nobody is in possession of the ultimate truth'.[12] In retrospect, many of the economic policy proposals flaunted at that time as 'gospel truth' were flawed.

The 1980s saw the emergence of international agricultural research organizations with a mandate to support Africa's development efforts. Supposed to champion Africa's green revolution, several of these organizations were grouped under the Consultative Group on International Agricultural Research (CGIAR). An implication of this arrangement was that resources that would have gone to national research institutions went to these international bodies, which were supposed to assemble the best minds to address specific agricultural problems. In addition, it sent a signal that someone else was adequately taking care of the research needs of the agricultural sector and that African policy makers need not worry. This further widened the gap between African researchers, the national research institutions and the policy makers.

Twenty years later with millions of dollars spent, questions are now being raised as to the impact of the CGIAR institutes. In reviewing the performance of these international research centres, it became clear that their envisaged relationships with national agricultural research institutions are often very weak. This weakness meant that the platform for transmitting the results of the research of the CGIAR centres to African farmers was broken. The top-down approach lacked the necessary sensitivity to national institutional set-ups, incentive structures and local conditions, and was devoid of an atmosphere that encouraged knowledge exchange and mutually reinforced learning. Bypassing the national research institutions was disastrous, as the CGIAR centres lacked adequate knowledge of African farmers and their socio-cultural environment. The outcome of this was a distorted relationship between policy makers, African researchers and the donor community in a manner that reinforced donor-driven research agendas.

5. Inept African leadership

True, there was coercion and almost a sense of infallibility among IMF and World Bank economists, but it also reflects the ineptitude of many African leaders, and their willingness to simply give up without any serious attempt to engage the 'opponent'. In fact, there is evidence that African government negotiators, if equipped with adequate information and supported by their best economists, could tilt the results of the negotiations with the two Washington institutions slightly in their favour. For instance, in its negotiations for a first structural adjustment package in the late 1980s, the Tanzanian government used an economy-wide model developed by a group of Tanzanian economists with support from Canada's International Development Research Centre (IDRC). The economists were part of the government negotiating team and used the model effectively to counter some of the policy proposals that were put forward by the Washington economists and, in the process, obtained a result that was reasonably acceptable to Tanzania.[13]

This is still not common practice. Most African government negotiators are civil servants who do not use the products of research to support their arguments. In many instances, they sign whatever documents have been prepared and busy themselves with personal matters as they travel on national assignments. Visits to Washington to negotiate with the IMF and the World Bank are regarded as favours, and come with perks that supplement their incomes. Larger national goals are often secondary to the private benefits. When technical assistance is required, governments have allowed the Washington institutions to recommend experts from abroad without seriously attempting to use their own research institutions or the technical expertise of their nationals. These foreign experts, who are often paid by the World Bank or IMF, and justified on the basis of lack of analytical capacity in Africa, reach the same conclusions and make similar proposals to those offered from Washington.

Over time, the intellectual dependence has deepened. Some independent-minded African researchers began to lose confidence, others turned to consultancy work, while yet others took a pragmatic and 'more rewarding' approach of doing research whose results were always in conformity with the Washington consensus, and thus guaranteed them a steady stream of assignments. More than anything else, this intellectual dependence has fostered the notion of globalized knowledge in a globalized world ... all 'sensible policies' worked well at all times and in all places. Worse still, the notion that knowledge is generated in the North and consumed in the South has been erroneously accepted.

In a climate where there has been no alternative view, no national vision, and a complete loss of policy autonomy, and where governments were inept and lacked confidence in the expertise of their own nationals, what would be the essence of policy research, and to satisfy whose demand? Strategically, it could be targeted at World Bank and IMF officials as an indirect route to African policy makers. Unfortunately, African researchers lacked an effective organizational framework that would have made this possible. Everyone accepted that the experts in Washington had all the answers, which were backed up with their own intellectual capital.

6. S&T policy research and Africa's economic renewal

For most of the 1980s and 1990s, in an environment preoccupied with market determinism and intellectual dependence, S&T policy research had no place in the scheme of things either in Washington or among African governments. First, science and technology policy implies interference in the normal functioning of the market. Once the economy was fixed, the doctrinaire proponents assumed, everything else would follow. But how could one have fixed an economy without the effective integration of science and technology plans with economic plans? Second, the weakened African states had lost their vision of industrialization, and hence paid no attention to science and technology that would have underpinned an industrialization process. Yet S&T-led development is a leadership-cum-state-led endeavour. Third, with rapid breakthroughs in global science and technology research leading to 'forced transitions' to knowledge-laden goods, services and processes, Africa lacked both the human and infrastructural capacity to interrogate, adapt, absorb or reject these changes.

Existing science institutions have not had the resources to conduct any meaningful research. Except in agriculture, science in Africa was not easily linked to production, as scientists and engineers did their work without considering what the market or the private sector wanted. The intermediation role of government in bringing together the knowledge and production sectors as perfected by the governments of Finland, the Netherlands and Taiwan was completely absent.

The Finnish model, as exemplified in the production of Nokia mobile phones, is most instructive.[14] The partnership between knowledge centres, including universities, research institutes and science parks on the one hand, and venture capitalists and the phone company on the other, with the government assuming a very strong steering role, created what became known as a 'national product' – the Nokia mobile phone. The reorganization of the government to recognize the cross-cutting nature of science and technology and its link to production led to the creation of the Finnish Science and Technology Commission, chaired by the President of Finland, with the Ministers of Education (higher education) and Industry as vice-chairs, thus emphasizing the link between knowledge and production.

In Africa, however, very few people inside or outside of government understand the wider importance of S&T policy and the need to re-engineer knowledge institutions to become product-driven. The scientific community has always been overly concerned with research and development (R&D) and declining budget allocations. While these concerns are legitimate, few researchers and policy makers understand the importance of generating technology from technology, the wider implications of technological innovation for Africa's economic renewal, or the need to re-engineer existing institutions to supply knowledge to the productive sectors. This latter concern is in the realm of social science and S&T policy analysis. But with little capacity in this field, it has been difficult to generate any demand for research or for senior scholars to assume the role of S&T policy entrepreneurs or champions. The first order of business has been to build institutional and research capacity in this field.

7. Creating the demand for S&T policy research

Given the importance of knowledge in development, and the critical importance of S&T policy research for Africa's economic renewal, there is an urgent need to create the demand for policy research, especially for S&T policy research. New opportunities are emerging in Africa that are likely to create a platform for improved demand for research, a more focused research agenda and stronger linkages between research and the productive sectors. But it will require a lot of work to take advantage of these opportunities. These include the national economic recovery plans or strategies being put together by many African governments, new visionary & nationalistic leadership, improved political participation and space for dialogue, and the framework of the New Partnership for Africa's Development (NEPAD). In addition, African governments such as those of Kenya, Nigeria and South Africa, have established economic and social advisory councils, appointed high-ranking advisers on policy and planning as well as on science and technology. These are new developments that augur well for a strong research–policy interface. The critical question remains whether the international community will respect these groups and individuals, and provide them the administrative and intellectual space they need to be effective.

The national economic recovery plans or strategies are particularly important because they are mostly home-grown, and are driven by the desire of the new democratic governments to deliver the 'democracy dividend'. The whole process of reclaiming the policy space from overt intrusion by donors is also engendering greater self-confidence. These elements provide opportunities for researchers to organize and influence the policy process proactively, including the S&T policy platform of NEPAD. These plans, which are put together mostly by economists, acknowledge S&T peripherally and assume, erroneously, in the neoclassical tradition, that you don't need proactive government intervention or a detailed S&T plan to achieve economic and social goals. Once this gap is identified, policy makers tend to be receptive to ideas about integrating S&T issues into their development plans.

Creating the demand for S&T policy research raises a number of capacity issues, however. First, policy makers need to recognize and appreciate the role of S&T in the development process, and able to integrate technology planning into economic and social plans. Second, researchers need to be trained and organized in a manner that will enable them to use state of-the-art knowledge, to adapt models that have worked elsewhere, and to influence policy processes. Finally, specific technological and entrepreneurial skills need to be developed using a reconstituted or new S&T infrastructure and organization that links science and technology to wealth creation, and knowledge to the productive sectors. These issues constitute the main preoccupation of institutions such as the African Technology Policy Studies Network (ATPS). This relatively new institution has a mandate to improve the governance of science and technology for Africa's development by supporting research, training and advocacy. Creating the demand for research will require the ATPS and other knowledge networks to create a market for ideas, to support the emergence of policy entrepreneurs, to instigate deeper reflection on the need to domesticate technology and knowledge in the context of African values and culture, and to create a cadre of African *intellectual freedom fighters* who are willing and able to use their knowledge to liberate the continent from poverty.

Notes

1. Dr Osita Ogbu (oogbu@atpsnet.org) is executive director of the African Technology Policy Studies Network (ATPS), PO Box 10081-00100, Nairobi, Kenya, www.atpsnet.org.
2. Weiss (1995).
3. Soludo et al. (2004).
4. Hart (1998).
5. Mazrui (1990).
6. Kinyanjui (1993).
7. Stiglitz (2002).
8. OAU (1980).
9. IBRD (1993).
10. Wade (1996).
11. Stiglitz (2002).
12. Soros (1998).
13. Internal IDRC documentation.
14. Castells and Himanen (2002).

References

Castells, M. and Himanen, P. (2002) *The Information Society and the Welfare State: The Finnish Model*. Oxford: Oxford University Press.

Hart, D. (1998) *Forged Consensus: Science, Technology and Economic Policy in the United States*, 1921–1953, Princeton, NJ: Princeton University Press.

IBRD (1993) W*orld Bank Policy Research Reports*, New York: Oxford University Press.

Kinyanjui, K. (1993) Culture, technology and sustainable development in Africa, *Asian Perspective*, 17(2): 269–295

Mazrui, A. (1990) *Cultural Forces in World Politics*. London: James Curry.

OAU (1980) *Lagos Plan of Action for the Economic Development of Africa 1980–2000*.

Soludo, C.C., Ogbu, O. and Chang, H. (Eds.) (2004) *The Politics of Trade and Industrial Policy in Africa: Forced Consensus?* Trenton, NJ: Africa World Press.

Soros, G. (1998). *The Crisis of Global Capitalism*. New York: Public Affairs.

Stiglitz, J.E. (2002) *Globalization and Its Discontents*. New York: W.W. Norton.

Wade, R. (1996) Japan, the World Bank, and the art of paradigm maintenance: The East Asian miracle in political perspective, *New Left Review*, 217.

Weiss, C.H. (1995) The haphazard connection: Social science and public policy. *Int. J. Educational Research*, 23(2).

REGIONALISM AND SCIENCE AND TECHNOLOGY DEVELOPMENT IN AFRICA

JOHN MUGABE[1]

Regional integration offers new and increasing prospects for Africa's scientific and technological development. If well organized and used, integration could provide the basis for developing and sharing infrastructure for research and development, and for mobilizing and using scarce expertise and financial resources. This chapter examines how science and technology considerations are being handled in the renewed efforts to promote regional economic and trade integration in Africa, and discusses new and emerging regional science and technology programmes.

1. Introduction

In the past four decades or so, most, if not all, African countries have adopted a large number of regional cooperation and integration schemes. There are currently more than 20 regional agreements concerning cooperation and economic integration at sub-regional and continental levels in Africa, with aims ranging from limited cooperation among neighbouring countries in specific areas of political and economic development, to the creation of a continental African Common Market. A common feature of these agreements is their appreciation of the role of science and technology (S&T) in national and regional economic development. Indeed, most regional trade, economic, political, environment and security agreements include provisions for S&T cooperation.

The integration of S&T considerations into regional agreements is based on the recognition that their individual economies are small and unable to marshal scientific and technological resources for development. Many countries are poorly endowed with the human, physical and financial resources necessary to develop and harness science and technology for economic change and growth. Thus, as economists would contend, economies of scale dictate that such countries pool their resources.

Despite the recognition of the importance of regional cooperation, there are so far very few tangible or concrete examples of how African countries have collectively harnessed and applied S&T to solve common development problems. S&T cooperation provisions have largely remained statements of intent. They have not been given practical expression through concrete projects and programmes. The few attempts to make the transition from policy (as embodied in regional treaties or agreements) to action have not been successful.

This chapter examines the reasons for the poor performance and limited levels of regional cooperation in science and technology. It shows that it is the absence of appropriate regional institutions and the failure to adjust regional economic bodies that make it difficult to realize or implement the S&T provisions of agreements or treaties. The situation is starting to change, however, with a new wave of regionalism characterized by deliberate efforts to design and implement plans for the application of S&T to development.

Section 2 describes the evolution of regionalism and its successes in sub-Saharan Africa. Section 3 discusses the various regional cooperation and integration instruments – treaties, protocols and programmes – and in each case highlights their S&T content. Section 4 examines two regional initiatives, and the R&D partnerships and networks that have evolved as a result. Section 5 focuses on the factors that make regionalism an effective mechanism for promoting S&T, and section 6 argues that the emphasis should be on institutionalizing science and technology within regional economic communities, rather than including such programmes as 'add-ons' to the broader agendas of economic and political integration.

2. The evolution of regionalism in Africa

Regionalism – the process of opening up and integrating national socio-economic and political systems – is receiving renewed interest in many African countries.[2] It is a cooperative process that is being used to build inter-state security and promote cross-border economic activities and exchange. Regionalism is not a new phenomenon in Africa, but can be traced to the

1960s when the newly independent states saw opportunities for economies of scale in production and trade from a larger regional economic bloc. In 2000 the African Development Bank (ADB) noted that '[t]he fragmentation of Africa into many nation states with scant economic coherence led African leaders, following political independence, to embrace regional integration as a central element of their development strategy'.[3]

By engaging in regionalism, particularly economic integration, African countries wanted to overcome three major barriers to development – the small size of their individual economies, their dependence on imports of high-value or finished goods, and their dependence on exports of a narrow range of low-value primary products, mainly natural resources.

Regionalism in Africa also emerged out of the pan-African political aspiration for a continental identity and unity, as well as the need to build hegemony that would intimidate the former colonial masters. The newly independent states wanted to ensure that the vestiges of the colonial past were dismantled or overcome. This aspiration was pronounced, and to some extent realized, with the creation in 1963 of the Organization of African Unity (OAU), which in 2001 was transformed into the African Union (AU). The process of transformation started in 1999 with the drafting and negotiation of a legal framework (now the Constitutive Act of the AU) to address Africa's development challenges. The Constitutive Act, adopted in 2001, provides for greater political unity and economic integration, and commits African countries to principles of democracy, respect for human rights, good governance, gender equality and people-centred development.

Following the creation of the OAU a plethora of regional treaties and institutions aimed at promoting regionalism emerged in the mid-1960s to the 1980s. These included the Customs and Economic Union of Central Africa (UDEAC, 1964), the East African Community (EAC, 1967–77; re-established in the early 1990s), the Southern African Development Community (SADC, 1980),[4] the Economic Community of West African States (ECOWAS, 1975), the Common Market for Eastern and Southern Africa (COMESA, 1995),[5] and the Arab Maghreb Union (AMU, 1989).

The UN Economic Commission for Africa (ECA), established in 1958, was instrumental in establishing the regional economic groupings and gave the bodies an economic orientation. The ECA acted as a catalyst in the movements that stimulated governments to take practical measures to promote economic cooperation. The main objectives of these regional groupings were the eventual elimination of all tariffs and barriers between members, the establishment of a customs union, a unified fiscal policy and coordinated regional policies in areas such as transport, communication, energy and other infrastructural facilities.

Many other factors have stimulated the regionalization of Africa, including the opening up of national economies, which has allowed for the natural pull of geography, common culture and tastes to take place. But policy-induced regionalization, or regionalism, has also played a role through the creation of regional integration agreements that have provided for, among other things, preferential elimination of tariffs among partners and more secure market access than that offered by the rest of the world.

Despite the aspirations and efforts of the 1960s and the 1970s, regional integration has remained elusive. A variety of institutional, political and geographical factors have made its attainment difficult if not impossible. These factors include weak regional institutions, rigidity in leadership's appeal to nationalism, intra-state conflicts and wars, the Cold War that pulled African countries to one or the other side of the East-West divide, and the structural barriers to trade and industrialization. As noted in a recent ECA report,

> Increased capacity to produce and trade manufactured goods is a cornerstone of regional economic communities' integration efforts – and one that should help boost Africa's unenviable 2% share of world trade in manufactures. Ultimately, Africa's regional integration efforts will be judged by the extent to which they help the continent pool its rich, and often rare, resource endowments to enhance economic prosperity, alleviate poverty, and improve its position in the world. The absence of industrial sophistication is one of Africa's greatest weaknesses.[6]

With regard to structural adjustment, Mkandawire and Soludo have argued that '[t]he debate on regional integration concentrates much more on complementarities than it does on product differentiation and competition within the larger market. There is a need to move away from the extreme emphasis on complementarities to a recognition that within the various regional schemes an array of products already exists that could be the basis for competitive markets. Regional arrangements can be used as a collective agent of restraint'.[7]

On the whole, past efforts to promote and use regionalism in Africa have not contributed to the economic transformation of the continent. The limited potential for increased trade among African states is frequently mentioned as an explanation of the lack of success of regional integration. The effectiveness of any economic integration effort is seen in terms of the relative size of gains owing to trade creation and losses from trade diversion. For intra-African trade to be mutually beneficial, in line with economic integration goals, the potential for trade among member countries should be substantial. If African countries are competitive in their production of similar goods, there will be many opportunities for the substitution of the commodities of one country for another, thus leading to more trade creation than diversion. Technology and technological change play a major role in stimulating and sustaining economic diversity and trade creation, and thus they underpin regional integration. Trade creation is unlikely to occur without technological progress.

Although their main objective is to promote economic integration of the continent, the various regional economic communities have spent the last three decades or so resolving political and social conflicts in some of its member countries, such as Angola, Burundi, Guinea Bissau, Liberia, Niger, Rwanda and Sierra Leone.

3. Science and technology in regional agreements and treaties

Regionalism is receiving renewed attention throughout Africa. The past several years have witnessed a growing number of regional economic and trade agreements, as well as a plethora of proposals for new bilateral and multilateral preferential trade arrangements. There is also greater recognition of the need for bilateral and multilateral S&T cooperation, and provisions for this purpose are increasingly being written into economic and trade agreements.

It is worth noting that the renewed interest in and efforts to promote regionalism are taking place at a time of the globalization of economic production and the associated rapid advances in technology.[8] Regionalization is being driven by advances in transport, information and communications technologies (ICTs), as well as in policy and politics. This is evident in the increasing transboundary movements of people, finance and products across the region. Intra-regional foreign direct investment flows are also increasing.

Africa has a wide range of regional instruments – policies, programmes, protocols and treaties – that articulate the importance of S&T cooperation. Most regional and sub-regional economic, political and trade treaties make explicit reference to the need to strengthen cooperation in various fields of science and technology. Article 13 of the Constitutive Act of the African Union gives authority to the executive committee of the AU to formulate policies that promote S&T cooperation.

The declaration and treaty establishing the Southern Africa Development Community (SADC) aims at promoting the development, transfer and mastery of technology. Article 21 (areas of cooperation) makes explicit reference to SADC member countries cooperating in science and technology. SADC's Protocol on Education and Training, ratified by at least eight countries, aims at promoting the development of a common S&T policy, establishing joint research facilities and regional centres of excellence, and facilitating the movement of scientists in SADC countries.

The treaty establishing the East African Community (EAC) contains several provisions on science and technology. Articles 5 (objectives of the Community), 80, and 103 are explicit on the role of cooperation in fostering the sub-region's scientific and technological development. Article 80(e) provides that the EAC shall 'promote industrial research and development and the transfer, acquisition, adaptation and development of modern technology, training, management and consultancy services through the establishment of joint industrial institutions and other infrastructural facilities'. In Article 103, member states commit themselves to 'promote cooperation in the development of science and technology within the Community through: (a) the joint establishment and support of scientific and technological research and of institutions in the various disciplines of science and technology; (b) the creation of a conducive environment for the promotion of science and technology within the Community; [...] and (i) the harmonisation of policies on commercialisation of technologies and promotion and protection of intellectual property rights'.

Similar provisions are to be found in the treaty creating the Common Market for Eastern and Southern African (COMESA). Article 100(d) calls on member countries to cooperate to promote 'industrial research and development, the transfer, adaptation and development of technology, training, management and consultancy services through the establishment of joint industrial support institutions and other infrastructural facilities'. The treaty also aims at promoting cooperation in the creation of an enabling environment for foreign, cross-border and domestic investment, including the joint promotion of research and adaptation of S&T for development.

Regionalism offers platforms on which scientifically and technologically weak countries can articulate their demand for technology, innovation policy and related institutional adjustments. If carefully configured and governed, such platforms provide a good foundation for restoring and enlarging Africa's confidence in its own abilities to generate and manage knowledge for economic change and human development.

African countries have signed and ratified a wide range of other multilateral agreements that contain provisions on international scientific and technological cooperation. At least 45 African countries are contracting parties to the Convention on Biological Diversity, the UN Framework Convention on Climate Change, and the Montreal Protocol on Substances that Deplete the Ozone Layer. Many are also members of the World Trade Organization (WTO), where issues of technical cooperation and technology transfer preoccupy most of the negotiations.

International cooperation in S&T is increasing in intensity and complexity. Several studies have shown that collaborative S&T activities have increased among developed countries and between some developed and developing countries.[9] This growth has been stimulated by a variety of factors, including globalization and increasing recognition of the benefits of collaboration. Most recent international and regional economic, trade, security and environmental agreements or treaties contain provisions on cooperation in S&T.

At the international level, many treaties emphasize cooperation in S&T, including the Vienna Convention for the Protection of the Ozone Layer (1985), the Montreal Protocol (1987), the Convention on Biological Diversity (1992), the UN Framework Convention on Climate Change (1992), the UN Convention to Combat Desertification (1994), the WTO Agreement on Trade-related Intellectual Property Rights (TRIPS, 1994), the Kyoto Protocol (1997) and the Cartagena Protocol on Biosafety (2001). They create obligations for their contracting parties to invest in joint S&T programmes and engage in cooperation through exchanges of expertise and information as well as sharing research facilities.

Agenda 21 – the United Nations programme on sustainable development adopted at the UN Conference on Environment and Development in Rio de Janeiro in 1992 – devotes a lot of attention to the need for international cooperation in S&T. For example, its chapter 31 (on the scientific and technological community) and chapter 34 (on transfers of environmentally sound technology, cooperation and capacity building) are largely dedicated to measures that promote such cooperation.

The Convention on Biological Diversity contains similar provisions. In particular, Article 18(2) states that 'each contracting party shall promote technical and scientific cooperation with other Contracting Parties, in particular developing countries, in implementing this Convention, *inter alia*, through the development and implementation of national policies. In promoting such cooperation, special attention should be given to the development and strengthening of national capabilities, by means of human resources development and institution building'. Article 18(5) requires the parties to 'promote the establishment of joint research programmes and joint ventures for the development of technologies'.

The Plan of Implementation of Agenda 21, adopted by governments at the World Summit on Sustainable Development in Johannesburg in 2002, is about the role of S&T in meeting sustainable development goals. Many of its recommendations are about mobilizing and directing science and technology to solve problems associated with energy deficiency, food insecurity, environmental degradation, diseases, water insecurity and many other sustainable development challenges. The plan calls on the international community to 'promote technology development, transfer and diffusion to Africa and further develop technology and knowledge available in African centres of excellence; and support African countries to develop effective science and technology institutions and research activities capable of developing and adapting to world class technologies'.

On the whole, there is increasing recognition and articulation of the role of cooperation in fostering the application of S&T for sustainable development. Scientific and technological development is a learning process that is largely achieved through cooperative or collaborative efforts of sharing experiences, information, infrastructure and other resources, such as human and financial. Today, no country can achieve scientific advances and technological progress without interacting with its peers and neighbours. The ability of countries and firms to innovate, both in technical and managerial ways, is largely determined by strategic alliances forged both within their industrial landscapes and across sectors. Furthermore, for industrial firms to become successful in generating new innovations, they often have to form strategic partnerships with public R&D institutions (this is clearly the case in such fields as biotechnology).

Cooperation in S&T can take various forms, including joint projects, sharing of information, conferences, building and sharing joint laboratories, setting common standards for R&D, and exchanges of expertise. For developing countries, particularly those in Africa, such cooperation can bring many advantages, including:

- providing access to new knowledge, foreign skills and training opportunities that may not be available at the national level;
- offering access to large and often expensive research facilities, including laboratories and libraries;
- avoiding the costs of duplication of research;
- enriching the political and social relations between countries;

- providing opportunities to establish multidisciplinary research activities and teams;
- creating a favourable basis for international funding; and
- building or strengthening domestic R&D institutions.

The importance of cooperation in S&T is also articulated in a wide range of declarations, statements and national policies. Many African countries have entered into bilateral cooperation agreements. For example, by 2002 Egypt had entered into at least 18 agreements, South Africa at least 27, Nigeria at least nine and Kenya at least five. South Africa's agreement with Nigeria, signed in early 2001, aims at enhancing cooperation between the two countries in fields such as biotechnology, environmental observation systems, materials science, space science, etc., and provides for exchanges of scientists engaged in joint projects.

South Africa has entered into bilateral cooperation agreements with at least seven other African countries, as well as with the European Union, Belgium, France, Germany, Hungary, India, Italy, Norway, Poland, the UK, the USA, etc. To implement its agreement with the EU, South Africa established a special Lead Programmes Fund and designated national institutions to be responsible for specific activities. This fund was established to enhance existing cooperation in the fields of biotechnology, new materials, ICTs, environmental management, rural development and urban renewal. During the first round (1999–2001), the fund successfully leveraged international R&D support and established viable consortia between South African Science Councils and Cirad (France), Alcoa (USA), Rolls Royce (UK), and IVL (Sweden), among others. The National Research Foundation (NRF) services the implementation of the agreements. Between January 2000 and March 2003 South Africa spent more than US$1.2 million servicing more than 27 bilateral and multilateral agreements.

Most, if not all, African countries recognize that international cooperation in S&T matters. With the exception of a few countries, however, there is no evidence that they have set up specific programmes or made institutional arrangements to implement the provisions of the agreements. Some of the reasons for this include the inadequate financial resources devoted to international and regional activities, the lack of explicit linkages between the S&T policies and foreign policies of most African countries, the limited capacity to negotiate effectively and monitor the implementation of cooperation agreements, and generally weak national S&T systems.

For African countries to be able to achieve high levels of scientific and technological development and thereby reap the benefits in terms of economic growth, poverty reduction, environmental sustainability, improved health, etc., they must place greater emphasis on pursuing S&T in regional and international contexts. Isolated national approaches, de-linked from regional and international programmes, will deny these countries opportunities to benefit from the globalization of science and related technological innovations.

African countries can benefit through increased regional cooperation because many scientific and technological advances are made in other regions of the world. A large proportion of scientific articles and patents are generated outside Africa. Most African countries do not have the necessary research facilities in areas such as genomics, since these tend to be relatively expensive. International and regional collaboration is necessary in order to enable African scientists to access such facilities. However, in order for Africa to be able to utilize and benefit from discoveries made and facilities located elsewhere, it needs world-class researchers who can communicate and collaborate with the best scientists around the world. The challenge for the continent, therefore, is to invest in creating a cadre of scientists who will be able to work with developed country scientists on specific international projects.

African policy makers and scientists recognize the importance of regional cooperation in S&T. This is explicit in the provisions of regional and subregional treaties, in the decisions of regional meetings and various statements. As noted above, however, little has been done to translate these provisions into concrete processes and S&T activities. Many African countries continue to work with isolated R&D systems, often with limited expertise and financial resources. The continent as a whole has spread its limited resources too thinly across the various fields. In many cases the existing science infrastructure of the better-off countries of the region is not accessible to others that desperately require it.

4. From policy intentions to practice: two examples

This section describes two examples of regional collaboration in Africa, involving agricultural research and laser technology.

ASARECA

The Association for Strengthening Agricultural Research in Eastern and Central Africa (ASARECA) is a non-political organization of the national agricultural research institutes (NARIs) of ten countries: Burundi, Democratic Republic of Congo, Eritrea, Ethiopia, Kenya, Madagascar, Rwanda, Sudan, Tanzania and Uganda. Based in Entebbe, Uganda, ASARECA's mission is 'to strengthen and increase the efficiency of agricultural research in East and Central Africa, and to facilitate economic growth, food security and export competitiveness through productive and sustainable agriculture'.[10]

This regional collaboration in agricultural research can be traced back to the early 1980s when scientists from national programmes began working together. To run these networks, and to consider and approve annual work plans, regional steering committees were put in place. The committee members included research coordinators and scientists from the NARIs. Over time, as these early networks evolved, they came to be regarded as one way to achieve economies of scale and to facilitate technology spillovers across national boundaries. This led to the idea of creating and building up a regional association.

ASARECA was established following the approval of the Framework for Action for Agricultural Research in Eastern and Central Africa, which was developed by the Special Programme for African Agricultural Research (SPAAR) in consultation with NARI leaders. ASARECA's three broad objectives were to improve the relevance, quality and cost-effectiveness of agricultural research; to establish and support regional mechanisms to reinforce and improve collaboration among the national agricultural research systems; and to improve the delivery of new appropriate information and technology. Given the many commodities and factors that each national system had to handle, and the need for greater efficiency and effectiveness in utilizing scarce resources, it was agreed that a regional strategy for agricultural research and research-related training be implemented. In September 1994, the Memorandum of Agreement that established ASARECA was signed, and in October the Executive Secretariat, based in Entebbe, Uganda, became operational

ASARECA carries out its activities through regional research networks, programmes and projects. However, it is important to note that there was already some collaborative research within the region before ASARECA was created. This was brought under the ambit of ASARECA and was continued by the first-generation research networks on potato and sweet potato, agroforestry, root crops and beans. The second-generation networks, established in 1990s, focus on banana, post-harvest processing, animal agriculture, maize and wheat, highlands, technology transfer, agricultural policy analysis, and improving access to agricultural information.

The African Laser Centre

The African Laser Centre (ALC), created in 2003, is another example of how regionalism is being used to promote technology development. Although originally an initiative of a few countries, the ALC has acquired a continental outlook and attention. Established on the basis that Africa can derive benefits from laser technology, the ALC's vision is to 'boost Africa into the forefront of science and technology'. Its mission is to 'enable African nations to collaborate with each other and internationally to play a major role in utilising light to advance science and technology, thereby contributing to the strengthening of their economies, their global competitiveness, education and welfare of their people. This cooperation will take place in the spirit of NEPAD and the African Union'.[11]

The ALC is a virtual centre of excellence for the continent. It has been designed as an open non-exclusive partnership to stimulate innovation, research and technology development in lasers and their applications. The ALC is actively promoting collaboration among laser researchers throughout Africa and between African institutions and their international counterparts. The six ALC facilities and their fields of specialization are listed in the table below.

Facility	Field of specialization
National Laser Centre, Pretoria, South Africa	Manufacturing, machining, and materials processing
University of Cheikh Anta Diop, Dakar, Senegal	Atomic and molecular physics and laser spectroscopy and processing
Laser and Fibre Optics Centre, Cape Coast, Ghana	Agricultural and environmental science
National Institute of Laser Enhanced Science, Cairo, Egypt	Medical and biological applications of lasers
Tunis el Manar University, Tunis, Tunisia	Plant and environmental science and molecular spectroscopy
Advanced Technologies Development Centre, Algiers, Algeria	Laser spectroscopy and surface studies

One of the novel aspects of the ALC is its reliance on African governments as the main sources of funding. The Centre was launched largely with funding from the countries that are hosting the facilities.

5. Harnessing science and technology for development

Africa entered the new millennium with a renewed determination to achieve sustainable development. After many decades of economic and social marginalization, political instability and conflicts, overdependence on the rest of the world for knowledge and finance, the continent and its people are now even more determined to eradicate poverty and to become fully integrated into the global knowledge economy. African leaders have set ambitious but realizable sustainable development goals, which are embodied in a new framework: the New Partnership for Africa's Development (NEPAD).

The creation of NEPAD is a clear indication of the determination of African leaders to institute measures to increase agricultural production and food security, stem environmental degradation, improve infrastructure and communications, fight disease, end conflicts and wars, and increase industrial production. In addition to setting the NEPAD agenda, African leaders have subscribed to the United Nations Millennium Development Goals (MDGs) and their targets. Realizing NEPAD's goals and the MDGs will require science and technology. Indeed, S&T can play a central role in meeting human development needs while maintaining the integrity of the natural environment. There is an explicit correlation between a country's scientific and technological status and its economic performance and affluence; indeed, the real income gap between poor and rich countries is largely accounted for by differences in the accumulation and utilization of S&T. Closing this gap will require deliberate measures to build the scientific and technological capabilities of poor countries.

In the past, African countries have done little to harness S&T for their development. This is demonstrated by the continent's enormous development challenges, which are largely a result of seven factors.

First, in most countries in Africa the links between scientific and political institutions are weak. Political organizations have not accorded S&T much attention in their manifestos and parliamentary activities. Yet technological change is a complex process that is influenced by many political factors. To engage in and manage this process, countries require the support of high-level political institutions. These institutions often determine the nature and levels of resources that go into public R&D activities, and the overall governance of science and innovation. There is, thus, a need to build strong political constituencies for S&T development in Africa.

Second, most African countries formulated their S&T policies in the 1970s and 1980s when development imperatives and technological opportunities were difficult, so that many of these policies focused on organizational rather than on programmatic issues. In recent years countries have been preoccupied with creating commissions or secretariats to promote S&T, and have paid little attention to the long-term programmatic aspects of S&T development. These commissions and secretariats have emerged to give an administrative view of the role of S&T in national affairs but they have failed to put in place the necessary programmes to anticipate and respond to emerging developments. Over time, some of these institutions have lost touch with reality – it takes more than administrative oversight to promote S&T development.

Third, African countries have devoted too little, and in many cases declining, funding to R&D. Most spend less than 0.5% of their GDP on R&D. This is so despite the declaration in the Lagos Plan of Action and in national S&T policies that each country would allocate at least 1% of its GDP to R&D activities. In agriculture, R&D funding has declined dramatically in the last decade or so, to the extent that the region's ability to achieve and sustain food security is being impaired. The low and declining expenditures on R&D are a clear indication of the low priority that countries have given to S&T.

Fourth, associated with the above three factors, the quality of science and engineering education is declining at all levels in Africa. Student enrolments in science and engineering subjects at primary, secondary and tertiary levels are also falling. These developments undermine the continent's aspiration to build up its numbers of scientists, engineers and technicians.

Fifth, Africa is losing some of its best scientific and technical expertise to other regions of the world. Growing numbers of African scientists and technicians are joining this 'brain drain', and are leaving the continent to work abroad for a variety of reasons, including the inadequate research infrastructures and poor remuneration packages. While other regions, particularly Asia, have developed and adopted strategies to mobilize and utilize their diasporas, Africa has not. The region can no longer afford to ignore this human capital – it needs to design ways to tap and use the enormous range of talents of Africans abroad for its own scientific and technological development.

Sixth, a further challenge faced by African countries relates to strengthening and/or building institutions dedicated to scientific and technological innovation. As a result of all the above factors, the R&D institutions in many countries are getting weaker. Most countries have not organized and mobilized their institutions in such ways to utilize their scarce financial and human resources in specific fields of science and technology. They have tended to spread their resources too thinly across the institutional terrain. As a result, the region has a whole has not been able to grow 'centres of excellence' in such areas as biotechnology, space science and ICTs.

Seventh, the links between public R&D institutions and private industry are generally weak. The results of public R&D activities are not often accessed and used by local industries, particularly small and medium enterprises (SMEs). In many cases there is a mismatch between R&D activities and national industrial development goals and strategies. For example, while the industrialization policies of most African countries have emphasized building and strengthening SMEs, the links between these enterprises and R&D institutions are weak.

6. Sources of optimism: commitments and actions

African policy makers and politicians have recognized that the barriers to the continent's scientific and technological development need to be removed if NEPAD's goals are to be realized. Thus, in November 2003, at the first NEPAD ministerial conference on science and technology, they embarked on a collective effort to develop a plan of action for S&T.[12] The conference generated a number of specific commitments and actions, as described below.

The first action was to establish the African Ministerial Council for Science and Technology. This high-level forum has started to critically examine and discuss emerging S&T questions and their implications for Africa's sustainable development. The Council provides policy and political guidance on the development and application of S&T in Africa.

The second major set of actions involved the creation and strengthening of networks and centres of excellence in science and technological innovation. In addition to establishing the African Laser Centre, which has received high-level political support, African countries launched the NEPAD Biosciences Initiative,[13] which aims to develop and apply bioscience research expertise to produce technologies that may help poor farmers to improve agricultural productivity. NEPAD has been instrumental in mobilizing resources to create or upgrade a network of world-class laboratories across Africa. The first of these centres of excellence, the Biosciences East and Central Africa (BECA), was launched in 2003 with an initial grant of C$30 million from the Canadian government. The reason for creating BECA was the fact that in the biosciences a critical mass of infrastructure, equipment, services and support technicians is needed to provide a suitable environment for high-quality research of an international standard. In view of the lack of such facilities in the subregion, it was recognized that it was not realistic in the short term to develop individual national institutions, and this led to the concept of a shared hub.

In subsequent discussions, spearheaded by NEPAD, it was recognized that for the hub to produce research outputs that would impact on development, a range of other laboratories with complementary capacities would also be required to transform those outputs into concrete products. The biosciences network was thus envisaged as composed of a hub, nodes and a broader set of members. The nodes would provide certain services to other members and receive critical investments to make them effective in their specific field. Members are entitled to access the nodes and the hub. BECA is an investment to enable the region to do strategic research that will have an impact on poverty. A similar effort has been initiated in Southern Africa, with laboratories dedicated to research and innovation in such areas as genomics and proteomics.

In addition to the above efforts, African countries have also committed themselves to improving science, technology and innovation policies. Specific actions they are undertaking include the establishment an advisory panel on biotechnology, a working group to design common African indicators or benchmarks for assessing the status of S&T, and a task force to encourage more African women to engage or participate in science and engineering. Each country has also committed itself to increasing national annual public expenditures on R&D to at least 1% of GDP. These efforts will be bolstered with the proposed establishment of a continental financial mechanism for regional research and innovation programmes.

Concerted efforts are now being made to promote S&T in Africa. Political and civil constituencies for S&T are emerging. African leaders have pronounced their commitment to ensure that science and technology are harnessed and applied to promote human development and the continent's integration into the global economy. What are needed are measures to sustain and build upon these developments in order to halt the growing human deprivation within the continent and its marginalization from the rest of the world.

7. Strengthening the S&T focus of regional economic communities

One of the reasons why past African aspirations to use regionalism for technology development have not materialized is the failure to institutionalize S&T programmes into the regional economic communities (RECs). Bodies such as SADC, ECOWAS and the EAC do not have offices or departments dedicated to S&T matters. Most of them have not created programmes to translate the provisions of their respective treaties into concrete actions. To enable them to build capacity for S&T, NEPAD has facilitated a series of regional workshops to identify specific projects and programmes. A key outcome of these workshops has been the establishment of 'science desks' in each of the RECs that will serve as vehicles for ensuring that regionalism is S&T driven. NEPAD plans to mobilize and provide resources for the establishment and maintenance of these science desks.

Another important factor is regional leadership. Achieving good governance of African economies and related politics will require investments in technology. Technology is crucial to increase the region's economic productivity and political stability. It is in this regard that African leaders need to put more emphasis on the role of technology in national and regional development. Establishing a culture committed to technological innovation and development requires political leadership. The experiences of many Asian countries in the process of industrialization and attaining economic competitiveness have shown that political leaders play a crucial role in establishing and sustaining a national vision and developing a strategy for technology-led development.[14] At present there is there is no such political leadership in any African country for such a strategy evolve or for technology considerations to be integrated into national economic and social strategies.

NEPAD is starting to play a role in building national political leadership for technological development. To play that role effectively, however, it will require support in terms of policy research and analysis. UN agencies and international universities, as well as regional centres such as the African Technology Policy Studies Network (ATPS) and the African Centre for Technology Studies (ACTS), can support NEPAD by making available policy papers on specific S&T issues.

Acknowledgements

This chapter is the product of collaboration with many institutions and individuals from a wide range of professional backgrounds. It brings together information and the views of many policy makers and representatives of regional economic institutions in Africa. I am grateful to all of them for their cooperation. In particular, I am grateful for the research support provided by Aggrey Ambali and Killian Munyuchi in the process of preparing this chapter.

Notes

1. Dr John Mugabe (john@nepadst.org) is the Science and Technology Advisor to the New Partnership for Africa's Development (NEPAD), and Adjunct Professor at the Institute of Technological Innovation, University of Pretoria, South Africa.
2. For a conceptual discussion of regionalism see Weiss (1999).
3. ADB (2000).
4. Formerly the Southern African Development Coordinating Conference (SADCC).
5. Formerly the Preferential Trade Area (PTA), established in 1981.
6. UNECA (2004: 95).
7. Mkandawire and Soludo (1999).
8. Goldstein (2002).
9. See the Advisory Council on Science and Technology (2000) and Wagner *et al.* (2000).
10. See www.asareca.org.
11. See www.csir.co.za and www.africanlasercentre.org.
12. NEPAD (2003).
13. See www.nepadst.org/programmes/prog_biosci.html and www.biosciencesafrica.org.
14. See Anyang' Nyongo and Coughlin (1991).

References

ADB (2000) *Economic Cooperation and Regional Integration Policy.* Abidjan, Côte d'Ivoire: African Development Bank.

Advisory Council on Science and Technology (2000) *Reaching Out: Canada, International Science and Technology, and the Knowledge-based Economy.* Report of the Expert Panel on Canada's Role in International Science and Technology. Ottawa: ACST.

Anyang' Nyongo, P. and Coughlin, P. (1991) *Industrialization at Bay: African Experiences.* Nairobi: African Academy of Science, p.vi.

Goldstein, A. (2002) *The New Regionalism in Sub-Saharan Africa: More than Meets the Eye?* OECD Development Centre Policy Brief No.20. Paris: OECD.

Mkandawire, T. and Soludo, C. (1999) *Our Continent, Our Future.* Dakar, Senegal: Council for the Development of Social Science Research in Africa (CODESRIA), p.124.

NEPAD (2003) *Outline of a Plan of Action for Science and Technology.* NEPAD Ministerial Conference on Science and Technology for Development, November.

UNECA (2004) *Assessing Regional Integration in Africa.* ECA policy research report. Addis Ababa: United Nations Economic Commission for Africa.

Wagner, C. et al. (2000) *International Cooperation in Research and Development: An Update to an Inventory of U.S. Government Spending.* Santa Monica, CA: RAND Corporation.

Weiss, B. (1999) *The Economics of Integration, the Politics of Regionalism: Interdependence and Integration Theory Revisited.* Graduate School of International Policy Economy, University of Tsukuba, Japan, Working Paper CIAO 3/99.

BUILDING A CRITICAL MASS OF RESEARCHERS IN THE LEAST DEVELOPED COUNTRIES: NEW CHALLENGES

LÉA VELHO[1]

Knowledge is at the heart of development and qualified researchers are necessary to produce a broad base of knowledge relevant to the solution of current and future practical problems. How to create and maintain a critical mass of researchers who are able to consistently and systematically contribute to and absorb such a knowledge base? This is the focus of this chapter, with special reference to the least developed countries. It is argued that it is very unlikely that LDCs will be able to build the research capacity they need simply by adopting the research training schemes developed in the advanced countries and offered by development cooperation agencies. The reasons for this are presented and illustrated with a case study of Nicaragua.

1. Introduction

There exists a common and widespread belief that a research career begins with a doctoral degree. Therefore, governments concerned with ensuring an adequate supply of highly qualified personnel are expected both to fund and regulate graduate training programmes. Training researchers has long been seen as the primary benefit universities can provide to an innovation-oriented productive sector, as well as to society.[2] In order to carry out this task, research training schemes were created in the advanced countries, in many developing countries, and are on the 'agenda for the future' of those poorer countries that have not yet been able to do much in this direction.

Despite differences in structure, organization and quality, graduate programmes worldwide have tended to converge on a model whereby the doctoral degree is granted to a candidate who has successfully performed original research in a specific scientific discipline – something that was once estimated to require at least four years.[3] Since this model was set up and became widely accepted, ideas and theories about knowledge production and use have changed. This chapter departs from the argument that such changes pose important challenges to the prevailing research training model. Specifically, it is concerned with the implications of the changes in knowledge production for the least developed countries and their task of achieving a critical mass of competent researchers.

It is a truism that knowledge is at the heart of development. It is also common sense that qualified researchers are necessary (albeit not sufficient) to produce a broad base of knowledge that is likely to form the background to the solution of current and future practical problems and to meet society's needs. Indeed, without such researchers, development strategies can hardly be knowledge based. How to create and maintain a critical mass of researchers who will consistently and systematically contribute to and absorb such a knowledge base seems to be a fundamental challenge faced by every country.

2. The changing nature of knowledge production and use

It is a recurrent idea in the literature that the research world is in transition, and a number of different models have been proposed to reflect this.[4] One such model that has become influential is the thesis advanced by Gibbons *et al.*,[5] that a new regime of knowledge production, called mode 2, is emerging alongside the more traditional and familiar mode 1, in which research problems are set and solved in a context governed by the interests of the academic community.

Mode 1 is a linear model in which research is seen as the starting point of innovation and there is a clear separation between knowledge producers (researchers) and users (firms, government, society at large). The model also assumes that research results produced in line with theoretical frameworks and prescribed methodologies of relevant disciplines ought to be utilized by end users because of their scientific validity. This validity is ensured through scientific peer review and reflected in publication of articles, preferably in mainstream journals.

Mode 2 knowledge production, in contrast, entails a broader conception of transdisciplinary knowledge, generated in the context of application.[6] It addresses problems identified through a process of continual negotiation between actors from a variety of settings. It is thus a systemic, interactive model in which knowledge is produced in the course of cognitive and social practices. It recognizes the existence of multiple knowledge sites, and of various skills and experiences that need to be brought together to solve particular problems. Quality is assessed by both experts and non-experts, not only in terms of scientific merit but also of the usefulness or relevance of the knowledge produced, being more socially accountable and reflexive.

Whether this transition from mode 1 to mode 2 refers to the actual dynamics of knowledge production, or to a change in our understanding of the process of knowledge production and utilization, or a mix of the two, is a matter of debate.[7] Some have even expressed doubts about the overall thesis put forward by this model.[8] However, one does not have to subscribe wholesale to the 'mode 1 and mode 2' vision to perceive a variety of ways in which the boundaries between academic and other worlds are becoming blurred, and to conclude that this is a growing trend. Actually, even the critics acknowledge 'the [uncontroversial] thesis of the diversification of the loci of scientific production',[9] the intensification of inter-sectoral collaboration, the increasing interdisciplinary character of contemporary science and the changing normative systems governing the work of researchers.[10] All such trends are in accordance with the features of mode 2 knowledge production. To this extent, there is significant agreement among authors that, in historical terms, we are witnessing a gradual shift in the relative space occupied by mode 1 and mode 2 knowledge production, with a steady expansion of the latter.

Under mode 1 knowledge production the task of S&T policy makers to ensure the supply of qualified researchers looked much simpler. It was agreed that governments had to devote resources (or obtain complementary resources from elsewhere) to help young people go into higher education, to maintain quality universities and graduate programmes, and to provide an environment conducive to research by putting in place competitive grant schemes and fostering a reward structure based on merit and controlled by reputable researchers. In terms of research (graduate) training, the task was to bring students to the research frontier of a particular discipline and to make sure that in this process they were socialized into the academic profession.[11]

The above directive was valid for all countries. For developing countries, the alternatives were to create their own graduate programmes along these lines, or to send their brightest and best young talents to be trained abroad, or a combination of the two. The latter was the path chosen by the better-off developing countries, including Brazil, China, India, South Korea and others, but even this strategy was fraught with difficulties. Most developing countries did not have the necessary resources either to establish their own graduate programmes or to send students abroad for advanced studies. But those talented young people who did go abroad were unable to find a favourable research environment on their return home, and thus the brain drain became a serious problem. What was needed was not in dispute: researchers were to be trained in postgraduate programmes and these were shaped by, and for the primary purpose of reproducing the academic profession.[12]

To the extent that mode 1 was the basis of university research and corresponding training structures, it is reasonable to say that mode 2 knowledge production calls for a 'reform' of the system. Actually, in the advanced countries, postgraduate education is increasingly influenced by the debate about the extent to which societies experience, or are expected to change, their mode of knowledge production. In the new regime (mode 2) research training is said to require the development of a broader set of capabilities, including communication and presentation skills, collaborative skills (with colleagues in other disciplines, or with actors in other sectors), understanding and management of intellectual property rights, and negotiation skills. Training in a scientific or scholarly specialty (and four years doing this on a master-apprentice model) as traditionally defined, is arguably much less relevant today.[13] The research training function of higher education and the transfer of knowledge through the young generation are thus loaded by a number of major debates about academic and scientific work, and about universities and their changing nature and roles. In policy terms, research training is being 'decoupled' from its strong association with academic careers and the reproduction of the academic profession.[14]

Obviously the above transition affects different countries in different ways. Those that have functional universities, established systems for training researchers (postgraduate programmes), a private sector that contributes to R&D and employs graduates, are talking about reform and adaptation. They are also discussing extending research training rights to other organizations such as private companies, hospitals and consultancy firms, and are training researchers to take jobs in the private sector, etc. But how does this debate on the changing nature of knowledge production and use affect research training in the least developed countries (LDCs), which have not yet been able to develop a critical mass of researchers, nor have the educational structures to train them?

This group of developing countries faces some major questions. Is it possible to create research capacity in mode 2 *only after* a country has established training structures in mode 1?[15] Is it possible to create capacity in mode 2 directly (is this leapfrogging, and if so, is it possible/desirable)? Would it be more appropriate to aim at the co-existence of both modes of knowledge production? The replies to these questions pose crucial challenges to LDCs that need to build their knowledge base and critical mass of researchers.

Another challenge for the LDCs is that their economic performance severely restricts their expenditures on S&T – and the increasing cost of scientific activity will probably widen the scientific and economic gap between them and the advanced countries. Thus, whatever replies a country gives to the above questions, the lack of resources may limit (or hinder) the implementation of a corresponding research training strategy. It is here that development cooperation has played an important role: capacity building in the LDCs has been the focus of many donors. However, what donors understand by capacity building and the form of support they offer depend on their views concerning knowledge production and utilization. Such views may be in line with mode 1 or with mode 2, and each influences accordingly the decisions made by the recipient country concerning the form and content of research training modes.[16]

The remainder of this chapter reflects on these questions and, in doing so, argues that creating research capacity in mode 1 in the LDCs, following the path of the advanced countries, is unlikely to be feasible. The reason is that it takes too long, it requires resources not available in those countries, and it does not attend to criteria of social relevance which are currently required of public universities. Moreover, as research capacity building in LDCs is somewhat dependent on development cooperation, the views and the educational structures of the cooperating Northern country tend to dominate the relationship and bring further complicating factors into the picture.

The argument is illustrated with an analysis of the case of research capacity building in Nicaraguan public universities with support from SAREC, the department for research cooperation of the Swedish International Development Agency (Sida). SAREC's modality of support to capacity building in the South has a cadre of followers in the donor community and is applied in many LDCs. This, added to the fact that the partnership between Swedish and Nicaraguan universities has been going on for over 20 years, makes it an illuminating case of the problems of research capacity development and the complexity of such effort.

The following sections present a brief picture of the socio-economic, political and university context of Nicaragua, the partnership, and its outcomes and impact, and the main problems with SAREC's modality of support to research capacity building. The concluding section draws lessons from the case study and proposes new grounds on which to build modalities of support to research capacity building in the South.

3. Cooperation between Swedish and Nicaraguan universities

The partnership between Swedish and Nicaraguan universities, as mediated and supported by SAREC, started in 1981. Over the last 20 years SAREC has fostered cooperation programmes between the four public universities in Nicaragua[17] and a number of universities in Sweden, covering a wide range of scientific fields in agriculture, engineering, medical sciences, geology and ecology.

SAREC's objective is 'to strengthen research capacity and support research which can contribute to the solution of important development problems of Nicaragua'.[18] In order to achieve this goal, SAREC has focused on providing opportunities for faculty members of Nicaraguan universities to pursue Masters and PhD degrees at Swedish universities, using the 'sandwich model'.[19] The latter is the name given to a type of graduate training that combines course work and periods of study at the Swedish partner institution with research work at the home institution, with the final degree granted by the Swedish university. Table 1 shows the contribution of the cooperation to the staffing situation of the four Nicaraguan universities in the last 20 years.

Table 1. Staff at Nicaraguan universities with MSc and PhD degreesobtained through the SAREC programme (1980-2000)

	Completed		Underway	
	MSc	**PhD**	**MSc**	**PhD**
UNA	22	2	-	10
UNAN-León	13	1	5	9
UNI	6	-	9	4
UNAN-Managua	-	-	-	5
Total	41	3	14	28

Sources: Synthesis documents provided by the universities.

It is difficult to judge the impact of such numbers, but it was certainly different at each university. At the National University of Agriculture (UNA), 25% of teachers with an MSc obtained their degree in the framework of this cooperation programme. At the older universities like UNAN-León, the impact of the SAREC programme has been much less impressive – only 8% of existing MSc holders in 2001. This contribution added to a larger effort by Nicaraguan universities during the 1990s to develop their human resources. Between 1990 and 2000, the proportion of faculty members with an MSc increased from 12% to 28%, and those with a PhD doubled from 4% to 8%,[20] although these figures are still well below Latin American average.

In addition, the analysis of the programme indicates that even if there was an increase in research capacity at the universities, the dynamics of knowledge production did not change very much during these years. Of course, the reasons lie mostly in the complexity of the problems faced by Nicaragua, including the economic crisis, institutional weaknesses and the political climate. However, the findings also point to a number of limitations of the model of research capacity building. The impact of the partnership on research capacity presents a number of problems derived from its own design and implementation.

4. Modes of knowledge production and research capacity

In designing the modality of cooperation in the early 1980s, SAREC recognized that a great deal of innovation takes place in the developing world, and thus it was essential to build local research capacity to support it.[21] Nonetheless, the process leading to innovation was believed to be a linear one whereby researchers must identify society's needs, translate those needs into researchable problems, work scientifically on them, disseminate the results to some kind of intermediary institution (a firm, government institute, extension organization, etc.), which would then make use of the results by incorporating them into an innovation. This, in effect, describes mode 1 knowledge production.

The new conception of mode 2 knowledge production has, *in discourse*, been adopted by some donors, including SAREC. Policy documents have referred to the 'focus on systems and a systems approach to development'.[22] 'Participatory methods', 'demand orientation', and 'local knowledge', have became the new buzzwords of development cooperation. The importance of linkages among stakeholders is also often highlighted.

In *practice*, however, donors find difficult to change their way of operation. On the one hand, the idea of the linear model is powerful and is upheld and forcefully defended by researchers, who are a strong interest group.[23] On the other, modalities of North–South cooperation that foster research capacity in mode 1 are much easier to implement, monitor and evaluate than those in mode 2. Selecting individual research projects on the basis of scientific criteria, monitoring the performance of graduate students, checking for publications in mainstream journals are well established practices in the research world. But the participatory methods necessary for mode 2 programmes are messy and difficult, the path from a practical problem to a research problem is not straightforward, and what is socially relevant is a matter of debate – in short, there is considerable uncertainty associated with mode 2 and donors prefer not to take risks. Ultimately, donors are accountable to their governments, and are usually required to adopt a results-based approach in their operations. By the same token, many recipient countries do not have a clear idea of how they want to go about building their research capacities. Research capabilities are often not included in national development plans, and are seen as questions to be decided by the universities.

Support to graduate education does not seem to allow much room for interaction between social actors. Yet it is generally believed that 'research training at doctoral level is the longest, most important and comprehensive form of training given to young graduates from developing countries to prepare them for careers and future leadership in research [...] such trainees provide the indigenous expertise and competence that all countries need for their national self-reliance'.[24] Without disputing the importance of highly qualified researchers for any country, it may be useful to reflect on the problems with this emphasis on doctoral training.

5. Problems with the emphasis on graduate education in LDCs

As far as the developing countries are concerned, there is no undisputable evidence that the number of Masters and PhDs, and the number of papers they publish in refereed journals, are related to either economic or social development. Brazil, for example, has made considerable investments in building and strengthening a scientific system since the 1960s. The graduate schools in Brazilian universities are regarded with a mix of envy and pride by all Latin American country neighbours: they produce over 6000 PhDs and 20,000 MSc degrees every year.[25] The scientific contribution of the country to mainstream science jumped from 0.4% in 1986 to 1% in 1999.[26] Yet, a recent analysis of the Brazilian experience in using knowledge for development concluded that 'Brazil's potential in the global knowledge economy remains largely unrealized. Its competitive position is weak and the country is definitely on the fragile side of the knowledge divide'.[27] In order to cross the knowledge divide, it continues, Brazil has to strengthen its innovation system, particularly 'by establishing effective links with industry and ensuring that results are turned into commercially viable products'. In terms of human development, in 2002 Brazil was ranked 73rd among 162 countries, far behind poorer cuntries like Colombia, Costa Rica and Venezuela,[28] illustrating that a strong scientific system does not lead automatically to innovation or social development.

A second problem with the emphasis on formal graduate training is that PhD research is not the most efficient manner to stimulate teamwork in the conditions that prevail in developing countries. Thus, if research is to be linked to innovation and social change, it must be a collective endeavour. In the advanced countries, PhD candidates usually work under the leadership of a professor who has a broad conception of a problem, promotes regular discussion, and encourages students to see the connections among their work. Nicaraguan graduate students in Sweden, however, carry out their research in Nicaragua, in the conditions of their own university, and are probably the only ones working on the topic. In addition, they have little opportunity to acquire tacit knowledge.[29]

A third problem is that not every research problem is an adequate topic for a PhD dissertation. Although there is no doubt that relevant research has to be of an acceptable scientific standard, not all relevant research meets the scientific requirements for a PhD. Thus, Nicaraguan faculty members are expected to select their research topics using scientific criteria rather than according to their social and economic relevance.

In addition, while PhD degrees serve a clear function in the advanced countries, this is not the case in most LDCs. In the former, a PhD is an important 'market' indicator and an entrance requirement for positions in academia and some industrial R&D labs. Basically, people in the North invest in a PhD in order to be able to pursue a career that would be unattainable otherwise. Therefore, a PhD candidate's incentives depend mainly on his or her career potential after graduating.[30] In Nicaragua, the title PhD has no functionality: candidates are already tenured university teachers, and obtaining the degree does not bring promotion. Therefore, while they may have some incentive to enter a PhD programme (personal pleasure of learning, opportunity to travel, enhance their visibility), they have no incentive to finish it.

Another problem is that, in the framework of the SAREC programme, Masters and PhD training take a sandwich format (multiple layers of course work in Sweden and thesis work in Nicaragua), and the degree is granted by a Swedish university.[31] This inevitably takes a long time, since it is a *part-time* enrolment for the PhD. When the Nicaraguans are at their home institutions, they teach, attend departmental meetings, supervise undergraduates, and have institutional duties. The sandwich model requires students to have periods of adaptation back and forth. It also makes it more difficult for them to work as part of a team while in Sweden and to participate fully in academic life there. It thus restricts their opportunity to acquire tacit knowledge, as discussed above. It is therefore not surprising that it takes the candidates a long time to obtain their degrees – some PhD candidates have taken over 10 years and MSc candidates take an average of six years.

A further crucial problem is the restriction of support to the degree being granted by the Swedish institution. This has a lot to do with the fact that part of the resources allocated to the programme must be spent in Sweden. Thus, the Swedish universities keep a sizeable proportion of the programme budget, paid as fees and expenses of Nicaraguan students.

Finally, it is possible to attribute most of the problems to the asymmetry in the relation between the partners. A consistent finding of this study was a persistent call from the Nicaraguan side for more autonomy in the choice of research areas, partners, tutors and budget allocations. Why they have not succeeded in achieving what they want has to do with belief, held by both sides that only SAREC funds research in Nicaraguan universities. It is necessary to point out, however, that the four universities involved in the programme receive 73% of a fixed proportion (6%) of government expenditures on higher education, plus additional funding for new buildings and reconstruction, plus exemption from all government taxes and utilities tariffs.[32] This, of course, is to the detriment of other spheres of public spending. In a country where 50% of the population live below the poverty line, and where only 1% of the population are able to attend government-supported universities, the commitment of a fixed budget to universities is a demonstration of the value given to higher education (and research, since most teachers are full-time and are expected to do research). This is true even if the budget of the universities is not enough to pay internationally comparable salaries and to fund research activities as desired by the university community. In view of the effort that is asked from society to fund local universities, it is to be expected that the latter will contribute to local development by training qualified human resources where and how the country sees appropriate, and by producing socially relevant knowledge. There seems to be little local awareness (among policy makers and the universities) of the fact that the partnership with Sweden can only take place due to considerable investment from local public funds.

6. Conclusions

In order to close the development gap, countries in the South need to develop their capacity to generate and exploit knowledge, including their capacity to do research. A major challenge for the LDCs is therefore: How to achieve such capacity – i.e. a critical mass of qualified researchers?. This challenge is magnified by two factors. On the one hand, the changing mode of knowledge production means that conventional training schemes are being questioned. On the other hand, the serious economic problems faced by the LDCs limit their internal options for building research capacity, and put them in a difficult position in their negotiations with international donors.

This chapter has argued that it is very unlikely that LDCs will be able to build their research capacities simply by adopting the research training schemes developed in the advanced countries and offered by development cooperation agencies. Such schemes are based on a mode 1 knowledge production and utilization that is, arguably, phasing out.

The collaboration between universities in Sweden and in Nicaragua, with support from SAREC, is a specific case of a North–South partnership for capacity building designed and implemented in line with mode 1. After 20 years, the partnership has produced 3 PhDs and 43 MSc graduates, and is currently supporting 14 MSc and 28 PhD candidates. Many of the latter started their training over 10 years ago, and it is likely that some will never finish. The problems they face to complete stem from the design of the sandwich scheme, the quality requirements of the Swedish universities, the lack of incentives attached to graduate degrees in Nicaragua, and the time constraints imposed by the heavy demands of teaching and administrative duties. In these circumstances, this modality of support offers a limited contribution to building a critical mass of qualified researchers that will be able to change the research environment of Nicaraguan universities.

Outside the universities, the impact of the programme is non-existent. The institutionalization of links with end users is not pursued given the prevalent view of the relationship between knowledge production and utilization implied in mode 1. A corollary to this argument is that, in order to have an impact on development, North-South partnerships should consider moving to forms of research training that are more in tune with mode 2 knowledge production. This would mean that capacity building would focus not only on graduate education, but also on creating opportunities for interactions among researchers and between them and other social actors, bringing together different types of knowledge that are necessary to address a particular problem. The latter would then be identified by directly involving research users and would be selected on the basis of their social relevance, incorporating mechanisms to ensure the quality of the research.

Obviously there are conceptual and methodological uncertainties in devising and implementing capacity building schemes in line with mode 2. In the context of Nicaragua, and of the new dynamics of knowledge production globally, research training has to prepare candidates for roles and skills that have not yet been clearly articulated. A major challenge facing schemes that aim to build capacity for socially relevant research, ultimately to produce useful knowledge that transcends disciplinary boundaries, is not only how to design the training and its contents but also how to measure, in qualitative and quantitative terms, the outputs of process-oriented research with multiple outcomes. For initiatives premised on mode 2 knowledge production, scientific value is only one dimension of quality – social relevance is another. Existing standards of science and scholarship exist to assess the former, including the number of masters and doctors trained, the number of papers published and the quality of research facilities. But capturing the nature of a specific development process that is largely invisible requires more than the usual research techniques. In addition to the traditional skills that the research community has imbibed, a nuanced reading of development that is iterative and gradual entails listening skills, the ability to combine an open and non-judgemental approach with enough understanding to make sense of and draw insights out of what one is observing and a capacity to reflect and intuit underlying movements. Clearly, the conventional quality indicators of academic research cannot grasp all the expected impact of schemes established in line with mode 2 knowledge production.

Concerning the donor–recipient relationship, conventional practice assumes that research capacity is best achieved through partnerships. Although the word 'partnership' suggests equal participation, in practice it is accepted that knowledge flows in one direction, from the North (in the case Swedish researchers) who have the knowledge, to the South (the Nicaraguan faculty) who have to create research capacity. As partnerships also embody the idea that both sides must share the benefits, it is assumed that experts (and other material resources) should be provided by the donor country. This limits considerably the recipients' choice of partners and feeds a passive attitude. A consistent finding of this study was the desire of Nicaraguan participants to enlarge their choice of training institutions beyond Sweden. The scheme offered by SAREC, however, does not allow such alternatives. And the Nicaraguans accepted that. Why?

That was a very intriguing question. But then there is a clear power relation concerning the control of funds and other resources. Donors and recipients (and the words are quite revealing) tend to assume that only donors pay for the partnership – therefore the rationale seems to be that those who pay, make the rules. What is totally forgotten is that Nicaragua contributes significantly, even financially, to the partnership. North–South partnerships always involve opportunity costs. Even 'free' outside assistance takes up local resources, demanding counterpart budgets and mechanisms, as well as the time spent on complying with donors' requirements. More to the point, in the Nicaraguan case, public funds do play an important role in the training of local faculty. Therefore, in order to meet the demands of the South, the 'partnership' assumption needs to be replaced by the notion of 'ownership by the South'. This means that donors must take up the idea of supporting capacity building without necessarily involving their own country's experts and institutions. This might not be an easy step for donors, since they are also constrained by their own domestic constituencies and provisions. It seems, nonetheless, to be an avenue worth pursuing when the general interest is development in the South.

The above assumes that countries in the South have the autonomy to decide what they need from donors, and how they prefer to go about meeting their own goals. The most important step towards ownership, however, belongs to the South itself. In Nicaragua considerable public funds are allocated to local universities. In practice, international collaboration is a way for the universities to augment their budgets, but there seems to be no awareness of this. The universities need to develop an holistic approach to international cooperation and to be pro-active when negotiating assistance within the framework of self-designed objectives. The most important challenge, however, is to have a long-lasting and widely agreed national innovation policy framework. This would spell out the role of the universities and how international collaboration could contribute to this. North–South partnerships must be recognized as a complement to the important national effort that Nicaragua makes in allocating public resources to maintain its universities and to build research capacity. Such recognition, however, must begin at home.

Notes

1. Léa Velho (velho@ige.unicamp.br) is Professor of Science and Technology Policy at the University of Campinas, Brazil.
2. Pavitt (1998).
3. Rip (2002).
4. For example, the 'triple helix' model (Etzkowitz and Leyderdorff, 2000); 'research systems in transition' (Ziman, 1994); 'national systems of innovation' (Freeman, 1988; Lundvall, 1992; Nelson,1993); and the 'post-modern research system' (Rip and Van der Meulen, 1996).
5. Gibbons *et al.* (1994).
6. 'Application is more than just product development carried out for industry […] and the processes operating to determine what knowledge is produced are much broader than is normally implied when we speak of taking products to the marketplace. The main idea of application is that knowledge is produced if, and only if, interests of various actors are taken into account. Actors are defined as industry, government and society more generally' (Gibbons *et al.,* 1994: 4).
7. Some authors contend that in practice mode 2 knowledge production has actually been predominant since the 18th century. They argue that mode 1 and its associated ideology of 'pure science', was promoted in the late 19th century and reinforced in the early 20th century as a way to 'defend and protect' the scientific establishment from external control. Since then, these two research modes have existed in parallel. Thus, these authors imply that what is in transition is our understanding of knowledge production, not the actual process (Weingart, 1997; Godin, 1998; Pestre, 2000; Etzkowitz and Leyderdorff, 2000). For a response of the proponents of 'mode 1 and mode 2' to the critics, see Nowotny (2000).
8. A major resistance to this thesis is related to its value judgement or normative character: mode 2 research is manifestly better adapted, more relevant and more efficient than mode 1, and thus should be used to inform policy making.
9. Despite disagreements with Gibbons and colleagues, Godin and Gingras (2000: 274) recognize the increasing distributed character of knowledge production and of intersectoral research collaborations. They found that in the 1990s the number of papers having non-university authors increased considerably, and so did the papers co-authored by researchers in different types of organizations.
10. There is plenty of evidence that the processes of allocating research funds and evaluating results have, in the last decade, incorporated other criteria than the judgement by peers (the sole *ex-ante* and post-evaluation mechanism in mode 1). For an overview of how research funding agencies have contributed to changes in the normative system of science, see Benner and Sandstrom (2000).
11. The process of socialization into the academic profession meant the internalization by the student that the 'most deeply held value of scientists is the extension of certified knowledge'. To achieve this, the researchers must behave according to a set of norms (Merton, 1973 [1942]). These norms are changing and thus constitute a new regime for science (Ziman, 1994; Etzkowitz, 1998). See also Ronayne (1997), Rip (2002).
12. Henkel (2002).
13. This argument has been put forward in a number of documents resulting from discussions between researchers and research policy institutions in the US and Europe. For a flavour of the arguments on the need for changes in graduate education see www.esf.org and CHEPS (2002) for Europe, and www.grad.washington.edu/envision for the US.

14. Blume (1995).

15. Some authors claim that academic training, excellence and standards of education can only be established through mode 1 (Krishna, 2004)

16. To the extent that sponsors influence the nature of research and the behaviour of researchers, it is to be expected that they have a considerable influence in shaping the conduct of research and the types of capacity being built in the countries where they operate (Benner and Sandstrom, 2000).

17. Universidad Nacional Agraria (UNA), Universidad Autonoma de Nicaragua-León (UNAN-León), Universidad Autonoma de Nicaragua-Managua (UNAM-Managua), Universidad Nacional de Ingeniería (UNI).

18. Sida/SAREC (2000: 6).

19. Sida (1998).

20. Porta (2004).

21. SAREC/IDRC (1991: 5-7).

22. Sida/SAREC (2000: 23).

23. Tait and Williams (1999); Benner and Sandstrom (2000); Etzkowitz and Leydesdorff (2000).

24. Nchinda (2002: 1705).

25. See CAPES (2002, http://ged.capes.gov.br/Agdw/silverstream/pages/frPesquisa Coleta.html). In 1999, the US awarded about 41,000 PhDs, 30% to foreign students (*Science and Engineering Indicators 2002*, table 2-26).

26. *Science and Engineering Indicators 2002*, table 5-43. Latin America saw the largest increase in scientific publications in the period 1986-1999, due to the Brazilian and Mexican contributions.

27. OECD (2001: 7).

28. UNDP (2001).

29. Scientific knowledge is created by a combination of codified (explicit) knowledge and tacit knowledge (Polanyi, 1958). Codified knowledge is contained and transmitted in books, articles, manuals, reports, etc. Tacit knowledge includes experience, personal skills, attitudes and scientific craftsmanship (Collins, 1995). To obtain tacit knowledge, one has to work with those who possess the knowledge, since it is not transmitted through codified sources

30. Mangematin (2000).

31. One motivation for the choice of the sandwich model is to foster links between Swedish and Nicaraguan researchers and thus develop capacities on both sides. Another motivation is to avoid the brain drain, as it is believed that if students do research work in their home country, they will work on a socially relevant topic under local research conditions. The sandwich model is also believed to contribute to institutional development because laboratories are built in the Southern institution for the researchers doing their thesis work (Sida, 1998: 29). The practice of sandwich PhD training for Southern researchers has become popular among donors such as DANIDA, NORAD and DFID, as well as the World Health Organization (Nchinda, 2002).

32. In 2001 the Nicaraguan government expenditures on higher education were US$35 million, of which US$25 million (73%) went to the four universities involved with SAREC. SAREC's contribution to the universities was US$800,000, about 3% of their budgets.

References

Benner, M. and Sandstrom, U. (2000) Institutionalizing the triple helix: research funding and norms in the academic sector. *Research Policy* 29: 291–301.

Blume, S. (1995) Problems and prospects of research training in the 1980s, in: OECD (Ed.) *Research Training: Present and Future*. Paris: OECD.

CAPES (2002, http://ged.capes.gov.br/Agdw/silverstream/pages/frPesquisaColeta.html).

CHEPS (Center for Higher Education Policy Studies) (2002) *Changing Modes of Knowledge Production and Labor Markets*. Proceedings of an international workshop, University of Twente, Enschede, the Netherlands.

Collins, H. (2000) What is tacit knowledge?, in: T. Schatzki *et al.* (Eds.) *The Practice Turn in Contemporary Theory*. London: Routledge, pp.107–119.

Etzkowitz, H. (1998) The norms of entrepreneurial science: cognitive effects of the new university–industry linkages, *Research Policy* 27: 823–833.

Etzkowitz, H. and Leydesdorff, L. (2000) The dynamics of innovation: from national systems and 'Mode 2' to the triple helix of university–industry–government relations. *Research Policy*, 29: 109–23.

Freeman, C. (1988) Japan: a new national system of innovation?, in: G. Dosi *et al.* (Eds.) *Technical Change and Economic Theory*. London: Pinter, pp.330–348.

Gibbons, M., Limoges, C., Nowotny, H., Schwartzman, S., Scott, P. and Trow, M. (Eds.) (1994) *The New Production of Knowledge*. London: Sage.

Godin, B. (1998) Writing performative history: The new New Atlantis? *Social Studies of Science* 28(3): 465–483.

Godin, B. and Gingras, Y. (2000) The place of universities in the system of knowledge production. *Research Policy* 29: 273–278.

Henkel, M. (2002) Current science policies and their implications for the concept of academic identity, in: CHEPS (2002) *Changing Modes of Knowledge Production and Labor Markets*. Proceedings of an international workshop, University of Twente, Enschede, the Netherlands, pp.55–69.

Krishna, V.V. (2004. Personal information.

Lundvall, B.-A. (Ed.) (1992) *National Systems of Innovation: Towards a Theory of Innovation and Interactive Learning*. London: Pinter.

Mangematin, V. (2000) PhD job market: professional trajectories and incentives during the PhD. *Research Policy* 29: 741–756.

Merton, R.K. (1973) [1942] The normative structure of science, in *The Sociology of Science*. Chicago: University of Chicago Press,

Nchinda, T.C. (2002) Research capacity strengthening in the South. *Social Science & Medicine*, 54: 1699–1711.

Nelson, R. (Ed.) (1993) *National Innovation Systems: A Comparative Analysis*. New York: Oxford University Press.

Nowotny, H. (2000) The production of knowledge beyond the academy and the market: A reply to Dominique Pestre. *Science, Technology and Society* 5(2): 183–194.

OECD (2001) *Using Knowledge for Development. The Brazilian Experience,* Paris: OECD.

Pavitt, K. (1998) The social shaping of the national science base. *Research Policy* 27: 793–805.

Pestre, D. (2000) The production of knowledge between academies and markets: A historical reading of the book 'The New Production of Knowledge'. *Science, Technology and Society* 5(2): 169–181.

Polanyi, M. (1958) *Personal Knowledge: Towards a Post Critical Philosophy*. Chicago: University of Chicago Press.

Porta, E.P. (2004) *Financiamiento de las Instituciones de Educación Superior en Nicaragua*, www.cresalc.org

Rip, A. (2002) Strategic research, post-modern universities and research training, in CHEPS (2002) *Changing Modes of Knowledge Production and Labor Markets*. Proceedings of an international workshop, University of Twente, Enschede, the Netherlands, pp.45–54.

Rip, A. and Van de Meulen, B. (1996) The post-modern research system. *Science and Public Policy*, 23(6): 343–352.

Ronayne, J. (1997) Research and the new universities towards mode 2, *ATSE Focus*, 98, www.atse.org.au/publications/focus/focus-ronayne.htm

SAREC/IDRC (1991) *Knowledge in the Pursuit of Change*. SAREC and IDRC.

Science and Engineering Indicators 2002. National Science Board, pp.5–7. www.nsf.gov/statistics/seind02/

Sida (1998) *Research Cooperation. I. An outline of Policy, Programmes and Practice*. Department for Research Cooperation, Stockholm, Sweden, p.37.

Sida/SAREC (2000) *Sida's Policy for Capacity Development*. Methods Development Unit, Stockholm, Sweden, p.26.

Tait, J. and Williams, R. (1999) Policy approaches to research and development: Foresight, framework and competitiveness. *Science and Public Policy*, 26(2): 101–112.

UNDP (2001) *Human Development Report: Making New Technologies Work for Human Development*. New York: UNDP, p.264.

Weingart, P. (1997) From 'finalization' to 'mode 2': Old wine in new bottles? *Social Science Information* 36(4): 591–613.

Ziman, J. (1994) *Prometheus Bound: Science in a Dynamic Steady State*. Cambridge: Cambridge University Press.

EPISTEMIC COMMUNITIES AND INFORMED POLICY MAKING FOR PROMOTING INNOVATIONS: THE CASE OF SINGAPORE

SUNIL MANI[1]

A group of developing countries, primarily in Asia, have emerged as important generators of new technologies. Among them, Singapore has shown one of the fastest rates of growth in generating local innovations. This chapter explains that to accomplish this, Singapore first developed a critical mass of research scientists and engineers, and then put in place a set of research grants to encourage both local and foreign enterprises to increase their investment in R&D. Singapore's impressive performance can be attributed not only to the existence of an innovation policy and the quality of the instruments of intervention in the technology arena, but also to the existence of epistemic communities within the machinery of government itself. In other countries without such communities to aid government policy making, most policy instruments fail to achieve the desired results. In the absence of informal professional networks, innovation policy making tends to be ad hoc and subject to political compulsion.

1. Introduction

An 'epistemic community' has been defined as 'a network of professionals with recognized expertise and competence in a particular domain and an authoritative claim to policy-relevant knowledge within the same domain or issue area'.[2] The existence of epistemic communities within otherwise bureaucratic bodies has enabled some developing countries to graduate from merely assembling goods to become the designers, manufacturers and exporters of high-technology products

This chapter discusses the role of epistemic communities in improving national innovation systems. Singapore was selected for two reasons. First, it has made dramatic improvements in its innovation system. Rather than replicating an elaborate bureaucracy in the form of a Ministry of Science and Technology, the country chose to create an epistemic community consisting of government officials, academics and international experts with domain-specific knowledge. Second, Singapore has successfully made the transition from being a manufacturer and exporter of electronic products, to one that is regarded as an important player in the international life sciences industry.

This chapter is structured as follows. Section 2 presents some evidence of the emergence of high-technology innovators in the developing world. This is followed by a brief discussion of the role of epistemic communities and their contribution to informed policy making. Section 3 analyzes the content and effect of Singapore's innovation policies, the instruments developed to implement them, and the impacts on the country's performance. Finally, section 4 offers some conclusions about the process of innovation policy making.

2. Epistemic communities and informed policy making

Innovation policies consist of a set of instruments, financial or otherwise, and institutions that are intended to lead to the creation of technological improvements in both products and processes. Innovation policies are usually designed by ministries of science and technology (or their equivalents) that are responsible for supporting technological change within national economies.

The success or effectiveness of an innovation policy depends not just on its design, but also on how well it is implemented. There is little discussion of the processes through which innovation policies are actually designed. There are no widely accepted standards or processes specifically for innovation policy making. In most democratic countries policy issues are subject to debate and discussions among stakeholders or components of the innovation system. In some cases these discussions take place through a policy dialogue that moves 'from green papers to white papers'.[3] Given the increasing complexities of policy design, even the preparation of a green paper requires considerable discussion and help from experts. Some countries bring together groups of experts variously described as national advisory councils or science technology advisers, while others rely on external experts or consultants.

It has been suggested that countries with sufficient internal expertise (for instance within national ministries or other policy-making bodies) are in a better position to design and implement good policies than countries that do not have such expertise. This is because the availability of experts will enable the policy-making bodies to process information, especially the technical information that is required to develop policy instruments, more effectively. In other words, countries may encourage the formation of epistemic communities that take the form of informal networks of professionals with recognized expertise and competence in a particular field, as well as an authoritative claim to policy-relevant knowledge about that field or issue. In less politically motivated cases, epistemic communities have a greater hand in the various stages of the policy-making process, including the introduction of policy alternatives, the selection of policies, and the building of national and international coalitions in support of those policies.

All organizations engage in some form of 'satisfying' or procedural rationality in their consideration of policy alternatives; 'if rationality is bounded, epistemic communities may be responsible for circumscribing the boundaries and delimiting the options'.[4] Epistemic communities need to be distinguished from bureaucratic bodies. The latter operate largely to preserve their missions and budgets, whereas epistemic communities apply their knowledge to a policy undertaking, subject to their normative objectives. Thus, members of an epistemic community are not policy entrepreneurs, although they may use the bureaucratic leverage they are able to acquire through their key positions within bureaucracies. Their behaviour is different from that of the individuals usually analyzed in terms of their bureaucratic constraints. They are often active in international policy dialogues and in national policy-making processes.[5] Therefore, the existence of epistemic communities within otherwise bureaucratic bodies has allowed some developing countries to graduate within a short time from being mere assemblers to designers, manufacturers and exporters of high-technology products.

3. The emergence of Singapore as a generator of high-technology innovations

Developing countries are not normally seen as generators of new technologies, but generally merely assemble or apply imported technologies. While this is certainly usually the case, a handful of developing countries have emerged as generators of new technologies. Although measuring and interpreting the outcomes of innovation is difficult,[6] the number of US patents granted to inventors from specific countries is a good indicator of the quantity and quality of innovative outputs. This is because it is extremely difficult, time-consuming and expensive to secure a patent in the United States, especially for developing countries where the largest firms are likely to be as big as most small and medium enterprises in developed countries. Consequently, there is a fair amount of self-selection by firms and institutions in developing countries who patent their best innovations in the US (see figure 1). Over the period 1985–2001, about 11 countries were awarded an average of 30 patents per year in the US.[7] These were Taiwan, Korea, Hong Kong, Singapore, India, South Africa, Brazil, China, Mexico, Argentina and Malaysia.

Singapore began to develop activities in the life sciences during the 1980s with the creation of a molecular biology research centre. It also increased funding for biomedical research at hospitals and universities, and established an ambitious training programme for life sciences researchers. Over the past few years, the government has intensified both science funding and industry promotion activities with the creation of a new Biomedical Sciences Research Council (BMSRC), and several new funds for supporting innovation and commercialization in the biotechnology and life sciences industries. Even though indigenous industry activities remain limited, the government is actively promoting Singapore as the preferred location for biotechnology and pharmaceutical companies in Asia.[8]

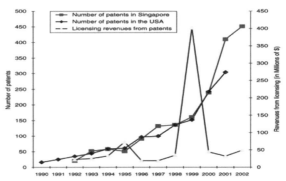

Figure 1. Patents granted to Singaporean inventors in Singapore and the USA, 1990–2001.
Sources: Agency for Science, Technology and Research (2003), USPTO (2003), World Bank (2003).

In the 1990s Singapore put in place a number of institutional and incentive systems designed to spur domestic technology-creating activities especially at the enterprise level. An examination of the performance of the domestic innovation system shows that the country has made significant progress in this direction, in both absolute and relative terms. The number of patents granted to Singaporean inventors has increased significantly – from less than 20 in the early 1990s to 300 in the USA and over 400 in Singapore in 2001. With high-tech products now accounting for more than 50% of manufactured exports, Singapore has the rare distinction of being a major competitor on world markets.

Singapore's innovation policies

The Singapore government introduced its innovation policies in two phases. During the first phase (1980–1991) the government played a passive role with respect to domestic technology development, and restricted its innovation policy to the development of small and medium enterprises and to engineering positive spillovers from foreign enterprises. During the second phase (since 1991) the government has been more explicit in its efforts to promote indigenous R&D by both foreign and domestic companies, and in establishing institutions such as the National Science and Technology Board (see table 1). This was also the time when Singapore's epistemic community was very pro-active.

Table 1. Singapore's innovation policy initiatives

1991	The National Science and Technology Board (NSTB) was established to develop the country into a centre of excellence in science and technology. The National Technology Plan set out the directions for promoting R&D in Singapore. A number of research institutes and centres were established.
1993	The Cluster Development Fund (CDF) was launched to catalyze the development of indigenous industries in high-growth clusters.
1995	The Innovation Development Scheme was launched.
1996	The Singapore Productivity and Standards Board (PSB), formed through the merger of NPB and SISIR, took over the role of SME development from the Economic Development Board (EDB). The National Science and Technology Plan (NSTP) and a US$4 billion R&D fund was launched to facilitate the development of S&T in Singapore. The Promising Local Enterprises (PLE) initiative was launched.
1997	The Committee on Singapore's Competitiveness was launched.
1998	Singapore One, the nationwide broadband multimedia infrastructure network, was launched.
1999	Industry 21, development blueprints for each manufacturing and exportable service clusters under the EDB, was launched. The Techno-entrepreneurship 21 Committee was established to develop and harness the potential of 'techno-entrepreneurs'. The Techno-entrepreneurship Investment Fund was launched to spur the development of the venture capital industry in Singapore.

| 2000 | The NSTB was converted into the Agency for Science, Technology and Research (A*STAR). |

Source: Economic Development Board.

The main institutional structure for S&T policy, the Singapore Science Council, was revamped in 1991 and renamed the National Science and Technology Board (NSTB) under the Ministry of Industry and Trade. Throughout the 1990s, the NSTB formulated and implemented all major policies with respect to innovation. In the recent past some of its tasks were transferred to another government agency, the Economic Development Board. Finally, in 2000 the NSTB was restructured and renamed the Agency for Science, Technology and Research (A*STAR), which comprises the Biomedical Research Council (BMRC), the Science and Engineering Research Council (SERC), Exploit Technologies Pte Ltd (ETPL), the A*STAR Graduate Academy (A*GA) and the Corporate Planning and Administration Division (CPAD).

Singapore's innovation policy instruments

Singapore has developed and applied a variety of policy instruments to promote indigenous science and technology research by both foreign and domestic companies. The first step was to increase the supply of technically trained human resources and to strengthen the technological infrastructure. In addition, the government has launched a variety of grant schemes and introduced fiscal incentives for companies to promote innovation. It has also encouraged the development of a venture capital industry to support technology start-ups, and has engineered positive spillovers from foreign direct investment (FDI).

1. Increasing the supply of technically trained human resources

Throughout the 1960s Singapore's emphasis was on a massive industrial training programme to upgrade the skills of its workers and to increase the supply of technicians and engineers who would eventually find employment in the numerous foreign companies that the state was in the process of encouraging. As the economy has developed, tertiary education has been expanded through two universities (the National University of Singapore and the Nanyang Technological University) and four polytechnics (Singapore, NgeeAnn, Temasek and Nanyang). Education has been a major item of public expenditure, accounting for about 22.4% of the government's recurrent expenditures,[9] since a substantial proportion of the cost of education is subsidized by the state. Over the decade 1989–1999 real expenditures on education increased by almost 20% per annum (see figure 2).

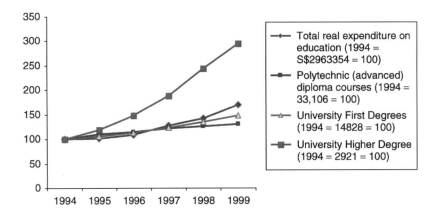

Figure 2. Expenditures on education, and enrolments at polytechnics and universities, 1994–1999.

Source: Department of Statistics (2000).

The education system in Singapore is biased in favour of science and technology subjects, and rightly so. Approximately 75% of enrolments at polytechnics and 62% at universities are in subjects such as engineering sciences, information technology, architecture and building technology, the health sciences and applied science and technology. Enrolments at both polytechnics and universities, in particular for higher-degree courses at universities, increased substantially over the period

In the field of science education, Singapore hopes to become the 'Boston of Southeast Asia' by developing the two universities to world-class standards. Substantial sums of money have been invested in improving their research facilities. The National University is in the process of setting up three specialized institutes linked to three areas in which Singapore has a comparative advantage – data storage, materials research and engineering, and medical informatics. The country is also supporting its graduates to undertake training abroad.

These policies on improving the quality of human resources have had two benefits: they have increased the supply of high-quality researchers, scientists and engineers, and have created a large pool of 'techno-entrepreneurs'.

2. *Strengthening the technological infrastructure*

A second policy instrument employed by the government of Singapore was the establishment of a number of research institutes and centres (RICs). Since 1991 the NSTB has established 13 RICs, each one concentrating on a specific area. These laboratories not only generate technologies themselves, but they also serve as a critical source of personnel for industry. The very existence of these institutes has encouraged local industry to collaborate with them in R&D projects. As noted above, R&D investments in these institutes have been increasing and now account for about 14% of the total.

It is interesting to note that Singapore established the RICs at a time when most other countries were rethinking the role of their own research institutes. The performance of these laboratories in Singapore has improved over time, although in terms of indicators such as the number of patents awarded and the revenue from them, no clear trends can yet be observed – it may be too early to assess them as a group. Among the 13 RICs, the most productive in terms of patents is the Institute of Microelectronics, which secured seven US patents in 1998-99. Some of these laboratories have linkages with both local and foreign firms through joint R&D projects.[10] These RIC–industry collaborations have resulted in the development of more than 70 new products and processes, some 20 of which have been commercialized, and have provided training for more than 580 researchers.[11]

3. *Incentive schemes: research grants*

Once it had achieved a critical mass of trained researchers, scientists and engineers, in 1991 Singapore began to employ a third policy instrument, the provision of grants for R&D. Today there are various grant schemes, including the Research Incentive Scheme for Companies (RISC), the Innovation Development Scheme (IDS), the Fund for Industrial Clusters (CDF), the Patent Application Fund Plus (PAF Plus) and the Technology for Enterprise Capability Upgrading Fund (T-UP).

Research Incentive Scheme for Companies (RISC)

The RISC encourages and assists companies and organizations to set up R&D centres and to develop in-house capabilities in strategic areas of technology in order to strengthen their competitiveness. Under the RISC programme a company can obtain a grant covering a maximum of 50% of its total research costs for a period of five years. There is no official maximum to the amount of grant. A company can receive RISC support only once, unless it changes course and decides to build up its research capacity in a different sector. In order to obtain a RISC grant, the company has to show a long-term research commitment, considerable research efforts and a perceptible growth in the number of researchers employed within the company. It is not known how many companies have benefited from this scheme.

Innovation Development Scheme (IDS)

The IDS is intended to encourage local and foreign companies to become more innovative. Under this scheme, companies are eligible to receive grants if their projects have not yet commenced at the time of application and involve product or process innovations that could lead to significant improvements in value added per employee, additional investments in new products or services, or the adoption of a new technology. The projects should also lead to significant contributions to the relevant industry or cluster. In the period 1995–1998, the IDS supported over 500 innovation projects (table 2). In 1996 alone, the scheme issued grants for 103 projects totalling US$80 million. For the period 1996–2001, these grants amounted to US$400 million.

Table 2. IDS grants by industry cluster (totals, 1995–1998)

Industry cluster	No. of projects
National Computer Board	154
Promising local enterprises	101
Electronics	73
Services	57
Engineering	56
Chemicals and life sciences	23
Other	49
Total	513

Source: Mani (2002).

Fund for Industrial Clusters (CDF)

The CDF is a special fund of US$650 million that was introduced in 1994 to support projects that carry too many risks for industrial companies to finance by themselves, and might thus not be realized. The fund is also used to create strategic alliances that will help secure investment projects in Singapore, to stimulate the growth of clusters of promising young industries, and to promote cooperation between Singapore and multinational companies. Since 1994 the CDF has spent US$325 million on 15 projects, in fields such as petrochemicals and other key industries. The government has announced its intention to increase the fund to US$1.3 billion.

Patent Application Fund Plus (PAF Plus)

PAF Plus is targeted at start-ups and helps defray the cost of patent applications, and thus encourages the diffusion of innovations. To be eligible to receive this grant, projects have two meet two conditions: the commercial benefits from inventions must accrue to Singapore and the project must not be receiving any other form of government assistance.

Technology for Enterprise Capability Upgrading Fund (T-UP)

T-UP is a grant fund that provides partial funding for research institutes to send research scientists and engineers on secondment to local enterprises for two years. It therefore helps local enterprises to develop their own in-house R&D capabilities. The scheme is open to all companies located in Singapore with at least 30% of their equity held by local investors.

4. Fiscal incentives

As the fourth policy instrument, the government offers five types of tax incentive for both foreign and domestic companies to promote local S&T research. These incentives include allowing companies to deduct some of the costs of in-house R&D from their income, to write off certain payments for R&D activities, and to offset the costs of acquiring patents. In addition, some royalty payments or technical assistance fees are payable to non-residents, including royalties, fees and contributions to R&D costs for the transfer of technology and know-how to Singapore. Thus, Singapore has created a comprehensive range of tax incentives for companies not just to create technologies through in-house R&D, but also to acquire technologies created outside the firm.

5. Venture capital

The fifth policy instrument the government uses is the promotion of venture capital. Singapore is one of the first developing countries to establish a thriving venture capital industry. The evolution of this industry can be traced back to 1983 when the first venture capital fund was raised.[12] Over the years approximately 60% of the total venture capital disbursements in Singapore have gone to technology-based entrepreneurs in the computer, electronics, information technology, biotechnology and telecommunications sectors. The government has supported the industry through a host of tax incentives. As a result, between 1995 and 2001, the volume of venture capital funds more than doubled, from US$6.2 billion to US$13.7 billion. The number of Singapore-based companies backed by venture capital doubled from 310 in 1998 to 635 in 2001.[13]

6. *Spillovers from foreign direct investment (FDI)*

Singapore has put in place some very imaginative policies intended to engineer positive spillovers from FDI to local small and medium enterprises (SMEs). The rationale behind these policies is to strengthen the technological infrastructure of the local SMEs and thereby make them attractive suppliers of inputs and other services to foreign companies. Under this programme, known as the Local Industries Upgrading Programme (LIUP), the government encourages multinational corporations to 'adopt' a group of SMEs and transfer technology and skills to them. The programme normally pays the salary of a full-time procurement expert to work for specified periods with the adopted firms and help them upgrade their production and management capabilities to the required standards.

In 1999, the LIUP focused on the development of new capabilities and talents to support key clusters in strategic areas such as total and integrated maintenance management for the process industry. Many multinationals in the process industry have adopted the outsourcing business model to reduce their overheads, and they are moving towards awarding larger and integrated maintenance contracts to local engineering companies with the required expertise.

Under the LIUP scheme, more than 3700 workers have so far been trained and certified in 13 critical skill sets identified by the process industry. A further 30 multinationals and 11 large local enterprises, government-linked companies and government agencies are partnering some 670 vendors in LIUP. Although this is an industrial policy instrument, Singapore has used it effectively to strengthen its SME sector.

A second scheme in this direction is a collaboration initiative wherein the Economic Development Board encourages collaboration and strategic partnerships among industry players, acting as a 'matchmaker' where appropriate. Promising local SMEs can benefit from collaboration with multinationals or other local companies by being able to access new technologies, products or markets. Likewise, multinationals can benefit from partnerships with promising local enterprises that can provide competitive products, original designs or equipment manufacturing.[14]

Singapore's performance

Singapore's performance cannot be explained solely by the fact that it has better schemes for financing innovation. Rather, it can be attributed to its earlier policy on human resource development, which led to substantial improvements in both the number and the quality of researchers, scientists and engineers. In addition, the Singapore government introduced its innovation policy instruments in exactly the right sequence. It first developed a critical mass of human resources, and once this was achieved, it put in place a set of research grants to encourage both local and foreign enterprises to invest in R&D. This was of course also facilitated to a large extent by these firms' strong demand for innovation, since most of their products were sold on international rather than local markets.

To elaborate on this sequencing, the government's innovation policies took into account both instruments and institutions both for creating technologies locally and for enabling local firms to derive maximum benefits from technology imports through both FDI and licensing. Both of these policies were in turn contingent upon other policies aimed at, first, increasing the supply of scientists and engineers, and then improving quality of training.

This policy, in turn, resulted in government support to innovations through two mutually exclusive routes. First, the government created an army of 'techno-entrepreneurs', supported by state grants, favourable tax policies and venture capital, who then established technology-based SMEs. The most promising of these SMEs were identified and given additional financial support to become the large companies of tomorrow through a grant scheme known as the 'promising local enterprises' initiative.[15] Second, an increase in the availability of technically trained human resources led to a phenomenal increase in the density of scientists and engineers.

4. Conclusions

Informed policy-making leads to better and more relevant policies demanded by the users – firms and research establishments. Most countries interpret innovation policies in terms of a variety of financial instruments. Although the availability of finance is an important requirement for technology-generating activities, its maintenance leading to optimal outcomes depends very much on the availability of a critical mass of qualified scientists and engineers.

Policy instruments have to be logically sequenced. This is much more easily said than done, however. In most countries innovation policies are designed (often very half-heartedly) by bureaucrats who may not be personally involved in design of the policy instruments for their implementation. Some countries seek the services of external experts (foreign or local) in policy design. But unless it is internalized by the agency responsible for implementation, the exercise is unlikely to be successful and cannot be replicated in the country over time. This is because policy instruments need to reviewed and redesigned in accordance with changing government priorities and the stage of technological development of the country.

The existence of an epistemic community or network of policy specialists who meet outside formal bureaucratic channels to discuss specific issues, set agendas, and formulate policy alternatives can in fact lead to informed policy making. Singapore has apparently managed to establish such a community within the science and technology administrative apparatus itself.

In Singapore, the epistemic community involved in innovation policy making is composed of the National Science and Technology Board (NSTB) and its recent incarnation, the Agency for Science, Technology and Research (A*STAR), which works in close coordination with the Economic Development Board (EDB). The agency's Corporate Planning and Administration Division played a coordinating role in getting this community up and running. The country has also made use of international experts from time to time. This has led to logically sequenced innovation policies and instruments that have produced very desirable outcomes. Singapore is unique among developing countries in that it has responded effectively to the needs of its innovation system.

Notes

1. Dr Sunil Mani (mani@cds.ac.in) is professorial fellow, Centre for Development Studies, Trivandrum 695011, Kerala, India.

2. Haas (1992: 3).
3. South Africa's 1996 innovation policy was designed through this mode of green paper to white paper (see Mani, 2002). However, when the recent innovation policy was announced (contained in the 2002 National R&D strategy) no such consultation took place.
4. Hass (1992: 16).
5. Edwards (2001) uses the notion of epistemic communities to analyze issues such as authority, hierarchy, recruitment and conflict in open source software communities (http://opensource.mit.edu/papers/kasperedwards-ec.pdf).
6. Smith (2004).
7. Mani (2002).
8. Asian Technology Information Program (2002).
9. Singapore Department of Statistics (2000).
For example, the Institute of Molecular and Cell Biology collaborates or has collaborated with pharmaceutical and biotechnology companies such as Pfizer (USA), Amylin (USA), Lynx Therapeutics (USA), Genzyme (USA), Milipore (USA), Glaxo Research Group (UK), Boehringer Mannheim (Germany), Applied Genetics (USA), Pharmacia Biotech (USA), and Terragen Diversity (Canada), and with Asian companies such as Wiltech Agro, Gene Singapore, Gene Singapore China and MediPearl.
10. Singapore Ministry of Trade and Industry (1999: 74-75).
11. Wang (2004).
12. Economic   Development   Board   website   (accessed   10   March   2004): www.sedb.com/etc/medialib/downloads/media_releases.Par.0010.File.tmp/Charts-Innovation%20&%20Enterprise.pdf.
13. Economic Development Board (www.sedb.com/edbcorp/sg/en_uk/index/ in_the_ news/press_releases/2002/economic_development4.html).
14. This grant scheme was introduced in 1995. There is a 'top 100 list' of 'promising local enterprises', selected by the EDB as possible Singaporean 'multinationals for the next century'. It strives to push each of these enterprises to a turnover of SGD100 million (US$60 million) by 2005. The list is intended to encourage innovation, and to help cultivate a new generation of entrepreneurs. The companies are then offered additional incentives. In 1999, 45 companies achieved sales revenues of more than US$100 million (up from US$31 million in 1998), and their average revenue was US$75 million (up from US$54 million). The scheme has also been successful in raising their productivity, which is now about 12 percentage points above the industry average

References

Agency for Science, Technology and Research (2003) *National Survey of R&D in Singapore 2002,* Singapore: Agency for Science and Technology Research.
Asian Technology Information Program (2002) *ATIP: 02.052: Life Sciences Promotion in Singapore*, Tokyo: ATIP.
Edwards, K. (2001) *Epistemic Communities, Situated Learning and Open Source Software Development.* Paper prepared for the workshop on Epistemic Cultures and the Practice of Interdisciplinarity, Trondheim, Norway.
(http://citeseer.ist.psu.edu/edwards01epistemic.html)
Haas, P.M. (1992) Introduction: epistemic communities and international policy coordination, *International Organization,* 46: 1–35.

Mani, S. (2002) *Government, Innovation and Technology Policy: An International Comparative Analysis,* Cheltenham, UK and Northampton, MA,: Edward Elgar.

Singapore Department of Statistics (2000) *Yearbook of Statistics 2000*, Singapore: Ministry of Trade and Industry.

Singapore Ministry of Trade and Industry (1999) *Economic Survey of Singapore*, Singapore: Economic Development Board

Smith, K. (2004) Measuring innovation, in J. Fagerberg *et al.* (Eds, 2004) *The Oxford Handbook of Innovation*, Oxford: Oxford University Press, pp.148–177.

USPTO (2003) *Patent Counts by Country/State and Year, All Patents, All Types, January 1, 1977–December 31, 2001,* Washington, DC: US Patent and Trademark Office.

Wang, C. (2004) The emergence of Singapore venture capital industry: investment characteristics and vale added activities, in A. Bartzokas and S. Mani (Eds, 2004) *Financial Systems, Corporate Investment in Innovation, and Venture Capital*, Northampton, MA: Edward Elgar, pp.225–251.

World Bank (2003) *World Development Indicators 2003*. Washington, DC: World Bank (on CD-ROM).

SCIENCE FOR TRANSFORMATION: RESEARCH AGENDAS AND PRIORITIES IN SOUTH AFRICA

JOHANN MOUTON[1]

How do research agendas reflect and represent the research interests of different constituencies? In South Africa, public sector research is currently being steered and shaped as a means to effect reconstruction and transformation in a society in transition. South African science is driven by a very broad and ambitious transformative agenda. One of the priorities is the reconstruction of the science system to address the needs and demands of the majority of citizens. This chapter assesses to what extent the government and its various S&T agencies are succeeding in this endeavour.

1. Introduction

In 1992, the African National Congress (ANC) commissioned a review of the state of science and technology in South Africa. Three of thee main conclusions of this study, sponsored by the IDRC, were that the science and technology (S&T) system inherited from decades of apartheid was fragmented and uncoordinated, did not serve the interests of all South Africans, and was ineffective and inefficient.[2] When the ANC government came to power in 1994, the new government used these and other findings as a point of departure in starting to reshape South African's S&T system. In its green paper (1995) and subsequent white paper on S&T (1996) the government committed itself to creating a new policy framework for public science, conducting a system-wide review of the national system of innovation in order to establish its strengths and weaknesses and future priorities, and establishing new structures to develop, implement and monitor the new policy framework.

The key motif of the 1996 white paper on S&T was the concept of a *national system of innovation*. More recently, in the National R&D Strategy (2002), the Department of Science and Technology explained this emphasis on a national system of innovation (NSI) as follows:

'The new government faced challenges in basic development. Having focused on the future for so long in the struggle, we now had to deal with the urgent service delivery needs of the present. Not surprisingly, the new funding scenarios required re-direction of the remaining technology competencies towards missions emphasizing quality of life and economic competitiveness. However, the emphasis was on reprioritization rather than the funding of new missions. Within this policy space, the White Paper on Science and Technology approved by Cabinet in 1996, established a policy framework for science and technology in South Africa based on the concept of a National System of Innovation'.[3]

Two key tenets of the notion of an NSI have 'guided' S&T policy, resource allocation and institutional 're-arrangement' since 1996. These are an emphasis on aligning the NSI with national socio-economic imperatives and frameworks, and the imperative to transform the system to reflect the larger demographics of the country. Underpinning both goals was a clear sense that the NSI should meet the demands and serve the interests of the entire nation, and not any specific sectoral interests.

This chapter addresses three specific questions. First, whose (research) demands are being addressed in South African science today, and to what purpose? Second, how are the research interests and demands of various constituencies in South African society articulated and represented on the national research agenda? Third, what modes of research (production) predominate in public sector R&D institutions in South Africa, and do these support a transformative agenda? The chapter then offers some observations about new, emerging forms of articulating research demand that suggest alternative modes of engagement between knowledge producers and users.

2. Whose research demands are addressed?

The South African science community is well aware of and recognizes the urgent need to undertake scientific research for development and in support of development objectives. The National Plan on Higher Education, released by the Department of Education in March 2002, emphasizes that research within higher education institutions should sustain current research strengths and promote the kinds of research and other knowledge outputs that are required to meet national development needs, and that will enable the country to become competitive in a new global context.[4]

The National R&D Strategy, published in the same year, states unequivocally that research and innovation should be aimed at poverty alleviation and improving the overall quality of life of South African citizens. It is significant that, in this statement, the department specifically mentions 'rural communities, women and the poor' as the primary end-users of innovations, and recognizes that 'innovations are needed to address poverty and that new (technological) approaches are required' in the process of sustainable rural development.[5] Even in developed and highly industrialized democracies where there are usually explicit structures and mechanisms to ensure fair distribution of access to knowledge production and its benefits, there is evidence that the 'fruits' of science and technology do not serve everyone equally.

In developing countries there is an added imperative to ensure that research serves the needs and demands of the poor, the illiterate and the marginalized. This is not only because of their more urgent needs and the potential greater benefit and value they can derive from the effects of research, but also because the demands of these groups are often not represented in national bodies and in organizations where decisions about research and research funding are taken. More often than not, the poor and marginalized have no access to such bodies; they are not well represented, or – in the worst cases – are unable to voice their concerns in a coherent and articulate fashion.

During the apartheid years, and specifically in the late 1970s and 1980s, various civil society organizations emerged to give voice to the disenfranchised and marginalized majority in South Africa. An interesting phenomenon was the emergence of numerous research NGOs and centres, many of them on the campuses of universities (predominantly historically black and English-medium universities), that deliberately and publicly aligned themselves with communities and interest groups in civil society (rural communities, rural women, underdeveloped and poorer areas). These organizations were 'hybrid' centres – they conducted research (usually in a participatory and critical fashion) but they were also deliberately activist and interventionist, constantly advocating the cause of the powerless and disenfranchised majority.[6]

These centres were characterized by the fact that they engaged in ideological and social critique utilizing participatory research methodologies (e.g. feminist and post-colonial approaches, participatory action research methods). They were closely involved with local communities to the extent that these communities had direct representation on their governing bodies. In particular, their research projects were defined in such a manner as to serve the interests of such local constituencies, usually involving a critique of apartheid policies and practices. As a result no public funding was available for these centres, and they were therefore funded by overseas donors and development agencies such as CIDA, Danida, DfID, IDRC, Sida, and the Ford and Mellon Foundations.

With the normalization of the research landscape in the post-apartheid era, many of these 'critical' research centres lost their overseas funding. Many universities decided that the centres had to be involved both in research and academic programmes in order to remain on campus. Most of them had no involvement in teaching and learning, and consequently lost their institutional base on university campuses. In addition, the national Human Sciences Research Council (HSRC) was transformed into a credible national research organization. This meant that the research previously conducted by these critical research NGOs was now increasingly being catered for by established academic centres, the HSRC and within some government departments. The death knell for many of these research NGOs came in the late 1990s, when the government decided that the majority of overseas development aid was to be channelled through government agencies or departments.[7]

By the turn of the century, the research NGO sector had shrunk appreciably, and applied and policy-oriented social and development research in South Africa was pretty much being conducted within government departments, the HSRC or academic centres on university campuses. Therefore, it is appropriate to ask whose interests and demands are currently being addressed in the current configuration of research organizations? In other words, are the interests of the poor and marginalized now adequately represented on the research agendas of South African university centres, government research departments and science councils?

In 2002, on behalf of the National Advisory Council on Innovation, the Centre for Research on Science and Technology (CREST) at Stellenbosch conducted a survey of the utilization of public research.[8] This survey targeted researchers in all fields of public science, including all universities and the science councils. Since one of the objectives of the study was to establish the nature and extent of the utilization of publicly funded R&D,

the respondents were asked to specify the major intended beneficiaries of their research programme or project. The results are shown in table 1.

Table 1. Intended beneficiaries of research programmes and projects (%) in 2002.

Intended beneficiaries	Type of research organization			Total projects	Cluster totals
	Science councils	Universities	Technikons		
Colleagues, peers in own discipline	18	32	31	27	39
Colleagues, peers in other disciplines	8	14	12	12	
Contracting agencies	10	6	7	7	47
Industry/firms	18	11	14	14	
Government	16	11	13	13	
Specific interest groups	17	12	13	13	
General public/ society/ community	13	14	14	14	14
Totals	100	100	100		
No. of options mentioned	1276	2317	366		

The responses in the first two rows (colleagues in own and other disciplines) typically refer to fundamental and basic research. If one ignores these responses, it becomes clear that a huge proportion of research across all types of research organization is carried out for specific contracting agencies, industry, government and specific interest groups. The percentages in the category 'general public, society and community' are slightly misleading as further inspection of the open-ended responses shows that most respondents interpreted this to refer to rather general and open-ended benefits. Most researchers who selected this option did not have a specific benefit or value in mind, but indicated that their research would 'in general' be of value to society or the public.

The other category of interest is the 'specific interest group'. Out of more than 175 open-ended comments and responses, the major beneficiaries listed here were health practitioners, teachers, consultants, community workers and organizations, donors and international funding agencies, farmers, unions, professional groups (engineers, dentists, doctors, lawyers) and industry associations. The number of responses was small, however, and in each case less than ten cases were listed.

This leaves three main categories of intended beneficiaries: specific contracting agencies, government and industry. Since the first is very likely to be a government department or company, it effectively reduces to two, government and industry. These findings are not that surprising if we look more closely at the main sources of funding for the projects documented in the CREST survey.

The science councils in South Africa (such as the Agricultural Research Council, Human Sciences Research Council and the Council for Scientific and Industrial Research) all receive annual block grants from parliament, and all of them augment these grants with contract research commissioned by government departments, business and industry (see table 2).

Table 2. South African science councils: main sources of funding, 2002.

Sources of funding	Total value of grants (R000)	%
Parliamentary grants	621 830	52.2
Business contracts	241 540	20.3
Government contracts	68 096	5.7
Other science councils	85 707	7.2
Sales of goods	53 102	4.4
Other sources, including international	121 653	10.2
Totals	**1 191 928**	**100.0**

Research at South African universities and universities of technology is for the most part funded by national agencies such as National Research Foundation (NRF), the Medical Research Council and the Water Research Commission, but, as table 3 shows, government contracts and industrial commissions are significant 'third stream'[9] sources of funding – business support constitutes 27% of all sources of research income. If one were to include other sources, which include government contracts, one would have to add another 28%.

It is clear that a significant proportion of public research in South Africa is both funded by and carried out for government and industry. The available information provides little evidence of many projects implemented directly for civil society organizations. This observation is not surprising. In most developed systems of innovation, the bulk of research funding also originates from industry or government. Similarly, research commissioned by a contracting agency is more likely to be of direct benefit to that agency. One could argue, of course, that many government-funded projects might be aimed at benefiting local communities and organizations, either directly or indirectly. However, another key question still remains unanswered: How, if at all, are the interests of these constituencies represented and articulated on the agendas of national S&T institutions? Are there adequate mechanisms in place to ensure that their 'authentic' interests are properly articulated on national research agendas?

Table 3. Universities and institutes of higher education: sources of funding, 2002.

Sources of funding	Total value of grants (R000)	%
National Research Foundation (NRF)/ Medical Research Council (MRC)		
Technology and Human Resources for Industry Programme (THRIP)	133 500	7.6
Innovation Fund		
University own funds	582 000	33.1
Business/private sector	480 000	27.3
Overseas donors	75 000	4.3
Other sources, including government	485 000	27.6
Totals	**1 755 500**	**99.9**

3. How are research agendas constructed?

The need for the transformation of South African science in the early 1990s was driven by the realization that the research interests of the majority of citizens were not being served by apartheid science. One of the most damning critiques of the apartheid regime was that it had developed one of the most sophisticated nuclear and defence R&D industries in the world, a vibrant energy research industry and various internationally competitive research niches, but was unable to provide shelter, clean water or basic services to the majority of its population.

The principal instruments through which national (and institutional) agendas are constructed and put into effect are policy 'statements' (symbolic measures), funding programmes (financial measures), evaluation and review processes (accountability measures) and performance-related processes (recognition and reward measures).

Policy statements, found in white papers, national acts (such as the founding act of the NRF) and national research strategies and plans – formulate and embody a national vision of where the system of innovation should be headed. Policies are normative discourses that specify desired end-states. As such, policies typically have symbolic value. So when the White Paper on S&T prioritizes poverty alleviation as the main end goal of science and technology, it sends a very strong signal to the research community. Similarly, when indigenous knowledge systems are identified as a specific new field of research on the national agenda, it signifies a new intent on the part of government.

However, policy statements are rather empty if the necessary tools are not put in place to give effect to these desired end-states. *Funding programmes, evaluations* and *performance-related measures* are generally recognized as three such measures of implementation. Since 1994, the South African government, through its funding agencies, has established various new funding programmes to give effect to its S&T policies.[10] With respect to evaluations and review programmes, the South African system of innovation currently has two major forms of research review[11] – evaluations by independent panels and the institutional audit review process.

The construction of research agendas can be approached from two perspectives. First, the *directionality* of agenda construction or, in other words 'who are the main actors driving the process?' Second, the degree of *interventionism* in agenda setting or the 'steering versus shaping' of research priorities.[12]

In South Africa, instances of predominantly government-driven and strongly interventionist agenda setting in public sector R&D can be witnessed. Policies, funding programmes, reviews and performance-related measures are all examples of government mechanisms put in place to give expression to its research goals and priorities. Even a cursory inspection of the governance structures of the major agencies (NRF/Innovation Fund/ THRIP/MRC) shows that government, higher education, business and industry are well represented on their governing bodies, whereas civil society and, especially, local communities are not.

There are a few spaces where 'alternative' setting of research agendas can be found. The most obvious ones are research in development issues – of which the South Africa–Netherlands Partnership for Alternatives in Development (SANPAD) initiative is the most significant, and research into HIV/AIDS. In both of these areas, somewhat ironically, overseas funding[13] has enabled local researchers to pursue more open research agendas outside formal government structures and funding regimes. From its inception in 1997, the SANPAD programme actively pursued ways and means to involve representative and diverse groupings in identifying research priorities and modalities.[14] One such mechanism was a stakeholder conference in November 1997, which attracted nearly 100 researchers, practitioners, policy makers and NGO representatives who shared an interest in 'alternatives for development'. The fact that the SANPAD could work outside the 'formal' government structures and funding paradigms made it possible for it to be more innovative in how it wanted to shape research and capacity building in this area. But initiatives such as these are few. The evidence overwhelmingly indicates that research agenda setting is increasingly dominated and directed by government.

Since 1994 the scientific community in South Africa has bought into the macro policy agendas and strategies of the post-apartheid regime.[15] There is clear evidence of what one could call the 'endogenization' of national priorities and goals in the research programmes and projects of many scientists in the system. The fact that the majority of scientists subscribe to the new national goals and priorities as inscribed in the new policy documents, is in itself laudable. However, it still does not mean that there is any guarantee that the pursuit of these goals and centrally defined agendas are in the interests of the poor and marginalized! In fact, this issue becomes even more problematic when one realizes that the demographic profile of the scientists in the system has not changed substantially over the past ten years.

When it came to power in 1994, the post-apartheid regime inherited a deeply skewed public science system. Various studies by CREST have shown that although there have been some positive shifts towards greater participation of female and black scholars (there have been huge increases in enrolment and, to a lesser degree, in graduations of black postgraduate students) and of female scientists across the system (although significant disparities remain). Although recent survey data show that the science councils now employ significant numbers of black and female researchers, the system is still heavily skewed and remains unrepresentative of the population.[16]

The production of scientific knowledge in South Africa continues to be dominated by white, male and ageing scientists. More specifically, The CREST surveys show that between 1990 and 2002, 80% of all peer-reviewed articles were published by men, although they constituted only slightly more than 60% of the R&D workforce. Similarly, 90% of all articles were produced by white scientists even though black scientists and academics constitute approximately 30% of the research workforce. The science system is also highly skewed at the institutional level. The weight of the South African science base – especially basic science – increasingly resides in a small number of historically advantaged institutions. The 'big five' universities (Cape Town, Natal, Pretoria, Stellenbosch and Witwatersrand) produce 64% of all scientific output (peer-reviewed articles), 53% of all PhDs, and are awarded 52% of all THRIP funding by the NRF.[17]

The scientific community in South Africa does not in any way represent the demographics of the country. Although there is evidence that this community has 'bought into' the new transformation agenda and is actively supporting many of the goals of the new national R&D strategy, their interests might not represent the real interests of the majority of the population. There is also evidence that those universities located in the rural areas – such as Fort Hare, North, Venda and Zululand – are increasingly repositioning themselves as universities *for* development. In an interesting repeat of history, these universities are increasingly – as did the Afrikaans universities in the 1930s and 1940s – defining themselves as institutions that need to meet the local demands of their surrounding communities. Historically, Afrikaans universities such as Potchefstroom, Free State, Pretoria and (to a lesser extent) Stellenbosch, saw themselves as 'volksuniversiteiten' that must first serve the training and educational needs of the Afrikaner nation, and then science in the wider sense. The same trend is noticeable with regard to the rural black universities listed above. If this trend continues, it might counteract some of the 'centralist' government initiatives on agenda setting outlined above.

4. What is the nature of knowledge production for social transformation?

The third issue to be addressed concerns the nature of research or knowledge production. As shown in section 2, the bulk of public science in South Africa is currently funded by and conducted for government, industry and business. Some authors have argued that these trends are in line with a shift from mode 1 to mode 2 forms of knowledge production.[18] The distinction between mode 1 and mode 2, introduced by Gibbons *et al.*,[19] points amongst other things to a shift from research agendas that are solely or mainly constructed by the scientists themselves (in universities and R&D laboratories) which is typical of mode 1, to research agendas that are developed in the 'context of application' (typical of mode 2).

The Gibbons thesis became very popular in South African S&T and higher education circles in the mid-1990s.[20] For some commentators, mode 2 equated with research that has its origins outside academia and more specifically within local communities and areas in which civil society is active. Mode 2 came to be identified (perhaps even somewhat idealistically) with collaborative and participatory modes of research. This thesis was so widely held that both the report of the National Commission on Higher Education (NCHE) and the White Paper on S&T, both published in 1996, alluded to it.

The NCHE report recommended that higher education institutions broaden their activities to encompass at least four types of research. These included *traditional research*, i.e. basic or fundamental research that seeks to extend the knowledge base within a discipline; *applications-driven research*, understood as discipline-based research directed towards resolving practical problems arising from social, economic or technological needs; *strategic research* commissioned by government or industry to mobilize a group, usually a trans-disciplinary group, to address an identified need or problem; and *participation-based research*, particularly research on social issues, that can only be effected through interactions and with the active participation of both the research group and the community it wishes to serve.[21]

The sentiments expressed in the NCHE report are echoed in many sections of the White Paper on S&T, but nowhere as clearly as in the following passage:

'Traditional ways of producing knowledge within single disciplines and institutions are being supplemented by knowledge generated within various applied contexts. This is knowledge that is collaboratively created within multidisciplinary and transdisciplinary research programmes directed to specific problems identified within social and economic systems. A national system of innovation benefits from "knowledge practitioners" being located in multiple knowledge generating sites and institutions such as higher education institutions, government and civil society research organizations. Setting up a national system of innovation in South Africa that will stimulate such collaborative, multidisciplinary, applications-based research will require new policy, funding and organizational arrangements, including provision for training a new generation of scientists and technologists oriented towards the solving of real problems'.[22]

The reality has turned out to be somewhat different, however. The Gibbons thesis posits a general shift towards application-driven research. But there are obviously various contexts for applying knowledge and research in a knowledge-based society: government, business, industry, multinational corporations, overseas donors and funders, NGOs and civil society. It would be a mistake to assume that the shift towards mode 2 necessarily means a shift towards more participatory and action-type community-based research. In fact, as the results of the CREST survey show (see above), the shift has been towards the poles of contract and consultancy-type research, rather than towards development and community-based research.

5. The homogenization of demand?

The cumulative effect of the trends discussed above can be described as the increasing homogenization of research demand in the South African S&T

system. One could even formulate this development as a more general thesis. The homogenization of demand occurs under the following conditions: where there is a tendency in S&T systems to steer the system either centrally or from the top, or both, and where, even within mainstream 'formal' science, there is an increasing blurring of boundaries between institutional missions.

The first condition, in effect, means that the research agenda is defined by central policy documents rather than driven from below by 'grassroots-level intelligence'. This is an ironic development given South Africa's political history. The vibrant system that was in place in the 1980s and early 1990s, with broad-based participation of community organizations and NGOs in national research initiatives, gradually gave way to developments in the mid-1990s that involved the 'decoupling' of these organizations from mainstream, academic and institutional science.

The second condition, the increasing blurring of institutional missions, is produced by two mutually reinforcing developments – the continuing pressure on science councils and universities to augment their incomes through third-stream funding. This has already led to a noticeable increase in the amount of contract and commissioned research within all these institutions. It is also driven by a kind of market failure – poor academic salaries, coupled with the lack of indigenous knowledge production and analytical capacity in government, have increased the demand for 'academic' (as opposed to freelance) consultants. Again, the agenda setting occurs within the commissioning agencies, i.e. the demands and interests of business and government are articulated and met, but not necessarily those of civil society and the public in general.

So who loses out with the increasing 'homogenization' of research demand? In one sense, it is the academics and scholars who do not have the money or time to pursue basic, fundamental and curiosity-driven research questions, and, of course, those in civil society who are still too far removed from institutional structures and networks to have their interests articulated and voiced.

There is a related dimension of these trends that should not be forgotten. The 'homogenization' of demand is not only about whose interests are being served, but also about the 'increasing conformity' or consensus that creeps into the system. The homogenization of demand could in practice also lead to a non-critical (articulation of) demand. Where the articulation of demand is increasingly steered by government and its agencies, and such demand increasingly represents the interests of government and industry, it is not too far-fetched to conclude that research interests that challenge and are critical of the consensus view are not reflected on national agendas.

6. Articulating the demand for research

The challenge can be articulated as follows: how can a developing country such as South Africa create/generate demand for research that is *heterogeneous* in terms of the range of interests it serves, *representative* of who is involved in the research, and *critical* in terms of the nature of the research to be conducted?

Instead of relying exclusively or depending on formal steering by government, other actors also need deliberately to pursue modes of interactive agenda setting. What are required are initiatives that strengthen the interface between research and the public sphere and incentive instruments that encourage more 'interactive engagement' between scientists and their 'publics'.

This rest of this section briefly examines a case that demonstrates new forms of such 'interactive engagement'. Following from the CREST survey on knowledge utilization conducted for the National Advisory Council on Innovation (NACI) in 2002, researchers identified examples of 'non-standard' forms of research.[23] They reported at least 10 research projects that utilized innovative organizational forms in engaging with funders, users and other stakeholders (e.g. practitioners).

One of these is the Arid Zone Ecology Forum (AZEF), an informal network that brings together, at annual conferences, researchers, conservationists, postgraduate students, farmers and other interested groups who are concerned with addressing and finding solutions to problems in the arid region of southern Africa, which extends from the Cape into Namibia and parts of Botswana. The AZEF network comprises 'people from state, provincial, educational and research institutions, as well as farmers and individuals from the private sector'.[24] Researchers and government officials come mainly from the departments of agriculture, environment and conservation in their respective institutions. One of the researchers associated with AZEF for some time commented on the value of the informal gatherings as follows:

> I think AZEF is a hugely important body for informally coordinating research, without rules, but just by mixing with fellow scientists and colleagues on a very friendly basis and listening to them and perhaps offering some constructive criticism on their projects and they on yours, you reach a much more effective goal, your results are much more effective in the end. AZEF plays a

major role in this and it certainly is growing amongst the Arid Zone scientists and the farmers who are qualified and can benefit from this sort of meeting. AZEF is increasing in stature and it is shown by the numbers who attend these meetings every year. (Interview with AZEF researcher)

These comments suggest that the AZEF does play a role, albeit a small one, in the process from knowledge production to utilization. Most pertinently, it provides a forum for researchers and practitioners to get together and share ideas about innovations and debate solutions to common problems. The value placed on informal interactions within the forum ensures that members feel comfortable talking about their work to people whom they know are interested in what they do and can give them constructive feedback. This 'homely' feel is further entrenched through the location of the annual AZEF meetings in small rural towns, as one of the organizers explained:

They are not in the major cities. ... it is quite nice because the meetings are very informal. And getting people together in a small town – they can't disappear to do other things at night. They are always forced to interact. The other thing I like about it is that taking 100-120 people into a small town does quite a lot for the economy. You fill the guesthouses and you use local caterers and hire the town hall, which is quite nice. And what we also do is we have a field trip in the middle of the meeting. So we go and look at specific projects that are being undertaken in the vicinity. The researchers introduce their work and we all discuss it. (Interview with Mark Anderson)

The location of the annual AZEF conference thus serves as a strategy to get participants to interact formally and informally, to network and also to engage with 'on site' research projects. The participants appreciate both the formal and the informal aspects of the meetings:

The formal part of the conference is usually two or two and a half days. This year because we got so many papers it will be two and a half days of presentations, talks as well as poster presentations. We also have what we call round table discussions, so this year we only have one. But if there is a topic we think needs input and time we will have informal round table discussions, usually in the pub over a few beers. Someone will introduce the topic and it is a more relaxed way. You find that people who generally wouldn't contribute in the meeting feel much easier about these round table discussions. (Interview with Mark Anderson)

In this context, the round table discussions serve as a specific strategy to get participants to talk and to share research ideas and possibly reflect on practical implications of the implementation of those ideas. This case shows how non-standard organizational forms are utilized in the production and utilization of research findings. The organization developed from its respective constituencies and is not directly related to government initiatives (although AZEF receives support from the National Research Foundation) and performs a strategic function in bringing together a wide range of knowledge producers and users at grassroots level. The nature of the engagements is such that the research interests of the diverse members arise 'naturally' from these interactions. There does not seem to be much in the way of central steering or top-down directives. The articulation of research demand occurs in self-organizing systems which in turn are embedded in other related networks.

Research demand can be articulated and developed in ways that complement and strengthen the more formal government-driven mechanisms described in the first sections of this chapter. The value of such 'non-standard' organizations is that they strengthen the absorptive capacity of informal research organizations and they also indirectly develop much needed capacity of civil society to act as knowledge brokers for their respective constituencies. In the final analysis, in order to ensure a more heterogeneous, representative and critical articulation of research demand that will serve the transformative agenda of a country such as South Africa, it is essential that the role of such intermediary agencies is revitalized and expanded.

Notes

1. Johann Mouton (jm6@sun.ac.za) is director of the Centre for Research on Science and Technology (CREST), Stellenbosch, South Africa.
2. IDRC (1993).
3. Department of Science and Technology (2002) National R&D Strategy, p.1.
4. Department of Education (March 2002) National Plan on Higher Education.
5. Department of Science and Technology (2002) National R&D Strategy, pp.42–43.
6. In an earlier paper (Mouton, 1995), I referred to these as 'critical' and 'oppositional' research centres. Centres such as the Centre for Adult and Continuing Education at the University of the Western Cape, the Centre for Health Policy at WITS and the Centre for Cultural and Media Studies at the University of Natal were established with the explicit intention to do research that challenged and opposed the apartheid policies of the Nationalist government.
7. For example, EU funding for technical support for education (including educational research) was to be channelled through an office within the national Department of Education.

8. Out of the 8000 questionnaires distributed to university and technikon researchers, and a further 2859 to science councils, 2058 were completed, constituting a response rate of about 20%. The complete report on the survey is available from the author.

9. The term 'third-stream funding' in the South African context refers to all research monies earned through contract and commissioned research, irrespective of whether this is for government, business, industry or other clients. The 'first stream' of funding refers to the parliamentary grant that all universities receive as part of the Education Vote, whereas the 'second stream' refers to grants and scholarships received through the national funding agencies such as the NRF.

10. The three most visible of these are the Technology for Human Resources in Industry Programme (THRIP), which is jointly funded by the Department of Trade and Industry and partners in industry, and is administered through the NRF; the Innovation Fund that aims to encourage new product and business development; and the NRF's Focus Area Programme, which has identified 10 areas for targeted funding.

The science councils and national research facilities are reviewed every five years by independent panels, whereas universities are reviewed every six years through the institutional audit review process of the Council for Higher Education.

11. Rip (1994 1997), Rip and Van der Meulen (1996).

12. Dutch funding for SANPAD and Wellcome Trust funding for HIV/AIDS.

13. The author was a member of the first interim committee of SANPAD, established in 1997, and of the first official South African programme committee, established in 1998.

14. Mouton (2001, 2002).

15. Department of Science and Technology (2004).

16. Mouton (2000, 2003).

17. Muller (1999).

18. Gibbons *et al.* (1994).

19. Ravjee (1999).

20. NCHE report, cited in Martin (1997: 98).

21. White Paper on S&T (1996, p.6).

22. The author wishes to acknowledge Jaamiah Galant's contribution to this section.

23. AZEF website: www.nrf.ac.za/azef/

References

Department of Science and Technology (2004) *South African National Survey of Research and Experimental Development 2001/02*. Pretoria.

Gibbons, M., Limoges, C., Nowotny, H., Schwartzman, S., Scott, P. and Trow, M. (1994) *The New Production of Knowledge: The Dynamics of Science and Research in Contemporary Societies*. London: Sage.

IDRC (1993). *Towards a Science and Technology Policy for a Democratic South Africa*. Ottawa: IDRC.

Martin, J.B. (1997) Research at the University of Cape Town. *Social Dynamics* 23(1): 88–101.

Mouton, J. (1995) Human sciences research at South African universities, in H. van den Berg *et al.* (Eds), *Directory of Human Sciences Research Organizations and Professional Associations in South Africa*. Pretoria: Human Sciences Research Council, pp.11–37.

Mouton, J. (2000) Patterns of research collaboration in academic science in South Africa. *SA Journal of Science*, 96(9/10): 458–462.

Mouton, J. (2001) Between adversaries and allies: The call for strategic science in post-apartheid South Africa. *Society in Transition*, 32(2):155–173.

Mouton, J. (2002) Research (with Ahmed Bawa), in: N. Cloete et al. (Eds.) *Transformation in Higher Education: Global Pressures and Local Realities in South Africa*. Johannesburg: Juta.

Mouton, J. (2003) South African science in transition. *Science, Technology and Society*, 8(2): 235–260.

Muller, J. (1999) *What Knowledge is of Most Worth to the Millennium Citizen?* Paper presented at the conference on reorganizing knowledge, transforming institutions: knowing, knowledge and the university in the 21st Century, University of Massachusetts, Amherst.

Ravjee, N. (1999) *'Modes' of Knowledge Production and Higher Education in South Africa: A critical review of the literature on the Gibbons thesis*. Report by the Centre for Interdisciplinary Studies, University of Stellenbosch.

Rip, A. (1994) The republic of science in the 1990s. *Higher Education*, 28: 3–23.

Rip, A. (1997) A cognitive approach to relevance of science. *Social Science Information* 36(4): 615–640.

Rip, A. and van der Meulen, B.J.R. (1996) The post-modern research system. *Science and Public Policy*, 23(5): 343–352.

NETWORKING KNOWLEDGE

SCIENCE AND TECHNOLOGY POLICIES THROUGH POLICY DIALOGUE

WIEBE E. BIJKER[1]

To formulate a science and technology (S&T) policy, one needs an adequate description and analysis of the research, technology and development situation in a country – a diagnostic study of S&T policies as well as the S&T landscape. This chapter discusses the development of a methodology and a toolbox for doing S&T diagnostic studies in developing countries.[2] The methodology is not intended to be used as a recipe, but rather as a set of guidelines and boundary conditions for carrying out such studies. An important reason for developing such a toolbox is to help generate S&T diagnostic studies that, because of their common methodological base, can contribute to the creation of a new cooperation strategy for science and technology that is shared by developing and donor countries.

1. Science, technology and society studies

Science, technology and society (STS) studies investigate the development of science and technology in their interaction with society.[3] One key result of these studies has been the re-valuation of indigenous knowledge. Scientific knowledge has been shown to be a specific knowledge system like many others. It does stand out for its specific characteristics, maintained through methodologies and checked by peer review, but these are social accomplishments, neither *a priori* given nor epistemologically different from 'other indigenous knowledge systems'.[4] Science has enormous value and potential, but this value is context-specific. There are situations in which scientific knowledge is irrelevant, and other types of knowledge more appropriate. This re-evaluation of indigenous knowledge and improved understanding of the process of scientific and technological work are two cornerstones of an argument for a specific strategy to stimulate the use of research and technology for development.

Zooming in on the process of scientific and technological work, a similar point can be made: scientific research and technological development are heterogeneous activities that do not have the purity that some philosophies of science have assumed in the past. Scientific knowledge is constructed in laboratories, on the land of small farmers, in the offices of funding agencies, at international conferences, and in editorial offices. It is not a matter of asking clever questions of nature, who then shouts back a clear 'yes' or 'no'.[5] Thinking about research and science must go further than the illusion that a combination of methodology and laboratories will automatically produce new scientific knowledge.[6] S&T policies must take into account a broad variety of aspects of scientific research – funding, technical infrastructure, social institutions, training and teaching styles, publication possibilities, national culture, and international scientific relations. Probably the most important result of STS research is *the very possibility* of a policy dialogue on the contents of an S&T policy agenda – within the standard images of science and technology, there is no point in consulting anyone other than scientists and engineers about the S&T agenda.

With regard to technological development, sociological and historical studies have developed a constructivist analysis of technology in contrast to the standard image of technology that was largely 'technological determinist'. The resulting social shaping models stress that technology does not follow its own momentum or a rational goal-directed problem-solving path, but is instead shaped by social factors. Therefore, constructivist approaches to technology, such as the social construction of technology,[7] start by defining 'relevant social groups', including technology users and consumers. Technical artefacts are described through the eyes of the members of these relevant social groups. The interactions within and among these groups can give different meanings to the same artefact. As a result of the involvement of these different groups, problems are defined differently and so are possible solutions, giving rise to different interpretations as to whether a problem has been solved or to the proper working of a technology. This interpretative flexibility demonstrates the necessity for a sociology of technology – it shows that neither an artefact's 'success' or 'failure', nor its technical 'working' or 'non-working', are intrinsic properties but are subject to social variables. Therefore, technology is not constructed merely by engineers, but also by marketing departments, managers, anti-technology action groups and users. Indeed, advocates of indigenous knowledge have argued that small farmers continuously experiment and are often more successful in improving agricultural techniques than are the large agricultural research institutions. It is therefore important to address issues in a wider cultural, political and economic milieu when formulating S&T policies.

It is important to stress that the employment of this sociologically informed constructivist image of science and technology in society does not discredit the work of members of other disciplines on S&T – such as that by economists, political scientists or policy analysts. It only puts the latter in a broadened and shifted perspective that allows us to identify the strengths but also the limitations of these bodies of work and thus provide a better explanation of how science and technology can be successful or unsuccessful in practice.

2. S&T in developing countries

In order to shed light on the questions why and with what consequences developing countries engage in scientific research and technological innovation, Shrum and Shenhav discuss three theoretical perspectives: modernization, dependency and institutional.[8]

The *modernization perspective* holds that science is strongly linked to technology, and thus improves the ability of a country to promote growth through the more efficient use of its resources. In order for a country to benefit, it is crucial that its economic infrastructure is able to absorb scientific research. Various studies have questioned this direct relationship between scientific research, technological innovation and economic growth. Particularly important for the argument in this chapter is to recognize that the modernization perspective erroneously assumes a linear relationship between science and technology. Rather, Shrum and Shenhav conclude, 'science penetrates the technological realm through a complex process consisting of several components but they do not occur in any determinate order. Often technological developments influence science'.[9]

The *dependency perspective* stresses that scientific research is another mechanism of domination of the developing countries by the industrialized countries, 'not just by producing the technological means for the subjugation of the masses (in some accounts) but also as an ideological force and an inappropriate developmental model. The creation and maintenance of scientific institutions not only absorb personnel and capital but constitute an irrelevant ideological diversion for countries without the resources or the connections to pursue Western, specialty-oriented science'.[10] Researchers in developing countries are often linked to international scientific communities and the scientific core in industrialized countries, which often also set the research agenda. The issue of formulating a country's research agenda is crucial. In a longitudinal study of 73 countries, in which a distinction was made between indigenous and scientific knowledge, Shenhav and Kamens showed that for less developed countries there is no relationship between scientific knowledge and economic performance, and even a mildly negative correlation in the case of the poorest countries. Industrialized countries do show a positive correlation between economic performance and scientific knowledge.[11]

The *institutional perspective*, which complements the dependency perspective, highlights the isomorphism of scientific institutions in developing and industrialized countries, which produces a shared orientation in values and organizational forms. 'Through mimetic processes by which successful existing systems serve as models, scientific institutions and beliefs are prescribed and diffused as key elements of the modern world system'.[12] This explains why all countries, despite the questionable economic benefits noted above, are committed to promoting (Western) science. It is important to note the implied warning that by adopting Westernized science and organizational forms, the comparability and compatibility of developing countries' research will be promoted, but solutions to local problems not necessarily so.[13]

While these three perspectives pertain to both science and technology, most of the studies of S&T in developing countries focus on technology. Technology has more direct relevance for dependency and development issues because it includes the development and improvement of industrial processes, the transfer or invention of artefacts, the establishment of information, communication and transportation infrastructures, the improvement of crops and food production, and the shaping of social institutions. Here again the key theme is the presence or absence of ties within and among countries.

Many authors have discussed the problems and advantages of 'technology transfer' – the movement of artefacts and/or knowledge between countries. Relations between countries are almost always relations between organizations, either public or private. Most technology transfer activities take place within and via multinational companies. 'Received wisdom regarding the R&D activities of multinationals suggests a variety of negative effects, centring on the generation of dependence in recipients'.[14] In the case of the RTD project referred to above (see note 2), the focus was on enhancing the S&T capacity within developing countries in a sustainable way. Therefore, technology transfer is a less desirable method because it may impair the development of domestic S&T capabilities that are appropriate to the country's stage and pace of socio-economic development.[15] State intervention and regulation are needed to support local firms in their relations with multinationals, and should be part of the country's science and technology policy.

However valuable the perspectives discussed in this section may be, for specific questions and situations, they all leave the content of science and technology untouched. They focus on the research system and institutions, rather than on the scientific knowledge and the technological artefacts and systems. The STS tradition introduced in the first section builds on an in-depth analysis of scientific and technological practices.

S&T policy

State action (including industrial, trade and S&T policy) is deemed crucial to the promotion of science and technology for development. Science and technology policy in socialist countries has received much attention; India, for example, has been studied in detail because of its relative openness and its active social scientific community. But studies of *how* science and technology policy is made in developing countries are still rare.[16] 'Increasingly it is recognized that state organizations compete with other institutions in less developed countries and that ... they are often too weak to implement unilateral change'.[17] In the 1970s R&D policies stressed the institutionalization of indigenous science and technology, while in the 1980s these 'self-reliant' policies were rethought and redefined.

Since the early 1980s, policy makers have realized that it does not make sense to conceive of development policy as a series of isolated projects. Often the positive effects of projects were nullified by poor macroeconomic policies or mismanaged institutions at the micro level. Hence, Szirmai notes, since the early 1980s foreign aid has increasingly been linked with a 'policy dialogue' aimed at improving macroeconomic policy and institutional reform, supported by the shift from project aid to programme aid. In this perspective, the dialogue element in programme aid focuses on establishing 'structural adjustment programmes aimed at macroeconomic stabilization and deregulation of the economy'.[18] Therefore, a broader conception of 'policy dialogue' should be adopted, one that is not restricted to this macroeconomic goal, but which also addresses the problem of the increased tension between national and local development and the possibly disruptive consequences of linking up with the high-speed environment of the global market.[19]

Policy dialogue

The concept of 'policy dialogue' was introduced into development policy discourse in the context of 'conditionality': setting conditions on foreign aid. These conditions referred primarily, though not exclusively, to economic policy. Respect for human rights, for example, might also be a condition, although Western policies have been very erratic in this respect. For the purposes of this chapter, it is more important to stress that both social policy and S&T policy can also be part of the policy dialogue. The arguments for this can be found in the previous sections.

Apart from bringing non-economic aspects to the table of a policy dialogue, the STS perspective has more radical implications that derive from its very different view of science and technology. The received view of policy dialogue builds on the necessary link between macroeconomic policy and development aid. We propose an extended conception of policy dialogue that, in addition, recognizes the socially constructed character of science and technology and therefore stresses the need to encompass a variety of other aspects as part of a successful research and technology for development policy. A policy dialogue as the basis for S&T policy should, for example, address the relations between 'Western' and indigenous knowledge; the conditions for endogenous development and reform of the country's institutional S&T infrastructure (rather than mimicking the institutional patterns developed in the industrialized countries); the conditions and formats for productive international cooperation via firms, universities, NGOs and government agencies; the various implicit conceptions of 'development' and 'beneficiaries'; the mechanisms that affect the distribution of benefits; the consequences of linking up with the global market and the ability to solve pressing local problems; and the country's educational and S&T capacities.

Finally, a further extension of the 'policy dialogue' concept is needed. The need to extend the subject matter to encompass a much wider variety of social, cultural, epistemological and political aspects has already been discussed. The dialogue should also be extended to other levels. Besides the dialogue between the donor countries and the developing nations, it is also necessary to stimulate a policy dialogue on a national level within the developing country, and on a regional level among developing countries. This is, again, supported by the previous analysis of science and technology. Science and technology do not develop in isolation, and hence a country's S&T policy needs to be fuelled by national discussions among stakeholders, policy makers, researchers, private companies and NGOs, as well as by inter-regional discussions among different developing countries.

3. A methodology for diagnostic studies of S&T in developing countries

To design an adequate strategy, one needs a good diagnosis of the situation. Similarly, to formulate an S&T policy, one needs an adequate description and analysis of the research, technology and development situation in a country – a diagnostic study. This comprises a diagnostic description of the S&T *policies* as well as the S&T *landscape*. If one wants to build an S&T policy *via a policy dialogue*, this sets specific additional criteria for such a study. This section identifies these criteria, and translates them into a methodology for carrying out such a diagnostic study.

The methodology is not presented in the form of rules to be followed simple-mindedly. Making a diagnostic study is a true scientific job to be carried out by experienced STS researchers with the necessary theoretical knowledge, empirical skills and tacit knowledge (see below). Instead, the methodology is cast in the form of a checklist that researchers can use to clarify the various dimensions and aspects they want to cover in their study. It also offers policy makers an instrument for discussing the plan for and results of a diagnostic study. All points on the checklist need not necessarily be covered by a particular diagnostic study, but the researcher should be able to argue why a specific point was omitted.

In the following paragraphs the insights from the previous sections are translated into clusters of checkpoints. The role of the checklist as part of a larger toolbox for generating diagnostic studies is discussed in section 4.

Concepts of policy and development

The argument for an S&T policy dialogue is founded on the recent rethinking of international aid and partnerships. It does not make much sense to conceive of development policy as a series of isolated projects; rather, it is necessary to link foreign aid with reform of macroeconomic policy and institutional infrastructure. The next step is to recognize that S&T policies need to address a wide set of issues. Technology policy cannot do without an economic reform policy, science policy cannot do without educational capacity building, and policies to reform the institutional infrastructure cannot do without an international collaboration policy. Such policies are destined to fail, and may even be damaging, if they do not properly fit with the socio-economic conditions and cultural particularities of the country concerned, and its desired direction and manageable pace of development. Such a broad scope is based on the observation that there are no neutral facts or technologies – all knowledge and all technologies are infused with politics and are thus value-laden. This also applies to the concept of 'development'.

Proper goals for a nation's development cannot logically be derived from some *a priori* principles, but need to be established in and through a policy dialogue. Nor is the impact of research and technology on development straightforward: explicit discussion of the strategic effects of science and technology on development is necessary.

Policy and development: issues to be addressed
1	<ul><li>Is S&T policy linked to a wider set of issues? For example:</li><li>research institutional infrastructure;</li><li>research funding structure;</li><li>foreign aid structure, private and government;</li><li>intellectual property rights and patent regulation;</li><li>international research collaboration, both among universities and via NGOs and multinational companies.</li></ul>
2	<ul><li>Is it recognized that all scientific knowledge and technological artefacts are value-laden? In other words, are specific technical and scientific accomplishments not used in naively neutral and objectifying terms?</li></ul>
3	<ul><li>How is 'development' conceptualized by the various actors involved?</li></ul>
4	<ul><li>How is the impact of science and technology on development viewed by the various actors involved?</li></ul>

The concept of 'policy dialogue'

The concepts of policy and development need to be complemented with the specific concept of policy dialogue, which has several elements.

First, we need to distinguish policy dialogue on three levels: *intra-national* (within the country and the government, involving national organizations and local stakeholders), *intra-regional* (among several developing countries in a region), and *international* (with donor countries). These three levels have implications for the types of actors and institutions that need to be included in a diagnostic study.

Second, to be a true *dialogue*, the policy dialogue must be interpreted as an ongoing, *open learning process*. *Open*, because policy goals and priorities are never fixed at the outset, but need to remain amenable to revision during the dialogue. *Learning,* because the policy dialogue should have the means to record the arguments, decisions, results, successes and failures of the process and make these widely available. And *process,* because the focus is on the process of reaching decisions on S&T policy rather than on the products of the dialogue. In other words, a policy dialogue is meant to strengthen the cognitive and infrastructural base for S&T policies in developing countries, rather than merely to 'sell' donor countries' ideas. In addition to products such as reports detailing the new policy, the mutual learning and the development of a shared understanding of problems and of trust among participants, achieved in and through the process, are also important results of the dialogue. In this perspective experts or consultants are process facilitators rather than providers of content.

Qualitative indicators of the *open* nature of the process include the variety of actors involved, and the existence of procedures to guarantee that the views of end-users and of the private sector are taken into account. For adequate *learning*, indicators are the openness of accounting and reporting procedures and styles, the development of trust, recognition and appreciation among the participants of each other's specific competencies and their willingness to discuss, recognize and (re)consider the implicit assumptions and limitations of each position, argument or approach. Indicators of the *process* character are a tolerance of failure, regular evaluations of progress and adjustment of goals, the flexibility of procedures and the eagerness to discuss whether the procedures include or exclude relevant groups, or favour or suppress specific positions or arguments.

Third, a policy dialogue on S&T should at least focus on developing new national S&T policies, formulating strategies to support institutional reforms of S&T infrastructures, and strengthening national S&T capacities. In addition to these enormous tasks, the dialogue should concentrate on the intensification of scientific cooperation at national, regional and international levels, and the identification of innovative funding mechanisms to develop and sustain appropriate S&T infrastructures. Moreover, the policy dialogue should address other issues such as ensuring a proper fit between S&T policies and the country's socio-economic conditions and cultural context, identifying the conditions and formats of collaboration that will help to meet national and local development needs, and to strengthen domestic S&T capabilities in the long term. Finally, the policy dialogue should explore strategies to address the consequences of linking the country to global markets, in particular to ensure a balance between the rapid pace of change in these markets (fuelled by the industrialized countries) and the pace of change that local and rural communities can tolerate without being disrupted.

Fourth, the S&T policy dialogue should allow for the participation of a large variety of relevant actors and groups. The dialogue should of course engage S&T communities such as universities and research institutes, and the public authorities responsible for formulating and implementing national

S&T policies and for reforming and strengthening public and private S&T infrastructures and capabilities. However, the intended end users of technologies, donor agencies, NGOs, private sector companies and local stakeholders from civil society (who may not be organized or represented at the national level) should also be involved in formulating the research and innovation goals at the earliest possible stage in order to ensure the best possible fit between innovation and implementation.

Policy dialogue: issues to be addressed	
5	Are different levels of policy dialogue distinguished? • intra-national • intra-regional • inter-national
6	Is the policy dialogue an open process? For example, by identifying: • a wide variety of actors and institutions involved • the procedures giving 'outsiders' access to the policy dialogue • the influence of end-users • the influence of the private sector
7	Is the policy dialogue conceived as a learning process? For example, by identifying: • procedures for accounting and checking the dialogue • procedures for reporting the results of the policy dialogue • positive strategic reactions to failures • flexibility in maintaining procedures and devising new ones • a reflexive attitude with regard to both the content and process of the dialogue • transparency of the policy dialogue process
8	Is the policy dialogue addressing key issues? At least: • the development of new S&T policies • reform of S&T institutions • strengthening of national S&T capacities • intensifying international S&T collaboration • innovation of funding structures • conditions for productive collaboration • fit with socio-economic and cultural context • pace of change in the global market and that of local communities
9	Are all relevant social groups, institutions and actors involved? At least: • user groups, potential users, local and national stakeholders • public authorities • donor agencies • S&T communities and institutions • NGOs • private sector companies

Description of the S&T landscape

A policy dialogue that is geared towards developing an S&T policy requires an adequate assessment of the current S&T landscape – the universities, private and public research institutions, funding agencies, NGOs and relevant regulatory agencies and other government offices. Such an assessment should focus on describing and analyzing indicators such as the numbers of scientists and technologists, the budgets at their disposal and their scientific and innovative activities.

The S&T landscape: issues to be addressed	
10	Is the S&T landscape described in terms of institutions: • universities • private and public research institutions • funding agencies • NGOs • relevant regulatory agencies and other government offices And in terms of relevant indicators: • science and technology workforce • financial budgets • scientific and innovative activities

Analysis of power relations

The parties involved in a policy dialogue are not neutral, without interests or agendas of their own. Therefore, in order to understand the dynamics of the policy dialogue and of S&T development in a country, the power relations between the various institutions need to be adequately described. Relevant aspects include economic, ethnic and political hierarchies, and national laws and international agreements relating to (intellectual) property rights, including patents.

Analysis of power relations: issues to be addressed	
11	Have the hierarchical relations between the various research institutions, donors, ministries, NGOs and multinational companies been adequately mapped?
12	Have national regulations that set conditions for R&D within multinational firms and national private businesses been described?
13	Have national laws and international agreements relating to (intellectual) property rights, including patents, been described?

Concepts of science and technology

After setting the general stage for policy making and policy dialogue, it is time to turn to the specific subject of S&T. It is important to avoid naive images of S&T, since they tend to deny the social, cultural, political and historical dimensions, and thus the possibility of an S&T policy that also aims to influence the research and innovation agenda substantially. To avoid these inadequate and ineffective images, it is necessary to take into account the results of the past two decades of STS research. In practice, this implies that all relevant social groups, not just engineers and scientists, need to be mapped. In doing so, special attention should be paid to the variety of cultural, regional and national sources of knowledge and technology (e.g. indigenous knowledge and traditional techniques).

Science and technology: issues to be addressed	
14	Have all the relevant social groups involved in a specific scientific or technological development been described?
15	Have all relevant forms of indigenous knowledge, craft knowledge and local expertise been described?

Fields of science and technology

A broad view of what constitutes new developments in S&T is crucial in order to exploit the potential of a country's scientific and technological capacity. Therefore, a policy dialogue should not only cover those areas most likely to contribute to the country's ability to link up with global markets, but should also explore areas such as biotechnology, ICTs, agricultural and marine technologies, and fields that are more likely to address local level development needs. Recent shifts in focus between fields of science and technology need to be highlighted in order to give an historical perspective to the science policy dynamics of a country. If a country already has an explicit policy on research and technology for development, it should be fully described.

Fields of S&T: issues to be addressed	
16	Have all relevant fields of science and technology been covered, including those that enhance the country's ability to link up with global markets, as well as those that aim to meet local needs? Has, for example, the trap been avoided of identifying technological progress with computers only?

17	Have the changes in focus between fields of science and technology over the past decade been documented?
18	Have the country's S&T policy plans been described?

Implementation of S&T policies

S&T policies need to explicate a strategy for demonstration and dissemination of research and innovation. In both the public domain and in private business, it is often assumed that once a new scientific finding is communicated or a new technical innovation is demonstrated, all the rest will follow automatically. Nothing could be further from the truth. Research findings and technological innovations need to be marketed and implemented. Marketing is not a straightforward process of launching the new fact or artefact into the wider world – continuous management, translation and coaching are also required. Hence, an S&T diagnostic study needs to pay explicit attention to such issues as demonstration, adoption-adaptation, implementation and diffusion. Here, it is important not to deny the existence of failures, since they may offer more interesting lessons than the successes.

Implementation of S&T policies: issues to be addressed	
19	Is the dissemination of scientific findings and implementation of technological innovations given sufficient attention? This may involve, for example, separate funding or management structures.

4. Generating diagnostic studies

The various checklist clusters presented above can be packaged in a toolbox for generating diagnostic studies that can be used in the formulation of policies to promote science and technology for development. Tools in a toolbox, however, can never stand alone, and even the best tools do not guarantee good work. Tools will only work if they are used by skilled people; they need to be accompanied by manuals, and to be handled with unwritten tacit knowledge. Also, they should be used by people with the relevant contextual knowledge and skills for doing social studies of science and technology in developing countries. This toolbox does not provide those basic knowledge and skills, although it does provide some means for acquiring and employing them. Even more crucial is *when* to pick up the toolbox in the first place. A necessary condition for applying the checklist is, of course, that the central role of S&T for development is recognized. It is equally important to recognize that such policy formulation should be done on the basis of a policy dialogue.

A diagnostic studies 'toolbox' should contain the following items: the checklist for designing and evaluating diagnostic studies, a workshop for training researchers, and advice to the relevant government agency to prepare the policy-making infrastructure. These items can best be described by following the process of promoting S&T for development. The first step in that process is to translate the overall political vision of the responsible agency into a concrete strategy. That means describing the policy problem in the right terms, and ensuring that the relevant politicians and policy makers agree on an adequate definition. Unless the general issue is framed in the right technocratic and bureaucratic terms, it will not survive. Once the political and administrative conditions are set, the diagnostic studies can be carried out. But to do that, researchers have to be trained to use the methodology. This can best be done in small, intensive workshops.

S&T diagnostic studies are the key element in the strategy to shape and stimulate S&T for development, and must be carried out by experienced and well prepared senior researchers, preferably with some experience in studying science and technology in society. They may have varied disciplinary backgrounds, such as the social sciences with some affinity to natural sciences and technology, or vice versa.

It is not enough, however, simply to hand these researchers the methodology. No methodology can be read as a recipe, but should be mastered in practice – learned 'on the job'. To save time, this learning can most effectively be done in a workshop where researchers who have already carried out diagnostic studies can share their experiences with new researchers.

Although the primary purpose of such a workshop should be to train the researchers who are to carry out the S&T diagnostic studies, it may be attractive and effective to use them for an additional goal as well. One of the recurrent themes in this chapter has been that science and technology should not be viewed as isolated activities in society. Rather, they should be viewed as part of the complex network that constitutes civil society – end users, funding bodies, small local companies, multinational corporations, policy makers, etc. Including some of these people in the workshop may serve several purposes. First, the policy makers and private business people will get to understand some of the basic concepts underlying the new strategy to promote S&T, and thus will be better prepared for what will be asked of them in the next steps. Second, the researchers will be confronted with some of the standard problems and objections they will encounter when talking to these various groups in society. Thus the workshop becomes a kind of 'learning laboratory' in which the researchers are trained almost as if they were really 'on the job', but efficiently concentrated in time and space.

The final step is to carry out the diagnostic study. The researchers contracted to do this have been trained in the workshop. To guarantee the process character of the diagnostic study, it is important to have in place an infrastructure of national and international contacts to support the researchers. At the national level, it may be wise to set up a kind of advisory committee that can help the researchers to reflect upon their findings. Such a committee could also be used to create, at an early stage, a base of support among politicians and government agencies, the research community and civil society. At the international level, a network of researchers who are involved in similar projects could enable them contribute to the modification and improvement of the methodology for carrying out S&T diagnostic studies.

Diagnostic studies will hopefully provide the kind of comprehensive inventory of relevant information and views that should form the basic ingredients of a policy dialogue on S&T policies. All relevant actors should be able to give inputs to, and make use of the outputs from, these diagnostic studies. The diagnostic study itself will be an instrument to help identify relevant actors, groups, and organizations to be included in this dialogue process. If conceived and carried out in this way, diagnostic studies will contribute to a democratization of the use of science and technology in developing societies.

Acknowledgements

The author wishes to acknowledge Dr Chris Leonards and Dr Ger Wackers for their inputs, and Rutger Engelhard for his valuable suggestions for the final version of this paper.

Notes

1. Wiebe E. Bijker (w.bijker@tss.unimaas.nl) is Professor of Technology and Society, University of Maastricht, the Netherlands.
2. The methodology was developed as part of an endeavour to stimulate a Research and Technology for Development (RTD) policy dialogue between the European Commission, the EU Member States and the African, Caribbean and Pacific (ACP) countries. The aim of the project (2000–2002) was to develop a framework for policy dialogue that would enable ACP countries to address the challenges and issues related to reforming their national RTD policies and strengthening their capabilities.
3. For an overview of STS studies, see Jasanoff *et al.* (1995).
4. See *Watson-Verran and Turnbull* (1995).
5. See *Latour and Woolgar* (1987), Collins (1985).

6. Even in such esoteric fields as high-energy physics, scientific knowledge has been shown to be influenced by the cultural, social and economic circumstances under which it is produced (Traweek, 1998).

7. See Bijker (1995) for an account of this social construction of technology approach. For a summary, see Bijker (2001).

8. Shrum and Shenhav (1995: 627–651).

9. *Ibid.*, p.630.

10. *Ibid.*.

11. Shenhav and Kamens (1991).

12. Shrum and Shenhav (1995).

13. See Turnbull (1989) for a study of agenda setting around the development of a malaria vaccine in an Australian-Papua New Guinea collaboration.

14. Shrum and Shenhav (1995: 637).

15. This is not to say that technology transfer can never play a positive role under specific circumstances. See Shrum and Shenhav (1995).

16. See Wieberdink (2004).

17. Shrum and Shenhav (1995: 639).

18. Szirmai (1997).

19. With a focus on Asia, a similar argument is made by Pinkney (1993: 5–17).

References

Bijker, W.E. (1995) *Of Bicycles, Bakelites, and Bulbs: Toward a Theory of Sociotechnical Change*. Cambridge, MA: MIT Press.

Bijker, W.E. (2001) Social construction of technology, in N.J. Smelser and P.B. Baltes (Eds.), *International Encyclopedia of the Social and Behavioural Sciences*, 23: 15522–15527. Oxford: Elsevier Science.

Collins, H.M. (1985) *Changing Order: Replication and Induction in Scientific Practice*. London: Sage.

Jasanoff, S., Markle, G.E., Petersen, J.C. and Pinch, T. (Eds.) (1995) *Handbook of Science and Technology Studies*. Thousand Oaks, CA: Sage.

Latour, B. and Woolgar, S. (1987) *Laboratory Life: The Social Construction of Scientific Facts*. Princeton, NJ: Princeton University Press.

Pinkney, R. (1993) *Democracy in the Third World*. Milton Keynes, UK: Open University Press.

Shenhav, Y.A. and Kamens, D.H. (1991) The 'costs' of institutional isomorphism: Science in non-Western countries. *Social Studies of Science,* 21(3): 527–545.

Shrum, W. and Shenhav, Y. (1995) Science and technology in less developed countries, in S. Jasanoff et al. (Eds.) *Handbook of Science and Technology Studies*. London: Sage, pp. 627–651.

Szirmai, A. (1997) *Economic and Social Development: Trends, Problems, Policies*. London: Prentice Hall.

Traweek, S. (1988) *Beamtimes and Lifetimes: The World of High-Energy Physicists*. Cambridge, MA: Harvard University Press.

Turnbull, D. (1989) The push for a malaria vaccine. *Social Studies of Science*, 19(2): 283–300.

Watson-Verran, H. and Turnbull, D. (1995) Science and other indigenous knowledge systems, in S. Jasanoff *et al.* (Eds.), *Handbook of Science and Technology Studies*. Thousand Oaks, CA: Sage, pp.115–139.

Wieberdink, A. (2004) *Troubled Waters: The Ambivalence of South–North Partnerships in Research for Development, A Case Study.* Utrecht: International Books.

FROM DEVELOPMENT RESEARCH TO PRO-POOR POLICY: EVIDENCE AND THE CHANGE PROCESS

JULIUS COURT AND JOHN YOUNG[1]

Better utilization of research in development policy and practice can help save lives, reduce poverty and improve economic performance. But bridging research and policy is harder than it looks. How can policy makers best use research for evidence-based policy? How can researchers promote their findings in order to influence policy? How can the interaction between researchers and policy makers be improved? These are challenges of growing practical and scholarly interest, in both North and South. This chapter provides a synthesis of the findings of recent work in ODI's Research and Policy in Development (RAPID) programme. It outlines an analytical framework for understanding the links between evidence and policy change, and highlights key issues in four areas: political context and the demand for evidence in policy processes; the quality and relevance of evidence; the importance of links and communication; and the role of external actors in developing countries. The chapter concludes with some practical guidelines for researchers who wish to enhance the policy impact of their work.

1. Introduction

Better utilization of research and evidence in development policy and practice can help save lives, reduce poverty and improve the quality of life. Since the publication of the 1998/99 World Development Report, *Knowledge for Development,* there has been greater acceptance that generating knowledge (i.e. research) is one key part of the efforts to reduce poverty.[2] A study by DfID cataloguing the value of research for development forcefully supports this view.[3]

Sometimes, however, it seems that researchers and policy makers live in parallel universes. Researchers cannot understand why there is resistance to policy change despite clear and convincing evidence. Policy makers and other stakeholders, on the other hand, often do not know what research exists, which policies are the most suitable, or how they can best be implemented in different contexts. They often 'regard *research* as the opposite of *action* rather than the opposite of *ignorance*',[4] and bemoan the inability of many researchers to make their findings accessible, digestible and available in time for policy decisions. However, policy makers may also be unwilling to act on the evidence, as has been the case with the HIV/AIDS crisis in some countries.[5]

Improving the use of research and evidence and the context in which they are used can enhance the ability of all stakeholders to influence policy, and in turn improve the effectiveness of development policy itself. Although research and evidence obviously matter, there is no systematic understanding of when, how and why they inform policy in international development. There are surprisingly few studies focusing on the development arena, despite the increasing emphasis on the need for evidence-based policy. Only in the last year have more focused and substantial studies emerged on the topic.[6]

This chapter is structured as follows. Section 2 outlines the context for recent and ongoing studies on bridging research and policy in the field of international development. Section 3 provides definitions of research and policy, and describes the analytical framework developed by the RAPID programme at ODI. Section 4 synthesizes the main findings of the RAPID programme, drawn from literature reviews, case studies, synthesis workshops, evaluations and in-country workshops, and section 5 outlines some priorities for future research. Section 6 provides some practical guidelines for researchers who wish to enhance the policy impact of their work, and section 7 presents our main conclusions.

2. Research and policy in international development

Researchers in many OECD countries have focused on the links between research and policy.[7] In 1977, Carol Weiss published the results of her seminal research on 'knowledge creep' and 'percolation', the process in which research findings and concepts are gradually filtered through various policy networks.[8] During the 1980s, the golden age of studies on knowledge utilization in the USA, it was recognized that although research may not have a *direct* impact on specific policies, the production of research may still exert a powerful *indirect* influence by introducing new terms and shaping the policy discourse. Since then, substantial investigations into research–policy linkages and evidence-based policy making have been carried out in OECD countries.

The failure to enhance the utilization of research and evidence in international development policy and practice is significant. Apparently, the diversity of cultural, economic, and political contexts makes it especially difficult to draw valid generalizations and lessons from existing experience and theory. Since the late 1990s, however, change has been in the air. For example, the International Institute for Environment and Development (IIED) identified a six-point programme for improving the impact of research on policy making.[9] The Overseas Development Institute (ODI) examined research–policy linkages, and provided a 21-point checklist of what makes policies happen.[10] The Global Development Network (GDN) is currently conducting a major study on the issue of the links between research and policy. The Canadian International Development Research Center (IDRC) has conducted a strategic evaluation of the influence of IDRC-supported research on public policy.[11] Over the last few years the International Food Policy Research Institute (IFPRI) has been measuring the policy impact of its research programmes, and how it can be improved.

An understanding of research–policy linkages in international development needs to take into account the wide range of contexts in which development policies are formulated. A number of emerging global trends are affecting both the generation of research and its use in policy processes. In the macro-level political context, four key challenges are democratization, markets, civil society and ICTs.

Democratization has been one of the most striking developments of the last decades. In 1901, no country could be considered democratic, according to the current definition of the term,[12] whereas in 2003 there were estimated to be more than 121 electoral democracies.[13] Between 1976 and 1999 the number of democratic regimes more than doubled, from under 40 to over 80, providing new entry points to the policy-making process. It is thought that democratic contexts better enable research to be conducted and communicated (due to freedoms), and provide greater incentives for policy makers to use research (due to accountability mechanisms).

Yet many developing countries, even if they appear to be democratic in form, still have unrepresentative political systems and weak structures for aggregating and arbitrating interests in society.[14] Policy-making processes tend to be centralized, and thus remote and inaccessible, with limited scope for wider inputs or participation except at the implementation stage.[15] Political leaders often view civil society inputs as illegitimate or inefficient, with the result that policy makers tend to increase their power whilst simultaneously isolating themselves from society. Policy formulation becomes responsive to the needs of elites rather than the majority, or the poor.

Markets are spreading and economies are increasingly open. Twenty years ago only 2.9 billion people lived in what could be termed a market economy, compared with 5.7 billion in 1999.[16] What does this increasing economic openness mean for research–policy linkages? Most obviously, it brings new actors into political processes. It also creates increased demand for research that can be accessed by those outside academia. Both firms and governments need research in order to be able to cope with a wide range of technical issues involved in economic policy formulation and regulation.

Civil society is generally considered to be opening up in many countries. The number of civil society organizations (NGOs, the media, think tanks, etc.) is growing, and their role in shaping national priorities is expanding. A theme common to many countries is the increasing importance of non-state organizations as actors in governance, although the input of civil society into public policy is still quite limited.[17] Civil society and the state often live rather separate lives, with governments continuing to set the policy agenda much on their own. There is still a tendency for many governments to silence or intimidate citizens who propagate views different from those in power.

Information and communication technologies (ICTs) have incredible potential to transform the generation and sharing of information. The poor are poor not just because they are marginalized or excluded from economic and political processes, but also because they are marginalized in information flows in society. ICTs can make information accessible to a far wider audience than before, and this information can potentially act as a catalyst for action, even for groups that have traditionally been marginalized. ICTs do not represent a miracle cure, however. The information gap is widening, and the need to be 'plugged in' to information networks in order to be able to influence policy may also exclude groups that fall outside the information society.

3. Analyzing research–policy linkages: a framework

In order to enhance *systematic* understanding of what, when, why and how research feeds into development policies, ODI's Research and Policy in

Development (RAPID) programme has developed a cohesive framework for analyzing research–policy linkages.

In the context of this framework, *research* is defined as 'any systematic effort to increase the stock of knowledge'.[18] Research therefore includes any systematic process of critical investigation and evaluation, theory building, data collection, analysis and codification related to development policy and practice. It also includes action research, i.e. self-reflection by practitioners oriented toward the enhancement of practice.

Policy is defined as a 'purposive course of action followed by an actor or set of actors'.[19] The focus is on *public policy*, with the understanding that this is not restricted to government policy. International organizations, bilateral agencies and NGOs also have policies, and often influence government policies. What makes policies public is not that they are adopted and implemented by government, but that they also affect or are visible to the public. Within the concept of public policy, there are a number of *sub-components of policy* that research may impact.[20] These are the agendas, arguments and policy horizons of policy makers, their policy objectives and their strategies to achieve them. Others include laws and regulations, institutions and their spending patterns, policy implementation activities, and policy capacities at different levels.

The RAPID framework for analyzing research–policy linkages is based on an extensive literature review, conceptual synthesis, and testing in both research projects and practical activities.[21] The framework consists of three spheres in which the issues to be taken into account for the analysis are clustered (figure 1). The first sphere, '*context*', clusters all issues pertaining to *politics* and *institutions*. The second sphere, '*evidence*', groups the questions that highlight *approach* and credibility, and the third, '*links*', brings together the concerns regarding *influence* and *legitimacy*. These three spheres are embedded in an environment and are affected by '*external influences*' such as international politics, economic developments and cultural factors.

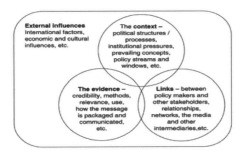

Figure 1. The RAPID framework: context, evidence and links

The framework should be seen as a generic, perhaps ideal, model. In many cases there will be little overlap between the different spheres, while in others the overlap may be considerable. The core of the analytical framework, then, should be viewed as a trio of floating spheres of variable size and degree of overlap, rather than as a solid mesh in which context, evidence and links are held as equally important, and equally overlapping, in every case.

Research–policy linkages are shaped by their *political context*. The policy process and the production of research are themselves political processes, from the initial agenda-setting exercise to the final negotiation involved in implementation. Political contestation, institutional pressures and vested interests matter greatly, as do the attitudes and incentives among officials, their room for manoeuvre, local history, and power relations.[22] In some cases the political strategies and power relations are obvious, and are tied to specific institutional pressures; in others the pressures are more vague, and are tied to broad discourses or paradigms that may exert a powerful influence on which ideas are noticed and which are ignored.

The framework suggests that the nature of the *evidence* is important for policy uptake. The research approach and methodology are important, as are the credibility of the evidence, simplicity of the message, how it is communicated and the degree to which it challenges received wisdom. The sources and conveyors of information may be as influential as the content; for example, people accept information more readily from researchers they trust. But the hypothesis is that good quality research, local involvement, accurate messages and effective dissemination strategies are important if the aim is for more evidence-based policy making.

Another set of issues concerns how evidence is *communicated*. The way new messages are packaged (especially if they are couched in familiar terms) and targeted can make a big difference in terms of how a policy document is perceived and utilized. For example, marketing is based on the insight that an individual's reaction to a new product/idea is often determined by the packaging rather than the content in and of itself.[23] The key message is that communication is a very demanding process and that it is most effective to take an interactive approach.[24] Continuous interaction is more likely to lead to successful communication than a simple or linear approach.

The RAPID framework emphasizes the importance of *links* – within and among communities, intermediaries (e.g. the media and campaign groups) and networks (policy communities, epistemic communities, advocacy coalitions, etc.[25]) – in effecting policy change. Issues such as trust, legitimacy, openness and the formalization of networks are important in relation to the speed and degree of research uptake. While some theory appreciates the roles of translators and communicators,[26] it seems that there is often an under-appreciation of the extent and ways that intermediary organizations and networks impact on formal policy guidance documents, which in turn influence officials.

Finally, the framework emphasizes the impacts of *external forces* and donor actions on research–policy interactions. While many questions remain, the key issues here include the impact of international politics and processes, as well as the impact of donor policies and research funding instruments. Broad incentives, such as EU membership or the Poverty Reduction Strategy Paper (PRSP) process, can have a substantial impact on the demand for research by policy makers.[27] Increasing democratization, market liberalization and donor support for civil society are also having an impact.

Much of the research on development issues is undertaken in the North, raising issues of access, perceived relevance and legitimacy. A substantial amount of research in the poorest countries is funded by international donors, which also raises a range of issues concerning ownership, whose priorities are being addressed, the use of external consultants, and perceived legitimacy. As policy processes become increasingly global, this arena will increase in importance.

The findings in this chapter are based on reviews of the literature and various studies conducted by the RAPID programme at ODI. These include:

1. extensive literature reviews, studies relevant to developing country contexts, analyses of communications issues and the influence of civil society organizations;
2. a synthesis of 50 case studies conducted as part of phase I of the GDN Bridging Research and Policy project;
3. four detailed case studies of the influence of research on specific policy changes: the adoption of the Poverty Reduction Strategy Paper (PRSP) initiative; the impact of the Sphere project on the performance of international humanitarian agencies; the spread of para-professional livestock services in Kenya; and the emergence and adoption of the Sustainable Livelihoods Approach (SLA) in DfID's 1997 White Paper;
4. strategic advice to phase II of the GDN Bridging Research and Policy project;
5. a sector study of the GDN Bridging Research and Policy project on HIV/AIDS in developing countries;

6. evaluations of the impact of research/policy papers on bilateral donor policy and practice, carried out for the SDC (Switzerland) and DfID (UK); and

7. workshops and seminars with researchers, practitioners and policy makers in Botswana, Morocco, India, Moldova, Kenya, the UK and the USA.[28]

4. A synthesis of findings

This section starts with a note on method and overarching principles, and some broad points about what our work says about existing models of research–policy linkages. We then discuss the three spheres in the RAPID framework – context, evidence and links – and the external influences. As we proceed, we indicate where our analysis supports some of the key strands of theory in the literature.

Method and overarching principles

The study of research impact and research–policy linkages is simply not amenable to a single conventional means of analysis. Nevertheless, there is a growing body of experience that indicates the value of using context-specific, triangulated combinations of qualitative and quantitative methods. The challenge is to find the middle ground between factors that are so context specific as to be irrelevant elsewhere, and those that are too generalized to be meaningful.

There are many methodological challenges in undertaking a study of research impact and research–policy linkages. It is difficult to define impact, since research can impact on policy in many different ways. Attribution is also difficult. Since policy processes are complex, multi-layered and change over time, it is difficult to identify the key factors that caused policy to change (or not) and to isolate the particular impact of research. Much of the evidence is qualitative and subjective. The issue of time complicates the analysis.

In the design of methodological approaches, two principles were adopted. First, triangulation – i.e. the use several research approaches to investigate an issue – would be required to ensure that the findings were robust. Second, the main findings of each part of the study would be peer reviewed both by researchers to assess the policy impacts of specific pieces of research, and by policy makers to assess the role of research in clear policy shifts.

Context: politics and institutions

Our work indicates that the political and institutional context is the most important sphere affecting the uptake of research into policy. Power relations, political contestation, institutional pressures and vested interests matter critically in all cases. The attitudes and incentives among officials and the local historical context also influence policy processes. In many political contexts in developing countries, the findings of research are often completely ignored. Our cases confirm the findings of Kingdon, who highlighted the importance of 'political streams' such as changes in government and public opinion, as well as of 'policy windows' – key moments when research can influence policy processes.[29] It is crucial to understand the political context in order to bridge research and policy.

The demand from policy makers is one of the main factors that determines whether research will be taken up or will have little impact. However, it is not just the demand for a solution to a problem that matters, but also consensus on the nature of the solution. In our PRSP case study,[30] for example, the most important contextual factor was the convergence of debates and controversies in the field of international development. The ODI and GDN case studies emphasize the problems for research–policy links when contexts become complex, highly politicized processes,[31] with increasingly polarized views developing in the different camps, and no mechanism for dialogue and resolution.

Policy is not just about statements and laws; it is also about implementation. RAPID's work certainly supports the view that 'street-level bureaucrats' (the employees of an organization responsible for implementation) can have an enormous influence on how policies are implemented.[32] All the cases indicate that paying attention to how new policies will be put into practice is an important aspect of policy change to which researchers often pay scant attention. The RAPID study of animal health policy in Kenya provides a powerful example of how street-level bureaucrats may be forced to deal with new problems, draw on available evidence, and therefore go through the process of policy adaptation before high-level policy makers. In this case, animal health care practitioners across Kenya's arid Northern region, finding themselves with virtually no operational budgets, adopted effective community-based approaches even though they were actually illegal, since they were the only way they could continue to provide any services at all.[33]

Evidence: credibility and communication

The findings for three sets of issues regarding research or evidence appear particularly robust. First, research appears to have a much greater impact when it is topically relevant. For an impact in the short term, research needs to relate to the policy issue of the day. Second, the perceived credibility of research is crucial for policy uptake. Many of our cases emphasize the importance of the credibility of key researchers or research organizations, and the approach used. Also, research that pulls together evidence from diverse sources can often help to foster uptake. But credibility also depends on the user. Third, it is clear from the case studies that the operational usefulness of research – whether it provides a solution to a problem – is critical. Research that had an operational orientation or action research seems to have an impact. Critical for uptake in many cases is that applied policy research focuses on providing recommendations for specific organizations. As formulated in the literature on marketing,[34] people buy products that provide solutions to problems.

But it is not just the content of the evidence that matters. How findings are communicated is crucial, since policy makers cannot be influenced by research unless they are actually aware of its existence. Our work confirms that the nature of communications efforts and the format of the research outputs matter critically for policy impact. Researchers could provide more clarity in expressing complex processes. Interestingly, the issue of credibility concerns not only the quality of the research but also the way it is packaged to make it palatable to policy makers.

It is hard to overemphasize the importance of targeting the message for a specific audience. Research needs to be communicated in a language that is accessible and relevant to the intended audience. Our findings emphasize the importance of communicating in different ways for different audiences. For non-specialists, reports need to use clear prose and graphics, as well as brief case studies, whereas technical guidance sheets are more appropriate for practitioners. The ODI cases also demonstrate the power of visual images. As has often been emphasized, 'seeing is believing'.[35]

There is evidence to support the view that it is best to take an interactive approach to communication.[36] It seems that continuous interaction leads to greater chances of successful communication than a simple or linear approach. The importance of interactions between researchers and policy makers is also emphasized in many cases.

The cases indicate how evidence can help to change the policy context. In our PRSP case, research evidence helped create a context in which the prevailing narrative was 'there is a problem with development policy'. This evidence, and the campaigns that used it, helped to influence the political contexts in a number of countries and at the international level. The evidence and operational research it spurred eventually resulted in a new policy context and policy shifts.

Links: influence and legitimacy

Much of the literature on bridging research and policy emphasizes that the links between researchers and policy makers are critical. Key issues include dialogue, feedback processes and collaboration between researchers and policy makers; the role of networks and policy communities; and issues of trust, legitimacy and participation. However, it is also apparent that many questions remain unanswered in this arena.

The case studies highlight the vital role of networks in policy change. As such they support the view of policy making as a series of negotiations that can be completed through formal and informal networks.[37] Many of them emphasize how such links maximize the sense of ownership and 'buy-in' in conducting evaluations and implementing the findings. They show how networks can facilitate knowledge sharing, coordination and cooperation. But a key question that remains is: what are the characteristics of networks that enable them to act as a bridge between research and policy? Epistemic communities – colleagues who share a similar approach or position on an issue and maintain contacts across their various locations and fields – can create new channels for information and discussion of new perspectives, and are particularly effective if they include a few prominent and respected individuals.[38] Such individuals can play an important role in bridging research and policy. Many of our cases describe how such individuals have been crucial in promoting pro-poor policies based on research.

The cases also repeatedly draw attention to the issue of the legitimacy of researchers and the research process. Researchers' links to the populations and communities that will be affected by the policies can also be important as a basis for legitimacy.[39] A recent paper for the Rockefeller Foundation emphasizes that social change will be more sustainable if the affected community owns not just the physical inputs to and outputs of policy implementation, but also the process and content of the communication involved.[40] Our work demonstrates that although it takes a great deal of time and work with local communities to develop effective and sustainable new approaches, this is essential to ensure their effectiveness and to acquire the legitimacy to advocate change.

External influences

In much of the work on developing countries, a set of factors has emerged that has had a decisive influence on the policy change in question and also on the spheres of context, evidence and links. These factors, loosely grouped under the heading 'external influences', include the impacts of international politics, the policies of donors, and the specific research funding approaches taken by donors.

In our PRSP case study it is clear that pressures felt by the World Bank and the International Monetary Fund have an impact not only on the institutions themselves, but also on most bilateral donors and, in turn, on all loan- or aid-receiving national governments. In other words, changes within these institutions form an external influence that can have substantial and far-reaching impacts on national policy processes and the use of evidence in policy processes. The effect of this external influence will be greater for recipient governments in the South than for others.

External influences also have a direct effect on the production and dissemination of research within international development. Broad incentives, such as EU membership or the PRSP process, can have a substantial impact on the demand for research by policy makers.[41] The processes of democratization and liberalization and increasing donor support for civil society are also generating demand for comparative analyses and for evidence-based recommendations. Donors are funding both research and communications and networking activities.

The increasing importance of international policy processes throws up a set of new research questions concerning transnational knowledge networks. Many of the RAPID studies involve fascinating elements of the transnational interactions of researchers, policy makers and donors. For example, the case of para-vets in Kenya involved the translation of a Chinese idea (barefoot doctors) into a different sector (animal health) in a different part of the world. How did this series of transnational interactions come about? Was there something about this sector that made it open to an idea transmitted across borders? Why did it occur in Kenya rather than somewhere else?[42] In a globalizing world, transnational knowledge sharing, both formal and informal, is becoming increasingly important.[43]

5. Some unanswered questions

Our work confirms that the political context has a critical impact on the uptake of research into policy. There is, however, very little evidence in the literature about the impact of democracy and good governance on the up-take of research into policy in the South. Much of the existing theory is from OECD countries and is based on assumptions of political and civil freedoms – especially academic and media freedoms. There is surprisingly little systematic evidence from contexts where these freedoms cannot be taken for granted.

We are left with some key questions: Do countries or organizations with good governance (accountability, transparency and responsiveness) use re-search more than others? Our work does suggest that democratic countries share a greater incentive, and are more likely, to use research in policy processes. The reasons why democracies would be more effective at taking up research into policy include factors on both the supply and demand side (and the relationship between them). In terms of supply, open political sys-tems allow evidence to be freely gathered, assessed and communicated. In terms of demand, democracies imply a greater accountability of govern-ments and therefore a greater incentive to improve policy and performance. Democratic contexts also imply the existence of more open entry points into the policy-making process. In contrast, autocratic regimes tend to limit the gathering and communication of evidence and have weak accountability mechanisms.[44]

In addition to general democracy and governance factors, some other is-sues are relevant here. Academic freedom is likely to be critical for re-search–policy linkages at specific policy level as well as the national level.[45] In some countries, for example, it is more feasible to conduct economic re-search than it is to undertake research on democracy or human rights. Media freedom is presumably a key factor influencing the communication of ideas into policy and practice. Freedom of information may be valued in its own right, but information and press freedoms have also been linked to the state's willingness to intervene in areas such as famine prevention, particu-larly in India.[46] However, there is no systematic data on the links between these issues and of the policy influence of research.

Civil society plays a part in most political systems – it is where people become familiar with and interested in public issues and how rules tend to affect the articulation of interests from society. Theories of social capital emphasize the importance of local associations in building trust and confi-dence both in institutions and among people.[47] Key issues here include the conditions under which citizens can express their opinions, organize them-selves for collective action and compete for influence. There is also evi-dence to suggest that civil society is an important link between research and policy.[48]

Given the importance of external influences on Southern policy contexts, a further pertinent question concerns the effects of uneven access to international research/policy networks for Southern institutions. Much of the research on development issues is undertaken in the North, raising issues of perceived relevance and legitimacy. Perhaps even more important, there is an imbalance between the relatively low priority given to research capacity building in Southern institutions in comparison to the research budgets spent by Northern-based institutions. Also, a substantial amount of the development research that is undertaken in the poorest countries is funded by international donors, which also raises a range of issues around ownership, whose priorities are being taken into account, the use of external consultants and, again, perceived legitimacy. As policy processes become increasingly global, this arena will increase in importance. In this situation, new questions emerge. Whose interests will guide research funding? And how will donor funding of research be evaluated?

Finally, we know that networks matter, but how and why? Out of the arenas in our framework, our understanding of such links remains the most limited. Although it is relatively simple to draw a 'family tree' of the key individuals and partnerships involved in a particular policy 'episode', it is harder to understand how more diffuse networks influence the research–policy process. The theoretical literature provides myriad typologies of 'formal and informal networks', 'epistemic communities', and 'downward links', all of which seem to be evident and important in the case studies. They do not, however, add up to a comprehensive analytical tool for understanding what makes links function. What are the characteristics of networks that enable them to act as a bridge between research and policy? Where, how and to what degree do networks actually make a difference to policy making? Networks have not been regularly evaluated until recently, which means there is a lack of comprehensive data on their roles and effects. Different assessment models are being developed to address this issue,[49] but the area remains in need of further research.

6. Towards practical guidelines for researchers

Although researchers can often control the credibility of their evidence and try to interact with and communicate with policy makers, they may have limited capacity to influence the political context within which they work, especially in less democratic countries. Resources are also often limited, and researchers need to make choices about what they do. Table 1 suggests what researchers and others with a stake in development research and policy need to do if they wish to improve research–policy linkages.

7. Conclusions

The work of the RAPID programme in the international development sector highlights the *indirect* influence of research on policy, through processes similar to the 'percolation', 'enlightenment' and 'knowledge creep' identified by Weiss. For example, the RAPID study of PRSPs emphasizes how academic research in the 1970s, 1980s and 1990s had an indirect influence by shifting the development discourse towards poverty reduction, participation and aid effectiveness. That research highlighted problems with development practices and set the stage for the policy reviews of the 1990s that led to the adoption of PRSPs by the IMF and the World Bank in 1999.

It often takes a *long time* for research to have an impact on policy. This was the case with the PRSPs, and with HIV/AIDS. In the latter case, by the time policy makers became aware of the significant number of deaths due to AIDS, the disease had already spread through much of the population. The key is that policy makers must understand the epidemiology of the disease in order to respond appropriately. The cases included in this study support Gladwell's arguments that changes in context and the influence of key individuals can lead to a '*tipping point*' when a relatively minor event galvanizes trends that have been building up 'beneath the surface'. In many cases there seems to have been a general context where it was increasingly apparent that change was needed, and where a specific issues then spurred a policy change.

Table 1. What researchers need to know, what they need to do, and how to do it

What researchers need to know	What researchers need to do	How to do it
Political context: Who are the policy makers? Is there policy maker demand for new ideas? What are the sources/ strengths of resistance? What is the policy-making process? What are the opportunities and timing for input into formal processes?	Get to know the policy makers, their agendas and the constraints under which they operate. Identify potential supporters and opponents. Keep an eye on the horizon and prepare for opportunities in regular policy processes.	Work with the policy makers. Seek commissions. Line up research programmes with high-profile policy events. Reserve resources to be able to move quickly to respond to policy windows.

What researchers need to know	What researchers need to do	How to do it
	Look out for – and react to – unexpected policy windows.	Allow sufficient time and resources1
Evidence: What is the current theory? What are the prevailing narratives? How divergent is the new evidence? What sort of evidence will convince policy makers?	Establish credibility over the long term. Provide practical solutions to problems. Establish legitimacy. Build a convincing case and present clear policy options. Package new ideas in familiar theory or narratives. Communicate effectively.	Build up respected programmes of high-quality work. Action-research and pilot projects to demonstrate benefits of new approaches. Use participatory approaches to help with legitimacy and implementation. Clear strategy and resources for communication from the start. Real communication – 'seeing is believing'.
Links: Who are the key stakeholders in the policy discourse? What links and networks exist between them? Who are the intermediaries and what influence do they have? Whose side are they on?	Get to know the other stakeholders. Establish a presence in existing networks. Build coalitions with like-minded stake-holders. Build new policy networks.	Partnerships between researchers, policy makers and communities. Identify key networkers and salesmen. Use informal contacts.
External influences: Who are main international actors in the policy process? What influence do they have? What are their aid priorities? What are their research priorities and mechanisms?	Get to know the donors, their priorities and the constraints they operate under. Identify potential supporters. Establish contacts with key individuals or networks. Establish credibility. Keep an eye on donor policy and look out for policy windows.	Develop extensive background on donor policies. Orient communications to priorities and in donor language. Try to work with the donors and seek commissions. Contact (regularly) key individuals.

While some of the existing theory does apply, our work indicates that care must be taken when applying such models to developing countries.

There is a need to adopt a broader framework than one that might be used in the OECD countries. The social, economic and political contexts may be different and more varied, and basic assumptions about political and academic freedoms may not apply.

Research *does* matter. Our work shows that the quality of evidence is crucial for policy uptake, although its influence can be slow and indirect. Academic research is more likely to have an indirect 'percolation' effect on policy language and the policy environment over time, while applied or policy-oriented research is more likely to have a direct and more immediate influence on policy. Impact can be enhanced and accelerated if research is topical and operationally relevant – and if communicated to different audiences via the most appropriate communicators, channels, style, format and timing. For impact, research communication needs to go far beyond the dissemination model that often prevails. Research is more likely to contribute to evidence-based and pro-poor policy making if researchers understand the political and institutional limits and pressures of policy makers, and is oriented to resonate with their ideological assumptions, or sufficient pressure is exerted to challenge them.

The political context is crucial, and many developing countries do not have contexts conducive to the uptake of research into policy. The level of demand for change, the extent of contestation and openness to new ideas are critical in terms of policy change and usually have a greater degree of impact over and above other factors. All stakeholders interested in enhancing research–policy linkages need to understand the political context and knowledge systems in which these interactions occur. In many cases, research–policy linkages will be enhanced by interventions in non-research components of systems. However, it is clear that whilst the political context at the moment of policy shift is a critical factor, the cases do not suggest that this context is immovable, unstoppable or deterministic of policy outcomes. Researchers, civil society groups and international actors can change the policy context. While policy processes in developing countries rarely conform to the classic policy cycle, making them more structured, transparent and predicable would help foster better uptake of research-based evidence.

The links between researchers and policy makers are critical. Key issues include feedback, dialogue and collaboration; the role of networks and policy communities; and trust, legitimacy and participation. Our work suggests that researchers are more likely to be influential if they interact with policy makers – as individuals, via mediators or through networks. It is worth noting the prominent role of 'policy entrepreneurs' – such as the connectors and salesmen identified by Gladwell. While we know that networks matter, we are not yet in a position to indicate clearly how and why.

In many developing countries, particularly smaller and poorer ones, international factors have a significant impact on research–policy linkages. Some of the major policy processes – such as the PRSPs – have led to an increase in the use of evidence in policy making. AIDS provides an interesting case: while the huge international push regarding HIV/AIDS has led many African leaders to 'speak the right language', the responses on the ground in terms of funding and activities to fight the disease have been mixed.

Our findings, although tentative, suggest that donor (or indigenous) initiatives to improve democracy and good governance as well as to promote civil freedoms have positively influenced the context for bridging research and policy. Our work is much clearer regarding the ways that donor research funding priorities affect the research undertaken in developing countries; for many countries, international sources provide a substantial share of research funding. It is less clear, however, whether this is more likely to feed through into policy. In some cases, international research enhances impact; in others it may hinder policy uptake. One clear conclusion is that donors should ensure that research is truly focused on the needs of a country (to enhance growth or reduce poverty), implying a greater emphasis on needs assessments. They should also ensure that research influences policy, implying engagement with policy processes and research as part of a package of measures (networks, capacity building, communications) rather than stand-alone. One way is to build local capacities around specific problem topics – of researchers, policy makers and mediators, depending on the subject and the context.

This chapter has provided a sketch of the critical factors, and the interactions between them, that influence whether some research findings are taken up and acted upon, while others are ignored. The analysis of the theory and the work in this area aimed to provide some useful insights and ideas, both analytical and practical, for researchers, practitioners, policy makers and others who wish to further evidence-based and pro-poor policy in their own work. While there will always be an element of unpredictability and surprise, these observations may help to maximize the impact of research on policy and practice in international development.

Notes

1. Julius Court (jcourt@odi.org.uk) and John Young are members of the Research and Policy in Development (RAPID) programme, Overseas Development Institute (ODI), London, UK.

2. World Bank (1999).
3. Surr *et al.* (2002).
4. *Ibid.*
5. The HIV/AIDS crisis has deepened in some countries because of the reluctance of governments to implement effective control programmes despite clear evidence of the causes of the disease and how to prevent it spreading.
6. Court *et al.* (2005), Court and Maxwell (2005).
7. See OECD (2001).
8. Weiss (1977).
9. Garret and Islam (1998).
10. Sutton (1999).
11. Lindquist (2003).
12. Democracy is defined as a political system with institutionalized procedures for open and competitive political participation, where chief executives are chosen in competitive elections and where substantial limits are imposed on powers of the chief executive (see Gurr *et al.*, 2001).
13. Freedom House (2003).
14. See Hyden *et al.* (2004); Grindle (1980).
15. Grindle (1980: 15).
16. Estimates included in a speech by World Bank President James Wolfensohn in 1999 (www.worldbank.org/html/extdr/am99/jdw-sp/jdwsp-en.htm).
17. Edwards (2004), Hyden *et al.* (2004).
18. This is based on the OECD's definition of research: 'creative work undertaken on a systematic basis in order to increase the stock of knowledge, including knowledge of man, culture and society, and the use of this stock of knowledge to devise new applications' (OECD, 1981).
19. Anderson (1984).
20. Weiss (1977), Linquist (2003).
21. See de Vibe *et al.* (2002), Crewe and Young (2002), Court and Young (2003; 2005). For more information about RAPID research and projects, see www.odi.org.uk/rapid
22. Kingdon (1984), Clay and Schaffer (1984).
23. Williamson (1996).
24. Mattelart and Mattelart (1998).
25. Pross (1986), Haas (1991), Sabatier and Jenkins-Smith (1999).
26. Gladwell (2000).
27. Court and Young (2003).
28. (1)de Vibe *et al.* (2002), Hovland (2003), Court and Pollard (2005); (2) Court and Young (2003); (3) Court *et al.* (2005); (4) www.gdnet.org/rapnet; (5) Court (2004); (6) Piron and Court (2004); (7) see www.odi.org.uk/rapid/meetings.
29. Kingdon (1984).
30. Christiansen and Hovland (2003).
31. Sutton (1999), Keeley and Scoones (2003).
32. Lipsky (1980).
33. Young *et al.* (2003).
34. E.g. Lambin (1996).
35. Philo (1996).
36. Mattelart and Mattelart (1998).
37. Kickert *et al.* (1997), Robinson *et al.* (1999).
38. Haas (1991); see also the chapter by Sunil Mani in this volume.
39. Fine *et al.* (2000).

40. Figueroa *et al.* (2002).
41. Court and Young (2003).
42. For a discussion of this case see Court *et al.* (2005).
43. Stone and Maxwell (2005).
44. For example, a case study from Uruguay charted the negative effect of the dictatorship on the use of research in health policy (Salvatella *et al.*, 2000).
45. For various pertinent aspects search www.aaup.org/
46. Sen (1999).
47. Putnam (1993).
48. Court and Young (2003); Court and Maxwell (2005); Pollard and Court (2005).
49. Church *et al.* (2003), Provan and Milward (2001).

References

Anderson, J. (1984) *Public Policy Making: An Introduction*, 3rd edn, Boston: Houghton Mifflin.

Christiansen, K. and Hovland, I. (2003) *The PRSP Initiative: Multilateral Policy Change and the Role of Research*, Working Paper 216, London: ODI.

Church, M. *et al.* (2003) *Participation, Relationships and Dynamic Change: New Thinking on Evaluating the Work of International Networks*, Working Paper 121, Development Planning Unit (DPU), University College London (www.ucl.ac.uk/dpu/WP121.pdf).

Clay, E.J. and Schaffer, B.B. (1984) *Room for Manoeuvre: An Exploration of Public Policy in Agricultural and Rural Development,* London: Heinemann Educational Books, p.192.

Court, J. (2004) *Bridging Research and Policy on HIV/AIDS in Developing Countries*, RAPID report. London: ODI (www.odi.org/rapid/).

Court, J., Hovland, I. and Young, J. (2005) *Bridging Research and Policy in Development: Evidence and the Change Process,* London: ITDG.

Court, J. and Maxwell, S. (2005) Policy entrepreneurship for poverty reduction: bridging research and policy in international development. *Journal of International Development,* 17(6): 713–725.

Court, J. and Pollard, A. (2005) *Civil Society Organizations, Evidence and Policy Processes: Annotated Bibliography,* Working Paper 249, London: ODI.

Court, J. and Young, J. (2003) *Bridging Research and Policy: Insights from 50 Case Studies*, Working Paper 213, London: ODI.

Court, J. and Young, J. (2005) Bridging research and policy in international development: Context, evidence and links, in D. Stone and S. Maxwell (Eds), *Global Knowledge Networks and International Development: Bridges across Boundaries,* London: Routledge.

Crewe, E. and Young, J. (2002) *Bridging Research and Policy: Context, Evidence and Links*, Working Paper 173, London: ODI. Available at www.odi.org.

De Vibe, M., Hovland, I. and Young, J. (2002) *Bridging Research and Policy: An Annotated Bibliography*, Working Paper 174. London: ODI.

Edwards, M. (2004) *Civil Society*, Cambridge: Polity Press.

Figueroa, M.E. *et al.* (2002) *Communication for Social Change: An Integrated Model for Measuring the Process and Its Outcomes.* Communication for Social Change Working Paper Series No 1. New York: Rockefeller Foundation (www.comminit.com/ stcfscindicators/sld-5997.html).

Fine, M., Weis, L., Weseen, S. and Wong, L. (2000) For whom? Qualitative research, representations, and social responsibilities, in N. Denzin, and Y. Lincoln (Eds.) *Handbook of Qualitative Research*, 2nd edn, Thousand Oaks, CA: Sage.

Freedom House (2003) *Freedom in the World*, Washington, DC: Freedom House.

Garret, J.L. and Islam, Y. (1998) *Policy Research and the Policy Process: Do the Twain ever Meet?* Gatekeeper Series no 74. London: IIED.

Gladwell, M. (2000) *The Tipping Point: How Little Things Can Make a Big Difference*. London: Little, Brown & Co.

Grindle, M.S. (Ed.) (1980) *Politics and Policy Implementation in the Third World*. Princeton, NJ: Princeton University Press.

Gurr, T., Marshall, M.G. and Kholsa, A. (2001) *A Global Survey of Armed Conflicts, Self-determination Movements and Democracy*. Center for International Development and Conflict Management, University of Maryland.

Haas, E.B. (1991) *When Knowledge is Power: Three Models of Change in International Organisations*. Berkeley, CA: University of California Press.

Hovland, I. (2003) *Communication of Research for Poverty Reduction: A Literature Review*, Working Paper 227. London: ODI (www.odi.org.uk/publications).

Hyden, G., Court, J. and Mease, K. (2004) *Making Sense of Governance: Empirical Evidence from 16 Developing Countries*. Boulder, CO: Lynne Rienner.

Keeley, J. and Scoones, I. (2003) *Understanding Environmental Policy Processes in Africa: Cases from Ethiopia, Mali and Zimbabwe*, London: Earthscan.

Kickert, W. *et al.* (1997) A management perspective on policy networks, in W. Kickert *et al.* (Eds) *Managing Complex Networks*. London: Sage.

Kingdon, J.W. (1984) *Agendas, Alternatives, and Public Policies*. New York: Harper-Collins.

Lambin, J. (1996) *Strategic Marketing Management*. Maidenhead, UK: McGraw-Hill.

Lindquist, E.A. (2003) *Discerning Policy Influence: Framework for a Strategic Evaluation of IDRC-supported Research*. Ottawa, Canada: IDRC (www.idrc.ca).

Lipsky, M. (1980) *Street-level Bureaucracy: Dilemmas of the Individual in Public Services*. New York: Russell Sage Foundation.

Mattelart, A. and Mattelart, M. (1998) *Theories of Communication: A Short Introduction*. London: Sage.

OECD (1981) *The Measurement of Scientific and Technical Activities: Proposed Standard Practice for Surveys of Research and Experimental Development* (Frascati Manual). Paris: OECD.

OECD (2001) *Science, Technology and Industry Outlook: Drivers of Growth: Information Technology, Innovation and Entrepreneurship*. Paris: OECD.

Philo, G (1996) Seeing and believing, in P. Marris and S. Thornham (Eds) *Media Studies: A Reader*. Edinburgh: Edinburgh University Press.

Piron, L. and Court, J. (2004) *Independent Evaluation of the Influence of SDC's Human Rights and Rule of Law Guidance Documents* (SDC Evaluation Report). Berne: SDC.

Pollard, A. and Court, J. (2005) *How Civil Society Organisations Use Evidence to Influence Policy Processes: A literature review*, Working Paper 249. London: ODI.

Pross, P. (1986) *Group Politics and Public Policy*. Toronto: Oxford University Press.

Provan, K. and Brinton Milward, H. (2001) Do networks really work? A framework for evaluating public-sector organizational networks, *Public Administration Review*, 61(4): 414–423.

Putnam, R. (1993) *Making Democracy Work: Civic Traditions in Italy*. Princeton, NJ: Princeton University Press.

Robinson, D., Hewitt, T. and Harriss, J. (1999) Why inter-organizational relationships matter, in D. Robinson *et al.* (Eds) *Managing Development: Understanding Inter-organizational Relationships.* London: Sage.

Sabatier, P. and Jenkins-Smith, H.C. (1999) The advocacy coalition framework: An assessment, in P. Sabatier (Ed.) *Theories of the Policy Process.* Boulder, CO: Westview Press.

Salvatella, R., Muzio, F. and Sánchez, D. (2000) Chagas disease and foot and mouth disease eradication in Uruguay, in *Lessons in Research to Action and Policy: Case Studies from Seven Countries,* Geneva: Council on Health Research for Development, pp.67–76.

Sen, A. (1999) *Development as Freedom,* New York: Random House.

Stone, D. and Maxwell, S. (Eds) (2005) *Global Knowledge Networks and International Development: Bridges across Boundaries,* London: Routledge.

Surr, M., Barnett, A., Duncan, A. and Speight, M. (2002) *Research for Poverty Reduction.* DFID Research Policy Paper. London: DFID.

Sutton, R. (1999) *The Policy Process: An Overview*, Working Paper 118. London: ODI.

Weiss, C. (1977) Research for policy's sake: The enlightenment function of social research. *Policy Analysis,* 3(4): 531–545.

Williamson, J. (1996) Decoding advertisements, in P. Marris and S. Thornham (Eds) *Media Studies: A Reader.* Edinburgh: Edinburgh University Press.

World Bank (1999) *World Development Report 1998/99: Knowledge for Development.* Washington, DC: World Bank.

Young, J., Kajume, J. and Wanyama, J. (2003) *Animal Health Care in Kenya: The Road to Community-based Animal Health Service Delivery,* Working Paper 214. London: ODI.

PRIORITY SETTING IN RESEARCH FOR DEVELOPMENT: A DONOR'S PERSPECTIVE

THEO VAN DE SANDE[1]

Dutch development assistance in research has taken the twin shape of technology transfer and research capacity building. In 1992 DGIS established a Research Unit to implement a new policy for utilizing and strengthening local research capacity on the basis of demand-driven research agendas. Some of the resulting Multi-annual Multi-disciplinary Research Programmes (MMRPs) developed into research organizations. Overall, the experience with the MMRPs has been rewarding in terms of utilizing local research capacity by funding local research proposals, and of enhancing the relevance of research by using a demand-oriented approach. In addition, the DGIS Research Unit supports a number of programmes where decision making is shared between Northern (mostly, but not exclusively Dutch) and Southern researchers. There is a broad consensus about the importance of supporting and utilizing local researchers and local research capacity to address local research agendas. Instead of a global research agenda with general priorities, a multitude of research agendas to address specific local priorities are emerging. In particular, the policy aimed to equip Southern researchers to address a Southern research agenda with practical research to address the priorities of the poor.

1. Introduction

In the post-war period research and innovation made a major contribution to economic growth in the industrialized world. This success gave rise to optimistic scenarios in which the apparently powerful tools of science could also be used to alleviate poverty and encourage development in the former colonies. Most of these scenarios were relatively straightforward, if not simplistic, and ultimately proved to be false.

The affluent society in the North was based on the carefully managed relation between mass production and consumption. Henry Ford was one of the first to recognize that he could pay his labourers a decent wage provided that they could be persuaded to use their increased purchasing power to buy products (such as the Model T Ford) that could now be produced cheaply, quickly and in large volumes. The success of 'Fordism' was based on a well defined division of labour, not only within the productive system, but also between the system, the government, civil society and science.

The role of science was to keep the engine of Fordism running by feeding it with innovations that would continue to increase productivity or economize on the use of raw materials, thereby contributing directly to profitability. Publicly funded research was to provide the basic capacity and ideas that privately controlled research could tap for innovations, aided if necessary by intermediaries like technological institutes. Within these boundaries, science and knowledge production were assumed to be objective, value-free, universal and curiosity driven. This traditional top-down, a-political, ivory tower image of research still persists as an attractive ideal to many, especially scientists and development policy makers.

The optimism regarding the role of science in development was therefore not surprising. Through the simple transfer of knowledge, technology or innovations from the North, the South could overcome poverty. If, in addition, the South invested in building a knowledge system roughly modelled on the ivory towers of the North, development was bound to be sustainable. Development assistance in research took the twin shape of technology transfer and research capacity building.

The picture sketched so far may seem exaggerated, but it provides an adequate framework for understanding the linearity mechanisms, methodologies, orientations and priorities of and in knowledge production. With the Green Revolution and the agricultural research system represented in the Consultative Group on International Agricultural Research (CGIAR) in mind, the picture becomes more concrete and vivid.

It soon became apparent that the Northern knowledge system was incapable of achieving the ambition of eternal growth. In order to meet the demand for innovation in the post-Fordist era, knowledge systems in the North were reorganized. The ivory towers were torn down, and knowledge became the product of teamwork, tailor made, flexible and multidisciplinary. To use the terms of Gibbons *et al.*, knowledge production shifted from mode 1 to mode 2.[2] It was in the midst of this shift, in the early 1990s, that a debate began in the Netherlands on the features of a new policy to support research for development.[3]

2. Dutch research policy

A crucial aspect of the Dutch policy on development research was that it did not aim for a science policy as such. The interest was primarily in development itself, with research as an instrument for development, or to get an analytical grip on the development process.

Basic elements

The first element of the research policy emerging at the end of the 1980s was the acknowledgement of the importance of domestic research capacity in developing countries. Various arguments were put forward to substantiate the relevance of fostering such a capacity, not least with a view to ensuring the sustainability of the contribution of research to development.

Until that time most research cooperation had involved the utilization of the research capacity in the North (the donor) rather than in the South. In the new policy, strengthening and utilizing Southern research capacity became more important, with the aim of building up a minimum critical mass of qualified local personnel at home rather than abroad. Research programmes in the South that were to be supported should therefore focus on developing human capacities, expanding the empirical knowledge base, and proposing and validating government policies.

The second element of the policy was that research should be based on the development priorities of local researchers and authorities in developing countries. In short, it should be based on local demand, and not on the interests of donors or Northern researchers. In order to make local priorities effective as research guidelines, efforts should be made to foster better relations between the scientific community, the private and public sectors and the political community.

One of the fundamental questions immediately raised was: whose demands or priorities should be used to guide the content and direction of research? Further, if there is no consensus among the scientific, economic and political communities in a developing country, who is to choose the priorities? The new policy made it clear that in resolving this so-called 'Ganuza dilemma',[4] foreign researchers and policy makers should not use the lack of consensus as an excuse for making such choices themselves. Neither could they disregard the priorities identified by a group in a developing country in favour of those of Northern researchers or funding agencies by referring to global problems such as the environment or new technologies, since developing countries were not involved in setting these research priorities. In addition to these Northern or global threats to local priority setting, it was realized that in most cases existing research capacity in the South inhabited ivory towers at least as high as those of their counterparts in the North. In addition, governments can make poor choices that do not adequately reflect the needs or the wishes of local people, in particular women and ethnic groups.

It was expected that the Ganuza dilemma could be addressed in three steps. First, identify the groups in the developing country whose interests should be served by a specific research programme, on the basis of development criteria. Second, identify local researchers who are closely affiliated with that group. Third, accept priorities that are the result of a conditioned demand orientation in a dialogue with the research and policy-making partners. In short, DGIS support to research activities in developing countries therefore required that the research agenda and priorities should be based on local demand, and that the agenda should be addressed by local researchers.

The MMRPs

In line with the new policy, in 1992 DGIS introduced a new instrument, the Multi-annual, Multidisciplinary Research Programmes (MMRPs). These programmes would support demand-led research focusing on the processes of change, development, transition and transformation in a specific country or region.[5] Established in ten countries, the MMRPs were intended to have the following characteristics:

- they would be designed, implemented and coordinated entirely in the developing countries;
- they would support locally relevant research, with contributions from various disciplines;
- the research agendas would be set in an autonomous internal policy dialogue between researchers and non-researchers (NGOs, grassroots movements, governments), free of external interference, in order to increase the relevance and societal impact of the research and ensure the utilization of the results;
- they would finance a wide range of activities, including networking, PhDs, workshops, training, methodologies, etc.; and

- once under way, they would be free to request support for monitoring, training, etc., from sources other than DGIS.

In each country, the local institution that hosted the programme, and the steering committee made up of representatives of major local stakeholders, enjoyed full decision-making autonomy. For these programmes a conscious attempt was made to create a sanctuary against the asymmetries of the global research world, leaving them free to make their own choices with respect to contacts, cooperation and support. Thus, the policy aimed to promote demand-led rather than supply-driven research. The Netherlands would supply the framework and the resources, while the research agenda would be formulated and implemented by the researchers in the South.

To prevent the programmes being usurped by special interest groups, independent intermediary organizations were identified that could be trusted to bear responsibility for facilitating the process of articulating local demand. Together with the selection of countries, the crucial choice of partners – the host organizations and chairs of the steering committees – were made by DGIS.

Continuity and change

In exchange for the opportunity to experiment with the new research policy and the MMRPs, DGIS also had to continue to service the clients of the old policy. The intention was to use the experiences with the MMRPs to reform those more traditional activities along the lines of the new policy. Thus, in addition to the changes, there would also be continuity.

DGIS continued to support multilateral research efforts through the CGIAR, albeit with a greater emphasis on reorienting them to reflect local research needs and priorities, and to strengthen research capacities in developing countries. DGIS hoped to strengthen inter-university cooperation programmes between the Netherlands and developing countries in line with the new research policy orientation. DGIS also aimed to increase expenditures on research to a target of 5% in its bilateral cooperation programmes.

3. Impressions and experiences

In 1992 DGIS established a Research Unit to implement the new policy. Given the importance attached to the MMRPs as instruments for utilizing and strengthening local research capacity on the basis of demand-led research agendas, the Research Unit devoted considerable time and effort to these programmes. Before addressing some of the lessons learned from these programmes, it is worthwhile sketching a broader view of the place of research in Dutch development cooperation.

In the early years the Research Unit attempted to quantify expenditures on research, not least with a view to assessing whether the 5% target was being reached (note that expenditures on traditional fellowship and scholarship programmes at higher education institutes in the Netherlands were not included).

In 2003 total DGIS expenditures on core research activities amounted to about €44 million per annum, or 1.1% of all expenditures on development cooperation, with a slight decline from 1.2% in 2000 to 1.1% in 2002. Almost 93% of this amount was spent on three categories: research/scientific institutions, agricultural research and forestry research. The annual budget of the Research Unit was €22 million, or one-half of DGIS expenditures on research. Most of the remainder originated from other ministries and directorates, such as the Environment and Water. Despite the target of 5%, bilateral expenditures on research were negligible.[6]

The activities supported by the Research Unit can be characterized in terms of the type of activity and decision-making power. Along the first dimension, a distinction can be made between support to research funding versus support to research activities and/or networks. Along the second, a distinction can be made between Southern versus shared North–South decision making. Support to the CGIAR is regarded as a separate category. Using these two categories, the Research Unit's expenditures in 2003 were as follows:

Research funding	Southern decision making (e.g. the MMRPs)	30%
Research funding	North–South decision making	22%
Research	Southern decision making	7%
Research	North–South decision making	16%
CGIAR		24%

The rest of this section describes the experiences with the various instruments in the context of the DGIS research policy.

The MMRPs

As can be expected, there are no easy or uniform lessons to be learned from the MMRPs (the latter as a metaphor for all research funding activities with

Southern decision making that received funds from the Research Unit). As a result of personal, institutional and organizational differences and differing local contexts, the experiences have been mixed. Nevertheless, an attempt can be made to draw lessons in terms of local research capacity, demand orientation and relevance, and resolving the Ganuza dilemma.

Local research capacity

The (Dutch) choice of the ten countries where the MMRPs were to be established was based largely on the assessment of whether there was an existing critical mass of researchers. It was considered to be beyond the means of the Research Unit to start building such a critical mass from scratch. In addition, it would be very difficult for a research-funding programme to function in an environment where the number and the quality of research proposals submitted for funding were likely to be low. In some countries there were serious doubts as to whether such a critical mass of researchers could be found.

Experience has shown that these doubts were justified. In some countries, despite serious efforts, it proved infeasible to establish an MMRP; in others it was decided to go ahead, despite doubts about the quality of the existing research capacity. These latter programmes were successful in organizing training courses for various target groups, but the research output has been very low and the impact remains even lower. The researchers involved and the scientific community at large appreciated the programmes, but they gained little support among civil society, NGOs or the poor since they were unable to deliver. Indeed, it proved to be beyond the means of the MMRPs to create a domestic research capacity.

Even the concept of research capacity building might have to be reconsidered. In several cases, the 'researchers' were in fact employed full-time as teachers or lecturers. University curricula and training programmes were insufficient to equip them as researchers. In some cases, professors or lecturers were not allowed to do research during the normal working week, so their work was confined to weekends. In other cases, teachers conducted their research on a consultancy or contract basis, in addition to their normal duties and teaching obligations. The more successful programmes, however, did provide opportunities for young researchers or senior researchers on sabbatical, by offering training in practical matters, such as how to write research proposals and methodological approaches.

In line with the demand orientation, the programmes developed their own ways of managing research, including generating research proposals, assessing proposals, monitoring and evaluation, and involving stakeholders. An inter-esting spin-off has been that some of the more traditional research institutes have shown interest in the management practices that evolved within the MMRPs.

In funding demand-oriented research activities in countries with an ade-quate critical mass, some programmes contributed to the process of rooting research capacity in their own society, by organizing workshops and confer-ences to present and discuss the research findings. The researchers were exposed to other stakeholders who took them seriously as partners, and be-came part of larger networks, perhaps also including farmers, NGO repre-sentatives, extension workers and policy makers. For the first time other stakeholders were able to hold them accountable for their results. In some programmes the concept of researchers was widened to include journalists or NGO activists.

From the perspective of the researchers, the most refreshing difference from normal research funding was the lack of bureaucratic ties and limita-tions. If available at all, research funding in developing countries is riddled with rules and is often highly politicized.

Demand orientation and relevance

Much of the disappointment in the performance of the research programmes in terms of development or poverty alleviation can be attributed to the ab-sence of links between ongoing research and the local demand for knowl-edge or innovations. In order to increase the relevance of the research sup-ported by the MMRPs, the DGIS policy had postulated demand orientation as one of the basic requirements for funding.

With hindsight, it is remarkable that in the design of the MMRPs so little attention was paid to identifying and prioritizing research to be supported. Neither DGIS nor the local programme partners made an effort to focus the research activities; the local steering committee was responsible for consid-ering and accepting research proposals. As a result, the research was spread too thinly, both geographically and thematically, and so had little impact. Partly as a result, it is equally remarkable that few stakeholders other than scientists and policy makers were involved in programme design or decision making. It appears that the networks of researchers identified to set up the programmes did not include NGO staff, extensionists or farmers. The pro-grammes' lack of focus prevented the meaningful involvement of other stake-holders. Thus, although DGIS and the local partners succeeded in preventing Northern concerns dominating the research agendas, too few efforts were made to involve other local stakeholders, and to encourage their contributions in order to ensure the relevance of the research. It was insufficiently taken into account that not only Northern, but also Southern researchers inhabit their own ivory towers.

From the results that were published, it can be concluded that those responsible for decision making did their best to support research that was relevant to the poor or powerless. Many studies were carried out that had an impact in terms of empowerment, development or poverty alleviation. Yet the involvement of other stakeholders would undoubtedly have added to the quality and the robustness of the programmes as a funding mechanism. The limited involvement of stakeholders also meant that the dissemination of the research results was not an integral part of the activities, but had to be organized by the researchers or the programme after the work was completed.

In order to do justice to the multi-faceted problem of poverty, it was assumed that the research would have to be multidisciplinary. Over the years, however, hardly any research supported by the MMRPs was multidisciplinary, let alone transdisciplinary. In some cases, it was only at the programme level that some degree of multidisciplinarity was achieved by combining the findings of various separate research activities. In terms of Gibbons *et al.*, knowledge production in the MMRPs turned out to be mode 1 rather than mode 2.

For many of the programmes, the preparatory phase extended over several years. Most of this time was spent assessing the adequacy of the research capacity and resolving institutional issues. In particular, choosing the right partners was considered to be crucial for success. These issues are discussed in the next section.

The Ganuza dilemma

The question of 'who will formulate whose demand' to be addressed by the MMRPs was crucial for ensuring the relevance of the research and its impact. The DGIS Research Unit, supported by the Netherlands Development Assistance Research Council (RAWOO), made extensive efforts to identify committed individuals and organizations (mostly NGOs) that would be able and willing to set up and implement the programmes. Fact-finding missions were organized and funds were made available for workshops to identify potential partners, to assess research priorities and discuss progress.

The institutional structure was supposed to consist of a steering committee made up of local stakeholders that would be responsible for decision making, an intermediary organization that would host the programme without interfering in the management, and a secretariat, headed by a coordinator who would be responsible for day-to-day management. In practice, the institutional design was defined by the coordinators, most of whom belonged to the network of the Research Unit. Depending on their position and ambition, the coordinators either established a new organization on behalf of the MMRP, or decided that the organization they worked for would host the programme.

Next, the Research Unit, in consultation with the coordinator, was to nominate the chair of the steering committee. Together, the coordinator and the chair were to decide on the orientation of the programme, and to identify the other members of the steering committee. The process of co-option was of course also heavily influenced by the networks of which the coordinator and the chair were members.

The Research Unit did little to encourage the development of effective checks and balances within the MMRPs. Sometimes, programme proposals were accepted before these checks and balances were in place, and little or no effort was made to encourage their emergence, or to insist upon written rules and regulations, criteria, terms of reference and a memorandum of understanding between the host organization and the steering committee.

The division of responsibilities between the programme elements were largely informal. In later years, the unclear position and role of the host organizations created confusion, not least for the coordinators who were often employed by them, who found their loyalties divided between the organization and the steering committee. In other cases the host organization took over – or at least tried to take over – the role of decision making from the steering committee.

In some cases a programme was registered as an independent organization with research organizations as members, who then assessed and decided on their own research proposals. In addition to the question of credibility of such a funding mechanism, this practice discouraged non-members from even trying to submit proposals for funding. Some MMRPs developed into research organizations rather than serve as a research funding mechanism, using project funds to carry out their own research rather than to support research activities or strengthen local research capacities.

The most intensive contacts between the MMRPs and the Research Unit were through the coordinators, at the annual coordinators' meetings. Thus, even though the steering committee was responsible for the programme, the members were not always involved in decision making and were informed only afterwards.

All of these factors have contributed to a very mixed picture with respect to the institutional design and the strengths of the MMRPs. What they share as institutions, however, is the vulnerability of decision making within the programmes and the extreme dependency on one or two individuals. From the perspective of the sustainability of the programmes, or of the use of research for development, this situation is one that must be avoided in the future.

Overall, the experience with and within the MMRPs has been extremely rewarding in terms of utilizing local research capacity by funding their research proposals, and of enhancing the relevance of research by using a demand-oriented approach. Southern researchers have used the opportunity provided by the programmes to show that they are capable of doing excellent as well as relevant research. The MMRPs have helped to build the self-confidence of the researchers involved, and have thus contributed to more equitable relations with their colleagues, either in reputable institutes in the South, or in international research institutes in the North. Local researchers have shown that they are capable of producing innovations, of contributing to the empowerment of the poor and of improving policies. In providing such opportunities, the MMRPs have contributed to the process of rooting research capacity in their local environment and establishing networks of stakeholders.

So far, these lessons have not been (sufficiently) translated into local attempts to influence research funding mechanisms, research policies or research funding. On a practical level, it is remarkable that none of the Poverty Reduction Strategy Papers refers to research as an effective instrument for reducing poverty. Of course, this is not the sole responsibility of the programmes, but at least it could have been expected that they would be able to make a successful case for the inclusion of research. In these respects the programmes are still modest and too inward looking.

4. North–South cooperation programmes

In addition to the MMRPs, the DGIS Research Unit supports a number of research funding programmes where decision making is shared between Northern (mostly, but not exclusively Dutch) and Southern researchers. Examples include the South Africa–Netherlands Research Programme on Alternatives in Development (SANPAD), the Indo-Dutch Programme on Alternatives in Development (IDPAD), the Netherlands Foundation for the Advancement of Tropical Research (WOTRO), and the International

Foundation for Science (IFS). More than 20% of the Research Unit's budget is devoted to such activities.

In the early years, the attention of the Research Unit was focused on gaining experience with the MMRPs in ways to strengthen research capacity in the South and to increase the relevance of research. The lessons learned from these experiences were also used to try to influence decision making in these programmes in the same directions.

It is even more difficult than with the MMRPs to draw conclusions about the success of these programmes. They are smaller in number, whereas their contributions on average have been greater. There are wide differences between them in terms of their geographical scope and thematic coverage. Some programmes have been established only recently, whereas others have a longer track record. In some cases the Research Unit is the sole donor; in others it is only one among many others.

Overall, however, the impression is that the experiences of these programmes in increasing the relevance of research and strengthening the local research capacity are not markedly different from those in the MMRPs. Perhaps at one stage the DGIS Research Unit may have been ahead of its time in terms of its research policy and main funding instrument, but over the last decade the donor community at large as well as the scientific community have been rethinking the concepts and basic principles of research, research cooperation and research funding.[7]

It is now widely accepted that increasing the local relevance of research is essential. The applicability of research (in production or policy), demand orientation, and stakeholder involvement in identifying priorities have become part and parcel of the vocabulary of all research donors, funding mechanisms and research institutes. In the same vein, there is a broad consensus about the importance of supporting and utilizing local researchers and local research capacity to address local research agendas. To a certain extent, a new division of labour between Northern and Southern research capacity is emerging. The major task of Northern capacity is to build and strengthen Southern research capacity (in addition of course to the production of knowledge to address their own challenges), whereas the Southern capacity is to produce knowledge that meets local needs and demands.

In this division of labour, a new dilemma is emerging. As a result of the emphasis on demand orientation and relevance in both the North and the South, research agendas are becoming increasingly localized. Instead of a global research agenda with general priorities, a multitude of research agendas to address specific local priorities are emerging. As a consequence, Northern expertise or technology transfer has almost by definition become irrelevant in terms of problem solving for the South. In addition, it is questionable whether, from a Southern perspective, capacity building in and by the North is meaningful. Southern capacity building might serve the purpose much better.

5. The CGIAR

The Research Unit's support to the CGIAR has a long history, as do the discussions on the necessity for and the pace of change within the Group and its Future Harvest centres. The Unit's experiences with the CGIAR have little to add to the foregoing discussion, except for the notable resistance to change with respect to the successes of the Green Revolution. For a long time, increasing productivity seemed to be the system's only possible answer to every problem.

A complicating factor in the case of the CGIAR is the rigidities that result from the institutional setup of its crop-oriented research centres with a global mandate. Increasingly these rigidities have proved to be a serious hindrance to the CGIAR in realizing its mandate, which is to increase food security and alleviate poverty.

Since the mid-1990s, however, the CGIAR has started to experiment with better integrated, more demand-led approaches in the form of the eco-regional programmes, system-wide approaches and, more recently, the Challenge Programmes. It is still too early to draw any conclusions about the functioning of the Challenge Programmes as funding mechanisms since they were launched only in 2003. The Centres are increasingly realizing that changes are necessary. For example, some five years ago, the suggestion by a few donors that there should be closer cooperation between the International Rice Research Center (IRRI) and the International Maize and Wheat Improvement Center (CIMMYT) caused an outrage. Yet at the CGIAR Annual General Meeting in 2003 it was announced that the two institutes had started open-ended discussions that might result in anything between close cooperation and a full merger.

6. Conclusions

At the 2004 World Social Forum held in Mumbai, India, some of the participants made it clear that there still is a wide gap between academics and activists on the one hand, and oppressed citizens and the poor on the other. It might be added that an equally wide gap could probably be discovered between academics and activists.

The ambition of the DGIS research policy was to close the gap between research and development, or at least to prevent the gap from widening. In particular, the policy aimed to equip Southern researchers to address a Southern research agenda with practical research to address the needs and priorities of the poor. Well functioning networks consisting of (representatives of) all the major stakeholders are a necessary condition for realizing this ambition.

Among the various activities supported by the Research Unit, there are many examples of successful linkages that have resulted in increased productivity, empowerment of women and ethnic minorities, employment, food security or improved policies. Thus an approach founded on the basic elements 'Southern capacity' and 'demand-led' research is capable of closing the gap. The evidence, however, is too haphazard to be convincing at an aggregate level. The MMRPs have been successful within the limits of their programmes, but were too inward looking. They have had little effect on the research policies or research funding principles in their respective countries. Neither they nor the Research Unit have been capable of putting research high on the policy agenda or to position demand-led research as an effective instrument for development or poverty alleviation.

One of the reasons seems to be that both the MMRPs and the Research Unit supposed that successful research activities would be sufficiently persuasive in and of themselves to influence research policy making. Rather than relying on automatic trickle down (or up) effects, the programmes and the Unit should have been more actively involved in policy making on research and networking.

Another reason seems to be related to the basic assumption that Northern dominance of research cooperation was the major cause of biases in the research agendas and the lack of relevance of research in the South. Once this dominance was removed and full autonomy was put in Southern hands, it was assumed that all problems would be solved. This proved to be a misconception. Research capacity in the South also resides in ivory towers and is not well rooted in the local context. It will require extensive efforts and shrewd strategies to persuade scientists to come down from their ivory towers and to become partners in networks and coalitions that respect and appreciate the contributions of other stakeholders in knowledge production.

Notes

1. Theo van de Sande (theo.sande@minbuza.nl) is policy officer with the Directorate General for Development Cooperation (DGIS), Netherlands Ministry of Foreign Affairs.

2. Gibbons *et al.* (1994), Nowotny *et al.* (2001).
3. Schweigman and Bosma (1990), Schweigman and Van der Werf (1994).
4. This dilemma was first articulated by Enrique Ganuza, a Latin American social scientist, during a conference on development research in Groningen in 1989.
5. Bautista *et al.* (2001).
6. These figures should be treated with caution since they relate to activities whose major or sole activity is research. Research expenditures within the framework of other activities are less visible and more difficult to quantify.
7. IAC (2004a,b).

References

Bautista, C., Velho, L. and Kaplan, D. (2001) *Comparative Study of the Impacts of Donor-initiated Programmes on Research Capacity in the South*. The Hague: DGIS.

Gibbons, M., Limoges, C., Nowotny, H., Schwartzman, S., Scott, P. and Trow, M. (1994) *The New Production of Knowledge: The Dynamics of Science and Research in Contemporary Societies*. London: Sage.

IAC (2004a) *Inventing a Better Future: A Strategy for Building Worldwide Capacities in Science and Technology*. Amsterdam: InterAcademy Council.

IAC (2004b) *Realizing the Promise and Potential of African Agriculture*. Amsterdam: InterAcademy Council.

Nowotny, H., Scott, P. and Gibbons, M. (2001) *Rethinking Science, Knowledge and the Public in an Age of Uncertainty*. Cambridge: Polity Press.

Schweigman, C. and Bosma, U. (Eds.) (1990) *Research and Development Cooperation: The Role of the Netherlands*. Amsterdam: Royal Tropical Institute (KIT).

Schweigman, C. and Van der Werf, I. (Eds.) (1994) *Development-Related Research Collaboration: A Second Look at the Role of the Netherlands*. Amsterdam: Royal Tropical Institute (KIT).

INTERNATIONAL COLLABORATION IN SCIENCE AND TECHNOLOGY: PROMISES AND PITFALLS

CAROLINE S. WAGNER[1]

International collaborations represent a growing share of scientific and technical activities. In contrast with national programmes and projects, connections at the international level are systems of communication, facilitated by ICTs, that are often difficult to identify. Policy makers are faced with the question of how to support, benefit from and exploit them. The networks created by international collaboration in science and technology (ICST) offer opportunities for developing countries to acquire knowledge for local development, but there are few guidelines on how to manage such networked systems. The potential for missteps and the obstacles to joining networks are significant. This chapter describes the dynamics of ICST, and offers a framework for decision making about how to use the opportunities they offer to provide the demand for development.

1. Introduction

Various studies have demonstrated that international collaboration in science and technology (ICST) is growing.[2] The number of citations to articles resulting from international collaborations has grown faster than those referring to domestic collaborations.[3] Much of the ICST is beyond the direct control of research funding agencies and donors, and the question of when and why these organizations choose to invest in ICST is discussed. Indeed, the bulk of funding commitments within scientific or technical projects are made without reference to their international or funding status.

This chapter argues that the bulk of ICST activities can best be presented and managed as a *network of communications*. It continues with a description of networked operations of collaboration at the global level and delineates steps to tap into this set of activities. Finally, it discusses the implications for the networked organization of ICST for future policy and research planning.

2. Why is international collaboration growing?

The growth in ICST is occurring within all fields of science and technology. Factors such as the ease of travel and access to ICTs contribute to, but do not cause this growth in international collaborations. ICTs and low-cost travel reduce the opportunity costs of linking together for joint experimentation and data sharing. Many of today's technology applications that facilitate international research collaboration, such as 'grid computing' for online engineering projects,[4] or open source software engineering, were not available 10 years ago. However, in order to justify the time and extra effort involved in international collaboration, researchers must see clear benefits in collaborative knowledge creation.

There appear to be five major reasons why researchers engage in international collaborative activities: (1) they can increase their visibility among peers and exploit complementary capabilities;[5] (2) they are able to share the costs of projects that are large in scale or scope; (3) they are able to access or share expensive physical resources; (4) by working together, they can achieve greater leverage by sharing their data; and (5) they need to exchange ideas in order to encourage greater creativity.[6]

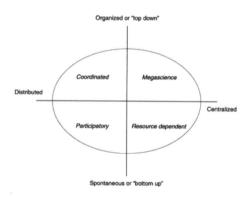

Figure 1. Schematic representation of factors relating to the organization of ICST.

Source: Wagner *et al.* (2000).

These sets of motivating factors are juxtaposed in figure 1. The vertical axis represents organizing features related to funding, extending from highly 'top-down' activities organized by institutions or organizations, to 'bottom-up' activities initiated by researchers themselves as they seek out partners for collaboration based on their own needs and interests. The horizontal axis represents the range of locations of research, from widely distributed to highly centralized. The juxtaposition creates four quadrants that can guide us in considering ways to understand and increase participation in international collaboration.

Researchers also self-organize 'spontaneously' into collaborative teams from the bottom up. They may work together to share, or may meet while accessing relatively rare or localized resources, such as botanists studying plants in a rainforest. This places them in the *resource-dependent* quadrant. Geophysics and soil sciences are two fields that might be considered as falling into this quadrant. Researchers can also self-select fellow collaborators independently of other factors like shared equipment, resources, or the interest of funding institutions, simply because the collaborator offers new ideas or complementary capabilities. This type of bottom-up collaboration, which could be termed participatory, occurs in fields such as mathematics or economics. It could also include cases where researchers of the same nationality living in different countries seek each other out. There are many cases of developing country scientists working abroad who collaborate with their compatriots.[7]

Each of these collaborative dynamics presents different challenges to policy makers or researchers who want to participate in ICST. Before exploring these dynamics in detail, it is useful to consider the motivation of the agencies that fund ICST, since they also influence the direction of research and the extent of collaboration.

3. Why do governments fund international collaboration?

Funding for ICST is committed by governments (through agencies, institutes, universities and special programmes), by quasi-governmental bodies that spend government money (such as the World Bank), and by non-governmental organizations (such as philanthropic groups). These three groups of 'funders' finance R&D for a variety of reasons, including the need to meet larger policy goals (national defence, foreign relations), to meet specific public missions (energy, health), and to promote knowledge creation (basic science or engineering), which is often tied to the rationale of enabling economic growth.

Funders spend some of their budgets on dedicated international collaboration, but in most cases, this tends to be a small percentage of their funding activities.[8] Research suggests that between 5 and 10% of all R&D funds are set aside for ICST. Quasi-governmental bodies with an international mission may spend a higher proportion of their budgets on ICST, but the net amounts for curiosity-driven research often are not high. NGOs commit considerable funds to S&T-related topics, but these are often highly mission-specific (such as malaria vaccine or crop research). The slice of funds available for open bidding and committed to 'open science' and technology is quite low.[9]

Figure 2 is a visualization of the role of funders in determining the subjects or organization of ICST. Funds dedicated to ICST, committed in projects such as the International Space Station or CERN, have been called 'corporate' partnerships or collaborations.[10] These are formal 'means to an end' research collaborations that are initiated by more than one group towards a common goal. When viewed in terms of overall spending, these activities represent a small percentage of all ICST – the 'tip of the iceberg' in figure 2. 'Team collaborations' are formalized through joint proposals or shared research resources, but they are not formally funded as such. Activities sponsored within the CGIAR centres or the international Human Frontier Science Program fall within this category. Finally, the bulk of ICST funds are spent within a diverse category of 'interpersonal collaborations' that includes informal partnerships, workshops, database development, fellowships, and many other activities.

Figure 2. Funding for ICST collaborations.

As ICST becomes less formal, governments and other funding agencies have less control over how funds are spent and who collaborates in the research. Thus, efforts to seek formal collaborations through foreign ministries are often disappointing because the funds available are very small. Even more disappointing is the fact that formal diplomatic-level S&T agreements often have no funds or authority attached to them. This is because the allocation of the bulk of the research monies is beyond the control of the diplomats. Even if they wanted to fund a specific programme with researchers from a specific country, the chances of finding and targeting funds in this way are minimal.[11]

4. Networking: a system of communications within ICST

If the bulk of ICST funds are allocated and spent by researchers as they take part in informal and team research activities, this has significant implications for anyone seeking to join these activities. How can these less formal activities be identified? How can policy makers and researchers find opportunities to initiate or join collaborations? How can interested researchers make themselves attractive candidates for membership on such teams? For the purpose of providing a framework for considering these questions, let us consider ICST as a system of communications.

When international science is considered as a series of communicating networks, it is possible to explain and even illustrate the dynamics of these relationships. Consider each co-authorship as representing a link between two researchers. Using this as a structure, it is possible to illustrate the network and then to 'see' changes in science and technology during the 1990s – changes that have significant and encouraging implications for developing countries. Between 1990 and 2000, at the regional level, researchers from more countries joined in collaborative research, as evidenced by co-authorships in internationally recognized peer-reviewed journals. Figures 3 and 4 show the network of linkages among African authors in 1990 and 2000, respectively. In 2000 the network is much better integrated, and shows the emerging knowledge hubs. Countries that were peripheral in 1990 are more closely tied into the network at the regional level in 2000.

The same pattern towards the integration of peripheral countries and the strengthening of links at the regional level can be shown to have occurred during the 1990s for all regions of the world except the Middle East.[12] This suggests a shift in the organization of science during the decade away from a 'centre-periphery' model with Germany, the UK and the USA at the centre of world science, with only a handful of industrialized countries as collaborators, to the emergence of hubs in all regions of the world. These regional hubs have served to draw in even smaller, more peripheral countries into an extended global network.

For researchers in developing countries, the benefit of joining a global network, even if only by linking to a neighbouring country, is that they are just a 'handshake' away from other members of the network. These networks create links in science so that researchers are only three or four steps away from each other in a broad global network of knowledge creators.[13] These links increase the chances of knowledge exchange in multiple directions, from advanced to developing countries, and vice versa. Local links also increase the likelihood that knowledge creation focuses on issues relevant to the developing countries rather than on issues that concern only scientists in advanced countries.

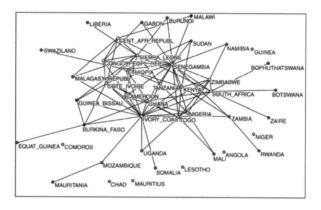

Figure 3. Network of co-authorships among African authors in 1990.
Source: Wagner and Leydesdorff (2003).

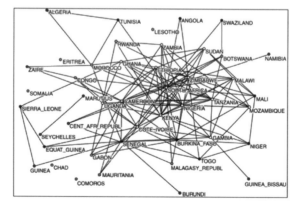

Figure 4. Network of co-authorships among African authors in 2000.
Source: Wagner and Leydesdorff (2003).

The networks operating at the international level are not 'flat', but have a structure and hierarchy. The largest and most scientifically advanced countries remain strong core members of the international system. However, the question for developing countries is not how to get into collaborations with Germany, the UK or the US, but how to take applicable knowledge from the network (no matter where it is located), make it relevant to local needs and problems, and tie it down. The process of tying down or retaining knowledge at the local level requires some institutional capacity.[14]

Within the overall structure of the international networks created by collaborative projects, the creation and communication of knowledge can be thought of as taking place at four levels:

- *Local:* building knowledge within laboratories and local research institutes that address local needs, e.g. a technical college that can help local farmers to solve problems.
- *National:* meeting national goals, building the economy, government-funded programmes to grow research capabilities.
- *Regional:* addressing problems, sharing knowledge among states with common problems, e.g. the APEC programme on environmental sustainability.
- *Global:* sharing resources, data and findings across national boundaries, e.g. 'megascience' projects such as the Large Hadron Collider and distributed collaborations like the Human Genome Project.

Figure 5 presents a visualization of these four levels of knowledge creation and communication.

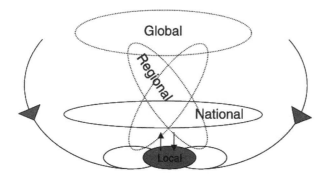

Figure 5. Science and technology collaboration operate on a number of levels, international collaboration is a system of communications on top of other levels.

As suggested by the dotted lines in figure 5, the 'global level' does not exist as a separate entity. There is no global ministry of science coordinating efforts at the international level. Relationships at the global level often self-organize through the initiatives of the researchers themselves. The links among researchers across nations operate through communications that tie the information and knowledge at the national and local levels, strengthening them. It is possible to use these ties to create a virtual neighbourhood of researchers who can share knowledge. For some new entrants to the network, however, the question becomes one of how to identify these links in the network, tap into them, and use the knowledge well.

5. Making strategic decisions for participation in ICST

The ability of any country or researcher to join the ICST network depends on two things – the resources they can bring to bear on a problem or question, and their attractiveness as a partner. While it may be possible to construct collaboration as a policy initiative, or to negotiate a diplomatic agreement to cooperate in science, these efforts will only be sustainable if they are supported by good science or solid technical skills. For this reason, policy makers or researchers seeking to develop an ICST strategy need to coordinate their plans with domestic efforts to improve domestic research and development. At the national level, in order to make the most of the international networks, government and research institutions should strengthen their links using face-to-face meetings and information technologies. Individual researchers should be regarded as 'stakeholders' in the process of decision making about ICST investments, since they are the ones who will be creating the connections to the broader network.

When making explicit plans for ICST, in order to be an attractive partner, it is important to build from strengths or to offer a unique resource. This is important because self-organizing networks look for partners rather than onlookers. 'Strengths' to offer can include, for example, a field of science or engineering where national researchers are publishing and being cited, a good database or a natural (or created) resource that scientists or engineers are interested in, or an innovative approach to a shared problem of interest to two or more countries.[15]

In any of these cases, selections must be made about where to place emphasis in order to build the critical mass to enable collaboration. Regional linkages can be highly productive and have the added advantage of involving less cost in terms of travel and cultural connections. Looking for and building regional hubs makes sense, and indeed, appears to be the way a number of countries have improved their connections over the past 15 years. Finally, bringing back the results of ICST to meet national needs is crucial to sustainability.

An ICST strategy needs both 'top-down' (government planned) and 'bottom-up' (interests of scientists and engineers) approaches. Identifying areas of common interest requires stakeholder analysis of where national capabilities lie, and determining what might be done with science or engineering. This can be accomplished through meetings that focus on identifying national needs, such as health care, security, energy, the environment, etc.

Once these ICST links are made, government policy can help to ensure that knowledge is made to flow back into local research institutes, and between them and industry. This feedback loop, or local network, is critical to being able to tie down the knowledge gained and maintain ICST participation in the future. This can be done by creating a database of developments and making it available on the web, or disseminating information in a newsletter or at public forums in order to gain recognition for the results.

Government influence over commitments and outcomes				
High ⟶ Medium ⟶ Low				
		Big Science	**Resource-dependent**	**Coordinated**	**Participatory**
High ↓	Government policy consideration	Care fully consider possible participation in strategic international collaborations already underway, such as genomics or physics research	Focus funds on a specific are a where Vietnamese expertise or unique resource would attract collaboration, such as fisheries	Examine research within the region where Vietnamese researchers could work virtually with others via the internet	Provide basic science fund, peer-revie wed, provided to best proposals for basic research; add funds for international conferences
Medium ↓	Actions for research institution to consider	Negotiate with other Vietnamese institutions about effective allocations of participation	Examine possibilities for creating centers of excellence in resource-dependent Science based on location, capabilities	Build broadband access to encourage virtual collaboration; built specialized database to support research	Create internal committees of researchers to review and support ICST activities
Low	Action at the level of the individual researcher	if big science is attractive, connect to regional researchers already working within the project	Create a team and seek funding from specialized non-governmental organization	Place good research on the Internet; seek to publish papers at the international level	Seek funds from the government or non-governmental organization to participate in international conferences and symposia; propose to host as well

Table 1. Special considerations for stakeholders in ICST decision making

6. Restructuring policy to tap knowledge networks

The knowledge networks that emerged during the 1990s and early 2000s now dominate relationships in international science and technology. Traditional policy approaches based on national systems of innovation and research, using a linear concept of knowledge creation (from basic research to the marketplace), and counting inputs (such as achieving 3% of GDP devoted to research spending), are inadequate to manage science and technology. Increasingly, ICST research is networked, spans disciplines and political borders, and includes participants from different sectors (such as university and industry researchers working on common projects). Each of these factors adds a measure of complexity to those seeking to do policy planning, monitoring and evaluation.

Indeed, the benefits to developing countries of the networked world of science and technology are twofold. First, knowledge may be easier to access. Researchers are more interconnected, creating the possibility that a 'local search' among professional acquaintances may turn up relevant information that can be useful locally. The marketplace of ideas is more accessible than it has been in the past. On the other hand, for developing countries using S&T to aid development, the network offers the possibility that many of the institutions that constituted a 20th-century concept of national systems of innovation – and that some countries with scarce resources have tried to imitate – are no longer needed in order to innovate. Some functions of an innovation system may be accessed virtually or shared with neighbouring countries in ways that reduce the up-front investment costs. (Does every scientifically advanced country need a synchrotron? A patent office? A metrology office?)

This chapter has argued that ICST for development should build on local strengths, be tied to critical domestic needs, and have a clear capacity building component. Selections should include a 'top-down' government perspective on national needs, and the 'bottom-up' interests of researchers. Identifying these areas of common interest, and building on knowledge-based motivational factors, will help to ensure that knowledge is tied down at the local level. Understanding and tapping into the network of interconnections among scientists and engineers at the global level can offer both knowledge and functionality to a developing country seeking to build an S&T base for development. Planning for interconnections at the local, national, regional and international levels, rather than thinking strictly about a 'national' system, will have the greatest pay-off in terms of providing demand for development.

Notes

1. Dr Caroline S. Wagner (cswagner@gwu.edu) is a research scientist at the George Washington University Center for International Science and Technology Policy, and a research leader at the RAND Corporation, Santa Monica, California.
2. Most of the studies have used the addresses of the co-authors of articles (Narin, 1991; Luukkonen *et al.*, 1992, 1993; Miquel and Okubo, 1994; Doré *et al.*, 1996; Georghiou, 1998; Glänzel, 2001; Wagner and Leydesdorff, 2005).
3. Persson *et al.* (2004), Narin *et al.* (1991).
4. Grid computing offers a means of solving massive computational problems using large numbers of computers arranged as clusters embedded in a distributed telecommunications infrastructure. Grid computing has the design goal of solving problems too big for any single supercomputer, while retaining the flexibility to work on multiple smaller problems (Centipedia.com).
5. Wagner and Leydesdorff (2005).
6. Wagner (1997; 2002).
7. Wagner *et al.* (2001).
8. The exception here is the EU, which spends most of its funds on international collaborations at the European level. While non-European countries are not restricted from participating, very few developing countries participate in EU-funded projects. There is a set-aside for development aid for research (see Wagner *et al.*, 2001).
9. Wagner *et al.* (2000), Wagner (2002).
10. Smith and Katz (2000).
11. Scientists themselves are often resistant to seeing funds set aside for targeted purposes or earmarked for work with a specific country, since they see this as undermining the peer-reviewed process of identifying and funding science based on excellence as the principal criterion.
12. In the Middle East, links have deteriorated at both regional and global levels (see Wagner and Leydesdorff, 2003).
13. Newman (2001).
14. InterAcademy Council (2004), UN Millennium Project (2005).
15. Clearly, for some countries that have little to offer in terms of strengths or indigenous capabilities, it may be the role of donor agencies to help develop capacities with the specific goal of encouraging ICST links. There are a number of cases where a developing country with a natural resource has been able to build this successfully into ICST.

References

Doré, J.-C., Ojasoo, T. and Okubo, Y. (1996) Correspondence factorial analysis of the publication patterns of 48 countries over the period 1981–1992. *J. American Society for Information Science*, 47: 588–602.
Georghiou, L. (1998) Global cooperation in research, *Research Policy*, 27: 611–626.
Glänzel, W. (2001) National characteristics in international scientific co-authorship relations. *Scientometrics*, 51: 69–115.

InterAcademy Council (2004) *Inventing a Better Future: A Strategy for Building Worldwide Capacities in Science and Technology*. Amsterdam: InterAcademy Council. www.interacademycouncil.net/report.asp?id=6258

Laudel, G. (2001) Collaboration, creativity and rewards: Why and how scientists collaborate. *Int. J. Technology Management*, 22: 762–781.

Luukkonen, T., Persson, O. and Sivertsen, G. (1992) Understanding patterns of international scientific cooperation, *Science, Technology and Human Values*, 17(1): 101–126.

Luukonen, T., Tijssen, R.J.W., Persson, O. and Silversten, G. (1993) The measurement of international scientific collaboration, *Scientometrics* 28(1): 15–36.

Miquel, J. F. and Okubo, Y. (1994) Structure of international collaboration in science, Part II: Comparisons of profiles in countries using a link indicator, *Scientometrics*, 29: 271–297.

Narin, F. (1991) *Globalization of research, scholarly information, and patents: ten year trends,* Proceedings of the North American Serials Interest Group (NASIF) 6th Annual Conference, June 1991, *The Serials Librarian*, 21.

Newman, M. (2001) Who is the best connected scientist? A study of scientific co-authorship networks. Scientific collaboration networks, I: Network construction and fundamental results, *Phys. Rev.* E 64: 016131; II: Shortest paths, weighted networks, and centrality, *Phys Rev* E 64: 016132; condmat/0010296.

Persson, O., Glänzel, W. and Danell, R. (2004) *Inflationary Bibliometric Values: The Role of Scientific Collaboration and the Need for Relative Indicators in Evaluative Studies,* Draft obtained from W. Glänzel, January 2004.

Smith, D. and Katz, J.S. (2000) *Collaborative Approaches to Research*, HEFCE Fund Review of Research Policy and Funding, Final Report, University of Sussex.

Wagner, C. (1997) *International Cooperation in Research and Development: An Inventory of U.S. Government Spending and a Framework for Measuring Benefits*. Santa Monica, CA: RAND.

Wagner, C. (2002) Science and foreign policy: The elusive partnership, *Science and Public Policy*, 29(6): 409–417.

Wagner, C., Brahmakulam, I., Jackson, B., Wong, A. and Yoda, T. (2001) *Science and Technology Collaboration: Building Capacity in Developing Countries?* MR-1357.0-WB. Santa Monica, CA: RAND.

Wagner, C. and Leydesdorff, L. (2003) Mapping global science using international co-authorships: A comparison of 1990 and 2000, in: J. Guohua *et al.* (Eds.), *Proc. 9th Int. Conf. on Scientometrics and Informetrics*. Dalian: Dalian University of Technology Press, pp.330–340.

Wagner, C. and Leydesdorff, L. (2005) Mapping the network of global science: Comparing international co-authorships from 1990 to 2000. *Int. J. Technology and Globalization*, 1(2).

Wagner, C., Yezril, A. and Hassell, S. (2000) *International Cooperation in Research and Development: An Update to an Inventory of US Government Spending,* MR-1248, Santa Monica, CA: RAND.

UN Millennium Project (2005) *Innovation: Applying Knowledge in Development*. New York: UNDP/Earthscan.

PRIORITY SETTING IN TECHNICAL COOPERATION: EXPANDING THE DEMAND FOR KNOWLEDGE-BASED DEVELOPMENT

JACQUES GAILLARD, ROYAL KASTENS AND ANA MARÍA CETTO[1]

The Technical Cooperation Programme of the International Atomic Energy Agency (IAEA) has the capacity to link scientific research and technical innovation to national, regional and global development priorities. The programme therefore provides a unique case study for science and technology-based organizations seeking to move from technology-driven to demand-based technical cooperation. This chapter examines the evolution of the programme over the last 40 years. It describes a sequence of conceptual changes within the programme in order to address the gap between science and development by fostering demand-led research, promoting technical solutions for national development priorities. The programme is also promoting cooperation between national scientific and technical institutions to encourage self-reliance and sustainability.

1. Introduction

The Technical Cooperation Programme of the International Atomic Energy Agency (IAEA) was conceived in the 1960s to close the technical capacity gap between industrialized and developing countries by promoting the transfer of technology and expertise. This technology-driven cooperation was expected to build and strengthen scientific and technical capacities in the 'recipient' countries. In some cases this approach was successful, but in many others it soon became apparent that the results of projects were unsustainable. The technical solutions and expertise 'transferred' from the North were often inappropriate or insufficiently adapted to the conditions in the South.

More recently, the setup of the Technical Cooperation Programme was reconsidered. Key concepts and tools were identified to underscore the importance of strong government commitment, of greater ownership of technologies by Member States and of sustainability of project outcomes for the success of projects and programmes. Thus, in 1997 a process was set in motion to redirect the programme – from supplying nuclear technology for its own sake, to building national capacities to meet priority needs through the application of nuclear science and technology (NS&T). This transformation of the programme's conceptual underpinning is still in progress.

This redirection required that the Programme's secretariat had to work differently. It had to create an understanding of the development constraints and opportunities that could best be addressed by applying NS&T, and to focus on supporting national nuclear agencies that wished to become more self-reliant. This redirection process provides the unifying purpose for strengthening cooperation among these agencies.

The Programme recognizes that for some years, the United Nations institutions have also been renewing their focus on institutional development and capacity building in Member States in the South. The emphasis on institutional self-reliance and sustainability implies a gradual but systematic transfer of UN management and technical responsibilities to qualified national institutions in developing countries and new regional cooperation models. This shift signifies important changes in the collaboration between developing Member States and UN organizations. It also implies a leadership role for the UN in promoting ownership and technical-managerial self-reliance, and a gradual evolution in relationships from 'donor–recipient' to genuine partnerships in science and development – a knowledge-based strategy for development. The Programme is now vigorously pursuing this vision.

2. 'Atoms for Peace': the origins of the Technical Cooperation Programme

The idea for the Technical Cooperation Programme was originally envisioned by President Dwight D. Eisenhower in his 'Atoms for Peace' speech in 1953, in which he emphasized the need to control the proliferation of fissile material while ensuring equal benefits and access to the power of nuclear science and technology.

The IAEA's objective is 'to accelerate and enlarge the contribution of atomic energy to peace, health and prosperity throughout the world'. The Statutes continue with the pledge to 'ensure, so far as it is able, that assistance provided by it or at its request or under its supervision or control is not used in such a way as to further any military purpose'.[2]

Under the Non-Proliferation of Nuclear Weapons Treaty (NPT), the Programme functions in both a political and technical environment and thus must fulfil its external role in accordance with the NPT. The Treaty brings into balance the IAEA's two main activities, the verification of peaceful uses of nuclear science and technology (also known as 'safeguards'), and their promotion for human development through the Programme. Until recently, the Member States have supported and maintained this balance between safeguards activities and technical cooperation programmes, thus helping to ensure relatively predictable funding for the Programme. It is important to note that these activities were carried out through two separate but coordinated programmes. The IAEA's Regular Programme of verification, inspection and regulatory activities, technical information exchange and coordinated research activities was financed from an obligatory assessment from all Member States. The Technical Cooperation Programme is voluntarily funded by Member States. The Regular Programme provides the management framework for the Technical Cooperation Programme, so that the latter does not have 'overheads' or administrative costs.

Article III of the IAEA Statute states that the Agency is authorized 'to encourage and assist research on, and development and practical application of, atomic energy for peaceful purposes', and to foster the exchange of scientific and technical information, as well as of scientists. The IAEA's research activities are designed to contribute to this mandate, by stimulating and coordinating research in selected nuclear fields by scientists in Member States. The research programme incorporates the concept of a lead laboratory, often in a developed country, but always representing advanced knowledge and technical competency to act as mentor for participating laboratories that are less advanced. Although laboratories in industrialized countries often function in a mentoring capacity, the research agenda, problems addressed and expected outcomes are expected to be driven by developing country laboratories.

The IAEA supports research mainly through coordinated research projects (CRPs) that bring together research institutes in developing and developed countries to collaborate on topics of mutual interest. These projects encourage the acquisition and dissemination of new knowledge and technology generated through the use of nuclear and isotopic technologies in the various fields covered by IAEA's mandate. The CRPs also provide an important foundation for the Programme because contract holders are often or later become the Programme's counterparts. The complementarity between the nuclear sciences (research) and nuclear-based technologies (applications) creates opportunities for IAEA to advance developments in key areas such as natural resources management and environmental monitoring, diagnostics of communicable diseases, human nutrition and micronutrient deficiencies, pest management, and energy production, including geothermal energy.

3. The first 40 years: transferring technology and expertise

In 1958 the Agency began its technical 'assistance' by offering a number of fellowships, and later by supplying equipment and experts. In the early years, the Programme supported just over 40 countries and disbursed less than US$2 million each year. By 2004, there were projects in 103 countries and an annual budget of over US$70 million.

Between 1958 and 2002 the emphasis was on human resources development. The IAEA trained more than 27,000 fellows. Throughout this period, the Agency planned and delivered project outputs worth more than US$1.2 billion in 103 Member States, while building technical competencies and scientific expertise in fields such as energy, safety, agriculture, industry, medicine, water and environmental protection.

Since the Rio Conference on Sustainable Development in 1992, the Programme has also supported national efforts to achieve key targets of Agenda 21, including human health, biotechnologies, atmosphere, land and agriculture, oceans and seas, freshwater, chemicals and waste, and energy and transport. Between 1993 and 2002, the IAEA supported 813 projects, valued at over US$210 million and involving 1853 national and regional scientific-technical institutions, 5787 scientists and technicians participating in 381 training events and training an additional 3082 fellows. This contribution to achieving Agenda 21 continues to grow.

4. Meeting national priority development needs and ensuring sustainability

The first major shift for the Technical Cooperation Programme occurred in the early 1990s, when 11 'model projects' were formulated to demonstrate how nuclear applications could respond to specific development needs. These projects were to reflect an indispensable role for the nuclear technology involved, have significant economic or social impacts, and produce sustainable benefits through strong government commitment. This 'model project' approach was endorsed by the Board of Governors in 1997, and became the core element of the initial strategy for redirecting technical cooperation towards meeting specific development priorities.

The present phase of the technical cooperation strategy began in 2002 with the introduction of mechanisms that function as priority setting tools. They include three major elements: the central criterion, country programme frameworks and thematic planning.

The *central criterion* establishes standards for project sustainability that require strong government commitment. Each project must meet a clearly defined national need, and produce significant economic and social impacts through the production of measurable benefits for end users. This commitment from national authorities helps confirm and validate the success of a technical application and ensure that the benefits are sustainable.

The process of preparing *country programme frameworks* (CPFs) involves a dialogue between the IAEA and the Member States to focus the technical cooperation on a few priority areas that can make significant contributions to achieving national objectives. The process is also used to help realize partnerships between national scientific and technical institutions and development authorities. Equally important is the role the CPFs play in assessing technical competence and capabilities and linking the relevant scientific-technical institutions to national development authorities and policy makers. The CPFs provide a useful framework for the formulation of the biennial project requests submitted by Member States to the IAEA.

Thematic planning, with the participation of experts from Member States, includes identifying best practices for successfully and sustainably applying nuclear technologies to development problems. Thematic planning also involves comparing nuclear techniques with conventional or emerging techniques, ascertaining the necessary preconditions to ensure the impact of outcomes in a particular thematic area, and identifying possible partners already working in that area. In addition, thematic planning influences the IAEA's coordinated research projects and provides a link between research activities and technical applications. One benefit of this process is that it provides opportunities for advancing and adapting nuclear science and technology to meet new or emerging needs, such as analytical tools for monitoring the HIV/AIDS pandemic and assessing vaccine trials, isotopic studies for coastal zone and river basin management, and analytical modelling for air quality management.

Priority setting for the Technical Cooperation Programme recognizes that the conditions and requirements in Member States determine the relevance of the IAEA's activities. The three elements provide a reasonable means of assessing and ordering information on conditions and requirements in Member States, and provide essential feedback for strategic direction. Thus, this approach provides a mechanism for the IAEA to periodically realign priorities with new requirements, time frames and opportunities, as well as justification for reallocating human resources as required by new priorities.

5. The role of nuclear science and technology in national development

The IAEA's focus on sharing safe and secure nuclear technologies in peaceful applications is given purpose through programmes that put advanced science to work to meet the needs of Member States, and facilitate collaboration in areas such as human health, agricultural productivity, water resources management and environmental restoration. Regional cooperation agreements play a vital role in fostering collaboration and expanding and sustaining its impact. These are formal intergovernmental agreements covering research, development and training, and provide opportunities for cooperation among national counterpart organizations.[3] The agreements work through regional resource units or other national centres of excellence, usually national nuclear science and technology institutions with comparative advantages in the region. They exercise a leadership role in specific thematic areas and provide technical and management services to other institutions in the region for a nominal fee.

The basic functions of the regional resource units are to provide analytical support to other members and supply experts as needed. The units also deliver standards or reagent kits to other countries and provide 'hands-on' training for IAEA trainees. They host regional training events and meetings, develop manuals and handbooks, and carry out IAEA contracts.

There is a strong association between nuclear science and technology and sustainable development. Many applications produce analytical outcomes that are knowledge based. At the World Summit on Sustainable Development in Johannesburg in 2002, the IAEA reported that over US$500 million worth of technical cooperation had been undertaken since 1992, with more than 800 projects valued at more than US$200 million specifically supporting the priorities of Agenda 21 such as human health, agriculture and food security, and water resources and environmental protection (see figure 1).

Examples of how nuclear science and technology contribute to national development can be found in every region. The following paragraphs offer some examples to illustrate the nature and scope of the benefits.

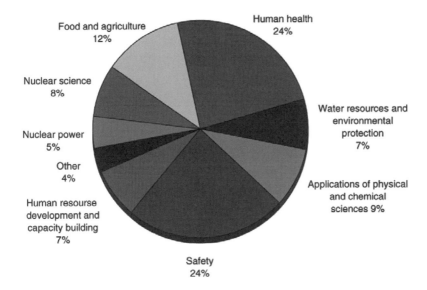

Human health: cancer diagnosis and therapy, variety of disease diagnosis, identification of drug resistant strains, sterilization, nutrition studies.
Agriculture and food security: development of new plant varieties, preservation of agricultural produce, control and eradication of pests.
Water resources and environmental protection: mapping of underground aquifers, water pollution, dam safety, environmental monitoring, management and remediation of contaminated areas.

Figure 1. Main areas of technical cooperation in nuclear applications in 2004; total disbursements US$73.3 million.

Human health

As can be seen from figure 1, human health is the largest area of IAEA technical cooperation, with an emphasis on radiotherapy as a valuable tool in the treatment of cancer. Building competencies and institutional capacity is becoming increasingly important as life expectancy and the incidence of cancer increase. The IAEA seeks to build up indigenous capabilities by training practitioners, improving the quality of equipment, and increasing the quality and effectiveness of treatment. One initiative, 'Management of the most common cancers in Africa', is promoting regional self-reliance by utilizing indigenous expertise in specialized teams that audit radiotherapy practices at national facilities. The initiative also aims to ensure the quality of therapy by applying management and control practices used by the regional designated centres under the African Regional Cooperative Agreement (AFRA).

At present eight regional centres are operational in Africa, all of which follow a process of pre-selection, auditing and appointment by AFRA representatives. They provide support in the fields of radiation oncology (Morocco and South Africa), non-destructive testing techniques (South Africa and Tunisia), radioactive waste management (South Africa), instrumentation (Egypt), radiation processing (Egypt), and mutation breeding and biotechnology (South Africa). The centres have been steadily increasing their contributions by hosting training events, providing expert services, and training African fellows. The IAEA is working with AFRA representatives to extend collaboration, particularly in promotional activities to help make full use of regional expertise and capacities. The IAEA periodically convenes project coordination meetings to review the portfolios of the centres, confirm regional priorities, discuss problems and possible solutions and procedures, as well as to identify new project activities that can be performed by the regional centres.

In many developing countries, particularly in Asia, micronutrient deficiencies can result in major public health problems. Despite the efforts of governments to eliminate micronutrient malnutrition, progress is still slow and patchy because of the lack of effective nutritional interventions. For many years, the IAEA and its Member States have contributed expertise and knowledge in research and technical cooperation to exploit applications of nuclear and related isotopic techniques as tools to solve nutritional problems prevalent in developing countries. The IAEA recently began an important collaboration with the Asian Development Bank (ADB) and five national analytical laboratories in Asia to evaluate and monitor ADB-sponsored food fortification intervention programmes and to develop rice mutants with low phytic acid from high-yield varieties. The management strategy calls for close collaboration between national laboratories and the regional food industry to produce bioavailability studies that will improve the formulation of processed foods by increasing iron, iodine and other essential micronutrients.

Agriculture and food security

In the area of *agriculture*, one example of South-South collaboration is the induced mutation plant breeding programmes that aim to produce crop varieties with improved yields, and the ability to tolerate specific environments. One such application in Pakistan involves an interregional demonstration project to support more productive use of saline groundwater and wastelands. Globally, some 77 million hectares are unproductive or marginally productive due to high salinity, and the problem is increasing. The basic technology package was developed through partnerships between the Pakistan Atomic Energy Commission and four national agricultural research institutes. For countries with large areas of saline lands, the applied techniques can be expanded at relatively low cost and thereby increase soil fertility, land value and, in some areas, reverse the process of desertification. The government of Pakistan is leading this project, providing IAEA with expertise to support seven participating countries. As a demonstration of its commitment, the government of Egypt recently allocated US$2 million to expand its programme to new regions of the country. To facilitate this collaboration, the IAEA has recently signed a partnership agreement with the International Center for Bio-saline Agriculture in the United Arab Emirates to promote the sustainable utilization of saline groundwater.

The African tsetse fly causes widespread economic damage and constitutes an ecological barrier to mixed farming and sustainable agricultural production. Its bite causes African sleeping sickness in both humans and animals. The sterile insect technique (SIT) uses radiation to sterilize healthy male flies that are released into the environment. They successfully compete with wild males for mates but being sterile cannot reproduce, which suppresses and eventually eradicates the tsetse population. The technical package sponsored by the IAEA for tsetse area-wide control activities was developed as a joint collaboration with the Tanga Tsetse Research Station in Tanzania. The SIT package has eradicated the pest from the island of

Zanzibar, and its use is now being extended under the mandate of the Pan-African Tsetse and Trypanosomiasis Campaign (PATTEC) of the African Union. The campaign is supported by the United Nations Fund – the organization set up by philanthropist Ted Turner to administer his donation of US$1 billion to foster UN system cooperation.

Another application of SIT involves the Mediterranean fruit fly (medfly) in a transnational project between Israel, Jordan and the Palestinian Authority. The project has effectively suppressed this pest in the Arava region and the Lower Jordan valley, allowing the export of vegetables to medfly-free countries without quarantine restrictions, with considerable economic benefit. The project has been expanded to cover Gaza, Israel's western Negev region, and fruit-producing areas in eastern Egypt. In this case, the fact that the scientific cooperation has succeeded even during civil unrest underscores the contribution of scientific cooperation to peace, security and international development.

Water resources and environmental protection

The management of *water resources* is a special area for knowledge-based cooperation because water is a shared resource that is held in a global trust. In every region, national nuclear institutions are applying techniques in isotope hydrology that are widely recognized as essential tools for understanding the entire water cycle and enabling sustainable water management. Most water projects are regional where scientists in developing countries are trained in isotope hydrology to map underwater aquifers, estimate groundwater resources, and combat the risk of pollution. In Africa, over 50% of IAEA expert assignments are carried out by local scientists and technicians, while in Asia and Latin America the figures are 60% and 70%, respectively.

In Ethiopia, for example, technical experts from South Africa trained counterparts in the use of isotope hydrology and helped tap a new groundwater field at Akaki, which now provides more than 40% of Addis Ababa's water supply. The expertise to implement this study benefited from the technical and scientific collaboration of seven North African countries in a regional groundwater management project. This expertise, along with related scientific and technical knowledge in Egypt, Kenya, Sudan, Tanzania and Uganda, provides the backbone of technical skills for a new initiative, 'Sustainable development and equitable utilization of the common Nile basin water resources', a capacity building activity linked to the Nile Basin

Initiative, supported by the Global Environment Facility (GEF) and the World Bank.

Due to the technical requirements and the transboundary nature of natural resource management, partnerships between scientific and development authorities are essential. In South America, the Agency has formed partnerships with the Organization of American States, the World Bank and the GEF to support the governments of Argentina, Brazil, Paraguay and Uruguay to protect and manage the Guarani aquifer. National authorities are carrying out groundwater assessments and are sharing the data through a technical coordination committee that is also developing system-wide modelling techniques for groundwater management. The Guarani, the largest groundwater aquifer in South America, contains enough freshwater, if protected in a sustainable manner, to supply the needs of over 300 million people.

The area of *environmental protection* is a relatively new and innovative area of cross-border collaboration among Member States. The Agency's Marine Environment Laboratory in Monaco has given priority to the use of nuclear techniques for sustainable coastal zone management. One of the most serious and visible problems facing coastal waters is related to a phenomenon known as 'red tide' or harmful algal blooms. The toxin produced by the algae causes paralytic shellfish poisoning, a condition that is deadly to aquatic animals and humans. Working with the Philippine Nuclear Research Institute and the Intergovernmental Oceanographic Commission, the Agency has developed a receptor-binding assay that is quick, sensitive and effective in determining seafood safety.

6. Looking to the future

The focus of Technical Cooperation Programme on sustainability and institutional self-reliance has set in motion a major shift toward increasing technical partnerships with national institutions that can play a leading role within regions with broader responsibility for technical cooperation involving mature nuclear technologies. For the IAEA this approach represents a different future for technical cooperation and a new model for organizing scientific research and technical applications that requires closer collaboration between the scientific and development communities. It also requires an evolution in relationships between more and less advanced institutions. It promises an alternative to the conventional model for technical cooperation that fosters peace, security and prosperity by strengthening the scientific and technological base for development.

Greater investments must be made in establishing and maintaining national scientific and technical infrastructures. Technical, scientific and managerial roles and responsibilities should be entrusted to qualified national and regional institutions. Scientific-development collaboration at the regional and sub-regional levels should be systematically promoted to enable lasting solutions to national development, and to set in motion scientific discovery and technological innovation. Establishing scientific-technical competencies at the national level, *as well as* institutional capabilities should be the focus. International cooperation should be transformed from over-reliance on technology transfer to knowledge transfer as the fundamental requirement for national development. New regional cooperation mechanisms for development should be encouraged, focusing on solving problems with cross-border consequences. For the IAEA, such problems include the control of communicable diseases, water and land resources management and pest control, particularly the ecological barriers presented by the tsetse fly and mosquito, as well as pests such as fruit flies and moths.

7. Conclusions

In setting the parameters for creating demand for knowledge-intensive policy preparation and priority setting in development-oriented research, there are two key questions: how can development strategies become more knowledge based? And how can research strategies be more demand based?

The IAEA experience suggests that by focusing on technical and scientific self-reliance at the institutional level, as a normative outcome for all technical cooperation activities, the emphasis in development strategies will shift from technology to knowledge transfer, because self-reliance requires specialist competencies – the confluence of skills, behaviour and knowledge within an institutional setting of capabilities. This shift will also require greater recognition of individuals as the custodians and brokers of knowledge.

The IAEA experience validates two possible approaches for making research strategies more demand based. First, the performance characteristics of technical applications should be periodically assessed against criteria such as efficiency and effectiveness, and the sustainability of outcomes and impacts. The acquired learning should be converted into requirements for new research or technical adaptations that will enhance the benefits of those applications. Second, analytical and planning processes should identify the most promising scientific knowledge and connect to the most pressing development constraints. Science and development partnerships work best in proximity to the problem where collective efforts can harness the labours of those most seriously affected with those capable of effecting the necessary scientific and technological advancements.

On a broader question, developing countries can create demand for research and knowledge-intensive policies by taking ownership of their development constraints and opportunities. They need to set national objectives and targets that call for solutions that are suitable to national circumstances, mobilize indigenous resources, and pursue national policies and programmes to achieve expected results.

The challenge to this notion is the strength of national science and technology institutions and their ability to lead or contribute to sustainable solutions. This is greatly determined by investment in such institutions, building and maintaining the necessary competencies, and the management of science and technology to produce high-value results. The question to be addressed by professionals working in international organizations and the scientific, academic and technical communities remains: are we working collectively to effectively enable and apply scientific and technological know-how at the national and regional levels?

Notes

1. Dr Jacques Gaillard (j.gaillard@iaea.org) is director of the Division of Planning and Coordination, Royal Kastens is Head of the Concepts and Planning Section, and Ana María Cetto is Deputy Director and Head of the Department of Technical Cooperation, International Atomic Energy Agency (IAEA), Vienna, Austria. For further information, visit http://www-tc.iaea.org/tcweb.
2. IAEA Statute, Article II (www.iaea.org/About/statute_text.html).
3. There are four regional cooperation agreements: (1) the African Regional Cooperative Agreement for Research, Development and Training Related to Nuclear Science and Technology among African Member States (AFRA); (2) the Regional Cooperation Agreement for the Promotion of Nuclear Science and Technology in Latin America and the Caribbean (ARCAL); (3) the Regional Cooperation Agreement (RCA) for East Asia and the Pacific; and (4) the Cooperative Agreement for Arab States in Asia for Research, Development and Training related to Nuclear Science and Technology (ARASIA).

References

Carnegie Commission (1992) *Partnerships for Global Development: the Clearing Horizon*, New York: Carnegie Commission.

Gaillard, J. (1999) *La coopération scientifique et technique avec les pays du Sud. Peut-on partager la science?* Paris: Karthala.

IDRC (1991) *Empowerment through knowledge. The strategy of the International Development Research Center*, Ottawa: IDRC.

Malcolm, S., Cetto, A.M., Dickson, D., Gaillard, J., Schaeffer, D. and Quéré, Y. (2002) *Science and Education Capacity Building for Sustainable Development*, Series on Science for Sustainable Development No.5, Paris: ICSU.

RAWOO (1996) *Towards a European Science and Technology Policy for Development.* The Hague: RAWOO.

Widstrand, C. (1993) *Donor Approaches to Research Capacity Building*, Working Paper prepared for the Donor Consultation on Agenda 21 Research and Capacity Building Initiatives, November 1993, Centre Rockefeller, Bellagio, Italy.

IAEA website resources:

IAEA Statutes, www.iaea.org/About/statute.html

Technical Cooperation Strategy, http://www-tc.iaea.org/tcweb/tcprogramme/ginf824.pdf

Water resources in the semi-arid areas of southern and eastern Africa, http://www-tc.iaea.org/tcweb/publications/otherpublications/sustainable_groundwater.pdf

Mutation Breeding Review, http://www.pub.iaea.org/MTCD/publications/newsletter.asp?id=55

Improved Nutrition through Nuclear Science, www.iaea.org/NewsCenter/Features/Nutrition/start.html

Science Serving People, www.iaea.org/Publications/Booklets/Ssp/index.html

IAEA Maps Out Programme of Action for Cancer Therapy, www.iaea.org/NewsCenter/Features/Radiotherapy/index.shtml

THE USE OF FORESIGHT IN SETTING AGRICULTURAL RESEARCH PRIORITIES

MARIE DE LATTRE-GASQUET[1]

Foresight activities can be useful tools in public decision-making processes, and in particular for agricultural science and technology priority setting. Foresight complements more traditional ways of looking at the future, such as projections and models. Foresight uses a systems approach that is appropriate for agriculture and can be embedded in research organizations. This chapter describes three foresight exercises. The exploration of possible futures for a commodity (cocoa) has helped defining new research priorities, partnerships and networks. The Dutch exploration of the challenges facing agribusiness, rural areas and fisheries, and the contribution of S&T to meeting these challenges, created new networks and led to actions. IFPRI's '2020 Vision' for food, agriculture and the environment led to interesting data and reached many researchers, but did not manage to generate consensus about research priorities. Finally, the chapter discusses the prospects for the use of foresight in developing countries, especially in Africa.

1. Introduction

A recent review of science and technology plans in Africa, Caribbean and Pacific (ACP) countries concluded that 'agriculture in general and agricultural S&T in particular do not have the priority which should be expected on the basis of the sector's importance in the countries' GDP. One may even ask to what extent tropical agricultural S&T development is surviving as a global public good'.[2] According to the *UNESCO Science Report 2002*, the state of S&T in most African countries has deteriorated substantially since the early 1980s. 'Severe cuts in government spending have pushed institutions of higher education and research centres into steep decline. National educational and research coordinating bodies, once focal points of reform for S&T, have lost much of their political power and influence. Indeed a significant number of these reform-minded bodies have been dissolved'.[3]

As noted by the Senegalese historian Mamadou Diouf, there has been a major shift in 'the tension between internal constraints (human and material resources, cultural capabilities and predispositions, historical circumstances), which it is believed can be eliminated by sound policies on the one hand, and by adequate institutional arrangements on the other, and by the opportunities that globalization brings at different times and in different circumstances'.[4] What can be done to reduce these tensions, to develop the power and influence of education and research coordinating bodies? In particular, what can be done not only to devise solutions but to define the problem?

We believe that foresight is a useful instrument for public decision making in many areas, in particular in the area of agricultural science and technology (S&T) policies. Foresight is a process that leads to defining problems, thinking about possible futures and making choices, and complements more traditional ways of looking at the future, such as projections and models. The chapter describes three foresight exercises that explored possible futures for a commodity (cocoa), for a country (agriculture in the Netherlands), and for food, agriculture and the environment (IFPRI's 2020 Vision). Finally, the chapter discusses the prospects for the use of foresight in developing countries, especially in Africa.

2. The use of foresight in agricultural S&T priority setting

Foresight has been described as 'the process involved in systematically attempting to look into the longer-term future of science, technology, the economy, the environment and society with the aim of identifying the areas of strategic research and emerging generic technologies likely to yield the greatest economic and social benefits'.[5]

Although the future is unpredictable, some developments can be foreseen and alternatives explored. Therefore, there is the possibility of preparing for the future (within limitations) or to try to shape it directly.[6] Foresight is neither prophecy nor prediction, but 'invites us to consider the future as something that we can create or build rather than as something already decided.

The philosophy behind the procedure is that the future is a realm of freedom, of power and of will. It is at once a land to be explored, hence the utility of vigilance and anticipation, and in particular of the exploratory perspective, and a land to be built on, hence the utility of investigating desirable futures and looking at the policies and strategies that can be adopted to achieve them'.[7]

Foresight assumes that there are numerous possible futures, any of which can be created through the actions we choose to take today. It is not so much concerned with predicting as with inventing or shaping a chosen future from the infinite range of possibilities. Foresight is not only understanding the system and looking into the future, it is also a collective learning process with a view to long-term strategic decision making. It therefore covers activities aimed at thinking about, debating and shaping the future.

The foresight process involves four stages. It starts with defining the problem, choosing the time horizon, setting the organizational framework and choosing experts. The second stage consists of constructing the system, identifying key variables, gathering data and drafting hypotheses. This stage is followed by an exploration of possible futures and scenario writing with the help of tree structures. The final stage involves outlining strategic choices, disseminating results and recommending a strategy (figure 1).

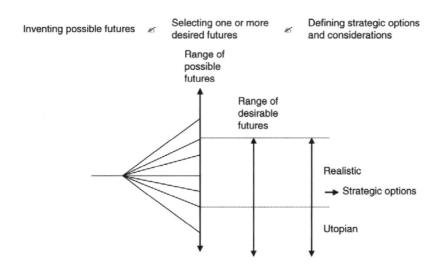

Figure 1. Strategic foresight (adapted from de Jouvenel, 2004).

During the process of exploring possible futures, the mental maps of the 'foresighters' must be stretched, since there can be a tendency for scenarios to strengthen existing beliefs. Creativity can be tempered by the need to be both credible and consistent. Often, final scenarios are judged by how well they fit with expectations about the future. Among all possible futures, some are desirable and others are not. Among the desirable futures, some are realistic and can help decision makers choose strategic options, while others are utopian. There is an almost natural inclination of participants to confuse the (un)thinkable (utopian) with the (im)probable or (un)realistic.[8] Once the strategic choices have been outlined, decision makers can examine their implications and take the decisions they find most appropriate (figure 2).

At the centre of the process is the interplay between anticipation, appropriation or collective mobilization, and action or strategic will.[9] For the participants, the foresight process can have a number of benefits, formulated as 'the 5Cs':[10]

1. Communication – among firms, industrial sectors, government and academia.
2. Concentration on the longer term – normally, day-to-day pressures force us to focus on the short-term, on 'firefighting' immediate problems, rather than contemplating what the world might (or could) be like 10-20 years hence.
3. Coordination – organizations can find out about what others are planning to do, and hence can coordinate their strategies more effectively.
4. Consensus – generating a shared vision of what sort of world we would like to create in the longer term.
5. Commitment – by involving knowledgeable and enthusiastic individuals in the foresight process, one can foster their commitment to convert new ideas into action.

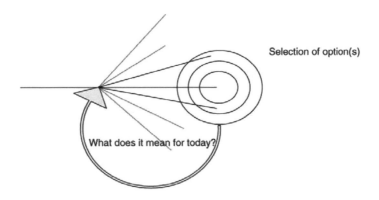

Figure 2. The decision-making process (adapted from de Jouvenel, 2004).

Agricultural forecasts, models and foresight

The future availability and prices of agricultural commodities are of interest to producers, national policy makers, traders, industry and international institutions. It is necessary to minimize and to cover risks, and to plan medium-term commodity policies. To understand what happened in the past and how it has affected the current situation, international organizations, national institutions and industry unions collect statistics on production, consumption and trade. Over the last 50 years there have been at least 30 quantitative estimates of future world food security, published regularly by the Food and Agriculture Organization (FAO) and the US Department of Agriculture (USDA), and occasionally by bodies such as the Organisation for Economic Cooperation and Development (OECD), the International Food Policy Research Institute (IFPRI), and the International Institute for Applied Systems Analysis (IIASA).[11] Although it is difficult to measure the precise influence of these forecasts on the actual policy debate, the fact that there are different players and models is in itself an indication of their perceived usefulness.[12]

To look at the future of production and exchange, most agricultural forecasts are based on two types of models: trend projections (or extrapolations) and world trade models.[13] In *trend projections* (e.g. of food supply and demand balances), relationships between variables lead to mathematical equations based on statistical series. The system is represented as it functioned in the past, and is used to project the future. There cannot be major changes from the past. These projections are useful for the short to medium term (one to five years).[14]

Trend projections are temping for decision makers because they provide relatively simple answers to their questions, but they have limits.[15] First, the description of reality provided by the model depends on the theory used. Behaviours are stylized in mathematical functions, so that the underlying hypothesis must be simple. However, as the hypothesis is not always available to the users of the model, they tend to anticipate changes that might not occur because the theories used do not correspond to reality. Second, trend projections for commodities represent only a part of economic reality. They cannot take into account the rest of the economy. If they do, through an economic model, the variables used are often exogenous. Third, in most cases, trend projections do not take into account risks – they deal strictly with the probability of things to come. At best, uncertainties are made explicit, but only in order to better isolate the statistical features of future developments. In the agricultural sector, there are many unpredictable risks such as climate variations, wars, price fluctuations, etc. Inaccuracies in the data are another reason for the divergence between the results of a model and reality. Official national statistics do not always reflect reality, as satellite data on surfaces and yields have shown. The difficulty in representing the passage of time is another reason for the divergence between model results and reality. Changes in consumption, for example, can be much faster or slower than expected. Trend projections are therefore good for the short term, but they remain valid in the medium term only if they are constantly adapted.

Models such as IFPRI's Impact model and the FAO's World Food Model are systems of equations developed to represent how variables interact with a subsystem that has already been isolated. Estimating models based on historical trends have the advantage of transferring to the future the structure of the interrelationships among variables that were consistent in the past. Over the years, the number of issues related to the supply and demand sides of the food balance equation that are taken into account has increased significantly. Modelling approaches have become more sophisticated, larger, and much more expensive.

Foresight could be an alternative way to look at the future of agriculture and agricultural research, using a systemic approach. When socio-economic conditions evolved slowly, when technological progress was rare, farmers used their experience and knowledge to improve production and manage their environment. When those conditions started to change, farmers could no longer deal with the new context and needed help, and researchers tried to develop new techniques that they hoped would improve yields. Because of failures in the adoption of such techniques, some agronomists started to adopt a systemic approach, considering the field as a system, and then looking at interactions between the techniques. The 'systems approach' to agriculture developed from there on. Doing agricultural foresight therefore means defining and understanding the system before building scenarios or looking at innovative activities. Defining the limits of the system on which the foresight will concentrate, and defining the different elements, is often difficult due to the numerous interactions between the agricultural and other sectors.[16]

Beyond agriculture, the notion has emerged of the national (or regional) system of innovation, which is made up of a number of actors and the links between them. Foresight offers a tool for getting the individual actors in the national innovation system to communicate, to discuss issues of long-term common interest, to coordinate their respective strategies, and perhaps even to collaborate. Foresight with scenario building, foresight models and trend projections complement each other. Once scenarios are designed, it can be useful to use a foresight model with the variables defined in the qualitative foresight, and to model the different scenarios.[17]

3. Technology forecasting and technology foresight

For many years, technology forecasting involved continuous monitoring of technological developments in order to identify promising future applications and assess their potential.[18] Over the last ten years, technology foresight exercises have been conducted in Europe and Japan to identify key or critical technologies. These exercises, often government-initiated, have involved wide ranging government–industry discussions and gathering expert opinions on technology futures, leading in some cases to blueprints and government actions. In the United States critical technologies have also been identified, but through a different process.[19]

S&T foresight looks at science in progress (*'la science qui se fait'*)[20] and fulfils a number of functions.[21] It provides a means for making choices in relation to science and technology and identifying priorities. It also offers a mechanism for integrating research opportunities with economic and social needs, and thereby linking science and technology more closely with innovation, wealth creation and enhanced quality of life. It can help to stimulate communication and partnerships among researchers, research users and research funders.

Drivers of S&T foresight

A number of reasons have been put forward to explain the growth of S&T foresight exercises, and of the various functions they are used to perform. Four major drivers have been identified.[22] The first of these results from globalization and growing economic competition. The growth of markets has put a premium on both innovation and knowledge-based industries and services. This in turn has given science and technology a greater importance and thus any tools that can assist in guiding investments in S&T have become important. Until the late 1980s, science operated under what might be described as the 'Vannevar Bush social contract'[23] – governments provided funding for scientific research in the expectation that it would ultimately yield benefits in the form of wealth, health and national security, but exactly what form those benefits would take and when they would occur were rather vague. Since the 1990s government expectations of their investments in science and technology have become much more explicit and specific, so that working with stakeholders to define and execute research activities has become indispensable.

A second driver is the increasing constraints on government spending, particularly in the public sector. Governments worldwide are faced with the twin forces of a declining revenue base (associated with high economic and political costs of deficit budgeting) and the growing public demand for services such as health and education. They therefore need to be able to justify any public expenditure and to show that it is a valuable investment.

The third driver results from the enormous changes in industrial production. Command and control management has been replaced by decentralized decision making, empowerment and teamwork. Attention now is on customer-supplier relationships, and the development of strategic alliances and effective networks. The drive for controlled high performance through quality management has been extended with the new emphasis on learning and knowledge organizations.

The fourth driver has been the change in the process of knowledge production, which has become increasingly transdisciplinary and heterogeneous.[24] The range of producers of knowledge has expanded, with an emphasis on knowledge constructed in the context of its application. In this model, there is a need for communication, networks, partnerships and collaboration in research, not only among researchers but also between researchers and research users in industry. One of the challenges facing (agricultural) researchers is to identify the potential beneficiaries or users of the results of their research, and to work with them to ensure that the results are exploited quickly and effectively to maximize the economic and social benefits.[25]

A fifth driver has been the rapid development and the growing convergence of technologies that are likely to have a revolutionary impact on economy and society in the coming decades. Frequently, however, technology foresight concentrates on identifying promising future applications and assessing their potential, rather than focusing on future research questions. In this approach, the possibility of developing new products following scientific discoveries are of central importance, as well as the conditions of emergence, development and diffusion of technological innovations.[26]

Embedded foresight

Defining research objectives, setting priorities and allocating funds call for a long-term view. Over the years, methods have been developed for setting research priorities.[27] Rather than continue to rely on opaque bureaucratic decision processes, S&T policy makers are starting to use S&T policy evaluation and foresight systematically to help them make choices.[28] There is a move towards embedded foresight.

Embedded foresight refers to individual and collaborative processes through which information about relevant technological, commercial and societal developments is acquired, produced, refined or communicated within research programmes, in order to generate shared understanding of and support for research and development activities. Embedding foresight means linking it to evaluation, programme planning and priority setting. It implies the replacement of rigidly designed programmes by more flexible and learning-oriented programmes in which the priorities are continuously negotiated and revised if necessary.[29] Such a combination enables research organizations to consider themselves not only as problem solvers, but also as the architects of new futures, and not only as researchers but as co-innovators who are involved in the implementation of future prospects.[30]

Increased interaction between research evaluation, foresight and pro-gramme planning can enhance S&T decision-making processes. These three processes involve at least three parties – the commissioners of the exercise, internal members (i.e. evaluation or foresight group members), and external members (evaluators, stakeholders and others) – who can thus support one another. This arrangement can facilitate the formation of a common vision and ambition in which no single party – policy makers, industries, produc-ers, community organizations or researchers – will dominate. It can create an atmosphere of dialogue and intelligent interplay between those involved, each retaining their own decision-making authority. Agreement can be reached on the division of tasks, and there can be increased cooperation in the financing, development and utilization of science and technology. This combination can enlarge perspectives and improve policy formulation and priority setting.

For a foresight exercise embedded within an agricultural research organi-zation, it is recommended that the objectives are clearly stated, shared within and outside the organization, and approved by a commissioning agency, usually a public decision maker with an interest in the work and who (co-)finances the exercise. This agency should appoint a steering com-mittee responsible for organizing and facilitating the foresight exercise, for choosing methodologies, and for compiling the final recommendations.

The foresight exercise should have a coordinator who activates potential participants, assists in the organization of workshops and seminars, monitors ongoing efforts, and provides information. Experts from a variety of backgrounds should be invited to contribute as members of panels or brainstorming sessions and as writers of essays. These experts should be selected as individuals but represent various communities, including:[31]

- the *research organization* hosting the exercise;

- the *science community* at large, both to ensure that the organization is receptive to new scientific trends and opportunities, and that new research strategies are pursued;

- *consumer interest groups,* since indirectly they will derive most benefit from technological change, and are potentially among the most powerful supporters of investment in agricultural research;

- *the rural development community*, since members of this group are confronted on a daily basis with the constraints to development and poverty alleviation, and may bring fresh perspectives to the key problems that must be addressed;

- *the farming community* – this is one of the most important groups representing the private sector, and the key reference group for most agricultural research. Farmers understand the problems and often have clear ideas about the feasibility of alternative research strategies;

- *agro-industry* – this is the other important group representing the private sector. In the process of agricultural development, farmers are increasingly integrated into the agro-industrial chain, through forward and backward linkages related to farm inputs, but even more to the processing and marketing of agricultural produce;

- *the 'public'* – agricultural research must relate to the problems as perceived by the public. Science journalists may contribute by identifying concerns that may be overlooked by experienced researchers; and

- *national, bilateral, and multilateral investment agencies* – agricultural research must be aligned with financial resource flows and agricultural investments so that research is linked to extension and development efforts.

The next three sections present three embedded foresight exercises that have been (co-)organized by research institutes in support of agricultural research and development activities.

4. Possible futures for a commodity: cocoa research priorities

In the 1990s, the cocoa commodity chain went through turbulent times due to accelerating technical, social and economic changes. International agreements aimed at price regulation and policy harmonization were questioned, and a new International Cocoa Agreement had to be negotiated in 1995. New relationships between public research and industry resulted in increasing vertical and horizontal integration within the sector. National research institutions faced many financial and institutional difficulties. New scientific discoveries required new research methodologies.

In this context, in January 1997 the Centre de coopération internationale en recherche agronomique pour le développement (Cirad) launched a cocoa foresight exercise to identify the research questions on which Cirad's researchers should focus, and to help them accept changes in their research priorities. The emphasis was as much on the process as on the results of the exercise.

A knowledge base, key variables and scenarios

A knowledge base covering both science and society was created, organized around four themes. Data sheets were prepared, providing information on current strengths and weaknesses, trends, possible breakthroughs and the potential for change. The data sheets were structured in such a way that would facilitate the identification of variables and trends that might influence future developments. The four themes of the knowledge base were as follows:

- *Countries.* The data sheets described the commodity chain in the producing and consuming countries, in order to assess the present situation, production trends, social needs and opportunities.
- *Actors.* The data sheets described the principal stakeholders – producers, marketing organizations, traders, industry, consumers, researchers, professional associations, international organizations, etc. – in order to assess their roles and attitudes.
- *Cross-cutting themes.* These included quality, prices, legislation, etc., in order to evaluate emerging themes for research.
- *Science.* These data sheets outlined the research results so far, current issues in various fields (genetics, agronomy, plant pathology, economics, etc.), as well as the state of scientific knowledge and the tools currently in use, in order to evaluate the situation of the research community and

emerging scientific and technical opportunities.

About 20 Cirad researchers analyzed the knowledge base in brainstorming and group discussions. During the *exploration phase* they listed and discussed potential variables. Some macro-environmental variables were characterized as 'uncontrollable' (e.g. climate, demographic trends, geopolitical shifts, economic growth and development, exchange rates). Other micro-environmental variables, such as market and industry trends, were characterized as 'controllable' by either Cirad or other actors. During the *selection phase* several controllable variables were identified as 'key variables' for the future. These variables were as independent as possible of each other, so that changes in one would not influence the others. The key variables for the cocoa chain were identified as: the balance between production factors (land, labour and capital), parasites and diseases, quality, consumption, and the operators of the commodity chain, especially professional organizations. Once these variables were identified, the researchers were able to prepare scenarios and to identify new questions for research.

The focus was on breakthroughs in order to develop contrasting scenarios that could provide a useful basis for the discussions. First, micro-scenarios were prepared for each of the controllable key variables that were considered to have the greatest influence on the commodity chain. Then, the compatibility of the different micro-scenarios was analyzed and three broad scenarios were prepared: the continuation of current trends ('business as usual'), an 'optimistic' scenario based on the sustainable development of the chain, and a 'pessimistic' scenario that detailed a production crisis and the virtual disappearance of the chain. The objective was not to present the future accurately, but to show extreme situations in order to encourage the participants to react, discuss and decide. Mathematical simulations of the three scenarios were produced using a world food analysis security model.

The participants then analyzed the roles of the many stakeholders in the cocoa chain – public and private producers, producer organizations, national policy makers, traders, industries, research organizations and intergovernmental organizations – and their relationships. This led to the proposal of a new typology for the countries involved in the commodity chain, and to the identification of new functions in the chain.

A collective view of the possible futures for cocoa

The cocoa foresight exercise involved a sequence of collective learning cycles that took place in two processes: through the compilation of the knowledge base and bibliometric studies, and discussions. The knowledge base led to the conversion of impressions into facts. It facilitated the identification of the variables that had influenced past trends and could perhaps affect future developments, leading to a collective and shared representation of the situation. A bibliometric analysis of two internal databases was carried out to assess the strengths and weaknesses of Cirad's cocoa research programme. A retrospective analysis of publications (articles, conference papers, reports, theses, etc.) and missions to partner countries covering ten years of activities was done. The scientists were encouraged to question the reasons for their presence in some countries and their thematic fields of research.

Discussions played an important role in the learning cycle. In a series of meetings, Cirad's researchers started to question their research activities and to wonder whether they were on the right track. They expressed some of their doubts and raised new ones. Slowly, a consensus emerged about a possible optimistic scenario for the commodity system, about changes that should be implemented, and new research activities. Outside experts were consulted on an *ad hoc* basis. For example, when groups of chocolate firms met, the foresight work was presented to them in order to obtain their feedback and to develop new networks. Operators in the commodity chain made useful comments that led to revisions in some hypotheses and scenarios. Individual contacts were often more constructive than group meetings because in meetings representatives of firms and policy makers would not give clear-cut opinions since they did not wish to reveal their strategies to competitors. Discussions contributed to changing opinions and to the construction of a common language.

New research priorities, partnerships and networks

After the foresight exercise, the collective view of the possible future of cocoa led to several changes within Cirad. Whereas the overall objective of the research programme had been to improve productivity, it would now focus on the sustainable development of cocoa production. This paradigm shift meant that in the future the programme would take into account economic as well as social and ecological aspects in an interdisciplinary approach. This was accepted because the researchers were aware that they had been on the wrong track.

The exercise led to the identification of threats and opportunities within the possible futures, to the definition of a desirable future, and the conditions necessary to reach it. This was a first step towards the establishment of a 'global cocoa programme'. The outcomes of the exercise were presented to stakeholders at a meeting in Paris in March 1999, and in June 2001 the Global Coordination Group on a Sustainable Cocoa Economy was officially launched. The 18 members of the group include representatives of farmers, governments of producing and consuming countries, national research centres in the producing countries, advanced and international research centres, the chocolate industry, and trade associations. Extra funding for research followed the establishment of the group. Linkages were developed between Cirad and the USDA. Since many operators in the cocoa chain were worried about future supply and consumer pressure to be environmentally friendly, they were sensitive to the added value provided by the scenarios so that they were adopted outside before internally within Cirad. All the operators decided to work in the same direction, even though each one might have had a different reason for doing so.

From a closed system into the political arena

Once the scenarios have been designed, the next challenge is to maintain the spirit and attention to outside events, and to continue to evaluate and correct ongoing activities. The foresight exercise may have ended, but the process of keeping database up to date, developing partnerships, keeping abreast of developments and, if necessary, formulating new research projects, continues. The experience of the cocoa foresight exercise shows that anticipation (prospective thought), appropriation (collective mobilization) and action (strategic will) keep up the spirit of thinking about the future, about projects and about networks.

Many research organizations tend to function as 'closed systems',[32] in which the goals are not imposed from the 'outside' and many staff seek to gain personal advantage, especially peer recognition. Before the foresight exercise, Cirad's cocoa programme was a closed system where researchers tended to think they alone were competent to analyze the sector's needs for innovation and to define their research priorities. They feared that the influence of stakeholder groups, especially agro-industrial firms, would limit their scientific creativity and manipulate them as researchers in a public institution. They feared being obliged to serve private interests. Evaluation and foresight pushed the 'closed system' into a 'political arena'. The differences between members of the coordination group – i.e. other stakeholders in the chain – became more apparent. The internal group became more politicized, and more concerned with its role in society. There were complex and reciprocal movements of power between the two coalitions. The foresight became the basis for a new type of discussion. Foresight and evaluation are indispensable instruments for the evolution of research programmes and for research institutions.

5. Possible futures for a country: agriculture in the Netherlands

In the Netherlands, the National Council for Agricultural Research (NRLO) is financed by the Ministry of Agriculture. Its task is to explore social, scientific and technological changes over the next 15-20 years using foresight studies to support strategic management in agricultural research.

Between 1995 and 1999, NRLO conducted a foresight exercise on the challenges facing agribusiness, rural areas and fisheries, and the contribution of S&T to meeting these challenges.[33] Most of the 1000 participants came from knowledge organizations (academia, research institutes, consultancy firms, etc.), national and provincial governments, societal organizations and the private sector. The participants shared a more or less well articulated sense of urgency that 'business as usual' was no longer tenable. Many were convinced that further modernization of farming practices would no longer suffice to make farming sustainable in social, ecological and economic terms.

The foresight process

In terms of content, the NRLO foresight process consisted of three themes. The first two, dynamics in society and dynamics in science and technology, were subjected to foresight. The third theme assessed the strategic consequences of the first two for the organization of innovation processes. Under each of these headings several sub-themes were defined. Most of the science and technology sub-themes were selected because of their expected relevance for coping with societal trends, in addition to their anticipated scientific or technological relevance (see figure 3).

Major themes	Dynamics in society	Dynamics in science and technology	Organizing innovation processes
Sub-themes	Agribusiness: • societal perspectives • globalisation • markets and consumers • agriculture and environment • animal health Rural areas Fisheries and aquaculture	Sensor technology Packaging technologies Veterinary epidemiology Molecular biology (animals and plants) Nanotechnology Production ecology Data processing Aquaculture Policy sciences and ICTs	Innovations at • systems level • large scale • multi-actor

Figure 3. The themes of the NRLO foresight process

In the design of the process, the idea was to alternate phases of divergence and convergence. Because dealing with uncertainty and making use of creativity are central, much room was given to generating broad arrays of possibly relevant ideas, insights, facts and strategic options. Selection phases were necessary to redefine the focus, but were again followed by phases of divergence. In most cases the divergence-convergence pattern was repeated two or three times, as illustrated in figure 4.

An additional requirement for the design of the process was to build agendas to give each foresight activity its own dynamics and provide a focus for the next step. Through such agendas, the aim was to ensure the commitment of members of the networks, as well as those who were involved only in the process. Therefore, at each step in the process, agenda-building questions were raised, such as 'what is really at stake?' (e.g. in the fisheries sector); 'what do dynamics in the societal, scientific and technological environment actually mean?' (e.g. for future options in the fisheries sector); 'how can the actors involved respond to those dynamics?' (e.g. what strategic conclusions can/should fisheries organizations and policy makers draw?); and 'how interdependent are individual strategies, and is there scope for collective action?' (e.g. do fishermen's strategies depend on what retailers want?).

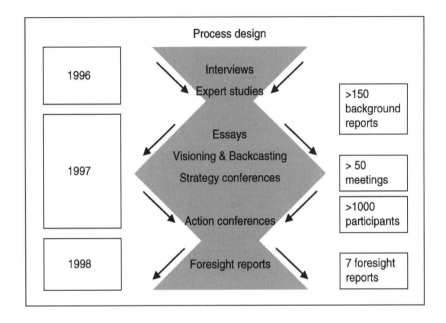

Figure 4. The NRLO foresight process: phases of convergence and divergence.

In the end, ten proposals for action were selected, including efforts to improve learning capacities, programmes for long-term system innovations and network development. These proposals for action were important results of the exercise. If well designed and implemented, the foresight process can encourage strategic, long-term thinking about an entire sector, like agriculture, and trigger decisions by different actors.

6. Possible futures for food, agriculture and the environment: IFPRI's 2020 Vision

In 1993, in collaboration with national and international institutions, IFPRI launched the 2020 Vision for food, agriculture and the environment. At that time there was considerable complacency regarding international food security. World grain stocks were high, and international prices were low, partly as a result of declining external assistance for agricultural development, and for international agricultural research. IFPRI decided to launch the initiative in order to refocus attention on agriculture and to stimulate debate on world food security.

The 2020 Vision initiative has two objectives. First, it aims to develop and promote a shared vision and consensus for action for meeting food needs while reducing poverty and protecting the environment. Second, it hopes to generate information and encourage debate in order to influence action by national governments, NGOs, the private sector, international development agencies and civil society. The initiative was intended for three audiences – researchers, educators and policy makers in the industrialized and developing countries – and is advised by a council of heads of state, Nobel Prize winners, chairmen or directors of donor agencies and researchers.

The process

The 2020 Vision initiative involves four major activities:

- generating information on key topics related to food, agriculture and the environment, paying special attention to emerging issues with long-term implications for world food supplies, alleviating poverty, and protecting natural resources;
- communicating the 2020 Vision challenges and the related action programme in order to increase public awareness of global food and environmental problems and what can be done to resolve them;
- facilitating forums for dialogue, debate, information sharing and consensus building among policy makers, researchers, and leaders in NGOs, the private sector and the media; and
- conducting pilot projects in research, policy communications, and capacity strengthening to support IFPRI's long-term strategy.

Looking back, one can distinguish three phases. Phase I (1993–96) consisted of writing papers and constructing Impact, a new global food model. In the first two years, under the 2020 Vision logo, IFPRI published many discussion papers and policy briefs, and organized 35 meetings to stimulate discussion and debate. In June 1995, at a conference in Washington, DC, attended by 500 people from 50 countries, IFPRI's director-general issued a powerful message that, as the world moves toward 2020, the global food situation might be safe but tremendous human suffering will continue, with hunger and malnutrition in large parts of the world, and rampant natural resource degradation. Although the world's natural resources would be sufficient to relieve this suffering by 2020, political will may be lacking. He argued that relieving this suffering would require, first of all, policies designed to improve the performance of developing country agriculture.

Phase II (1997–2001) saw the improvement of the Impact model, international communication and consensus-building efforts, as well as helping developing countries to design and implement their strategies at national level. This phase ended with a conference on sustainable food security for all, in Bonn in September 2001. The 900 participants, from the public and private sectors and civil society, discussed the goals, solutions and actions necessary to end hunger in the next two decades, and considered the critical driving forces to achieve food security and priority areas of action at global and national levels.

In phase III (since 2001), more studies were published, and conference, 'Assuring food and nutrition security in Africa by 2020', was held in April 2004. It brought together more than 500 traditional and new actors and stakeholders from more than 50 countries to discuss how to bring about change and action to assure food and nutrition security. A new tone marked the conference: the dramatic situation in Africa was clearly presented; doubts about the capacity of Africa and the world to address the present and future crises were expressed, but at the same time the participants expressed their political will to find solutions rather than to wait for funding from OECD countries. As one participant put it, 'The strength of the conference was the mixture of delegates from political, academic, administrative and activist backgrounds, which enhanced the quality of the debate. Its weakness was in the broad spectrum of issues covered, and hence the inability to go into any issue in any real depth'. A statement on the way forward shows that the conference is part of a longer-term consultative process on real action toward food and nutrition security in Africa. The steps forward must focus on implementing action and on developing a process of learning and change. Specific 'road maps' for change must be developed at regional and national levels, building on existing strategies where appropriate, and facilitated by an organic process.

Impact assessment

In 1999, an external impact assessment of the 2020 Vision initiative[34] evaluated the capacity of the initiative to reach the three audiences, to achieve consensus, and to catalyze action. Although the initiative had reached a large number of researchers and educators within universities, research organizations, international financial institutions, private companies, think thanks and NGOs, it had not managed to generate consensus among researchers (e.g. about research priorities) and had therefore had little impact on them, or on developing country policy makers, probably because the objectives were too broad.

7. Foresight for Africa

Over the last 50 years agronomic research has helped to transform French agriculture. After the Second World War, France was not self-sufficient in food, even though more than one-third of the population worked in agriculture. Today, France is the world's second largest exporter of agricultural produce and agro-food products. Three factors have contributed to this success: the development of public policies with substantial budgets for their implementation; the emergence of a social movement within the agricultural sector that developed and encouraged modernization; and the creation of a dynamic public research system, strongly supported by development and training institutes.[35]

Over the last five years, the European Commission and EU Member States have worked to develop, through foresight, the policy and research capacities in the ten new Member States, and to assist their integration. In the developing countries, especially in Africa, despite even greater challenges, foresight could be used to identify agricultural research objectives. The drivers are there: African agriculture is among the world's most globalized and at the same time the most subsistence-oriented;[36] it relies on exports of unprocessed agricultural commodities; and it produces part of its food requirements and imports the rest. In view of the enormous agro-ecological, economic and sociological diversity and complexity a systems approach is essential. The number and the diversity of actors are increasing – producers and producer organizations, national and international companies, NGOs, public enterprises, universities, research institutions, etc. The relationships between research and trade policies are developing due to international agreements and developed country policies. There are also risks: despite international efforts, policies for agricultural research and development are inadequate, and the state of S&T has deteriorated substantially in most African countries. National educational and research coordinating bodies have lost much of their political power and influence – there was virtually no recruitment throughout the 1990s and salaries are inadequate. Despite the lack of institutions and of political commitment, foresight could help foster commitment to the future and encourage debates among actors.

In public institutions, researchers from different disciplines have learned to work together and to develop multidisciplinary research projects. They have also adapted their methods of work to local conditions and are increasingly working with farmers (participatory methods) to identify demands and to develop producer organizations. More work must be done for researchers to work with the rest of civil society, especially consumers and politicians. Cooperation between researchers from public organizations and in the few private companies interested in Africa could also be increased. Foresight could help this movement.

Foresight is not a panacea. It is a time-consuming process, but it can help in discussions about complex systems and in the formulation of demands. It forces the participants to be inventive, to make linkages among variables, and to take appropriate decisions. Striking a balance between global analysis and strategies for a commodity on the one hand, while remaining practical and specific, and using the results to reorientate policies and research programmes on the other, is not easy.

Experience indicates that it is important to maintain a balance between pressures from the inside (research staff) and the outside (stakeholders, especially the 'powerful' ones, such as agro-industrial firms) and to acknowledge weaknesses, but at the same time to be reasonably ambitious. Foresight should be seen as a contribution to a global effort, and stakeholders should be explicitly informed that the final choice of strategic options will be made by the decision makers.

Notes

1. Dr Marie de Lattre-Gasquet (marie.de_lattre-gasquet@cirad.fr) works at the Centre de coopération internationale en recherche agronomique pour le développement (Cirad) in France. At present, she is special adviser to the Director General of Cirad on questions of foresight and strategy.

2. Box *et al.* (2003).

3. Gaillard *et al.* (2002).

4. Diouf (2003).

5. Martin (1995).

6. See Cazes (1986), Hatem (1993), Gonod and Gurtler (2002), Cornish (2004).

7. De Jouvenel (2004).

8. Van der Meulen *et al.* (2003).

9. Godet (1977).

10. Irvine and Martin (1984, 1989).
11. McCalla and Revodero (2001).
12. Paarlberg (1999).
13. McCalla and Revodero (2001).
14. Griffon (2004).
15. Godet (1977).
16. Researchers at the Institut National de la Recherche Agronomique (INRA) have developed their own method of foresight and have carried out exercises on oilseeds, vegetable and animal proteins, forestry, water, etc.
17. Following the cocoa foresight exercise, a simulation using a world food security analysis model developed by Cirad provided information on the impacts of changes in cocoa production on prices and trade.
18. See ESTO (2001) and http://esto.jrc.es/monitoring_list.html.
19. Wagner and Popper (2003).
20. Latour (1995).
21. Johnston (2001).
22. Martin and Johnston (1999).
23. The legislation creating the National Science Foundation in effect established a social contract under which the government would pay scientists to engage in research of their own choosing, on the understanding that significant benefits would come back to US society in the forms of military security, public health and economic prosperity (Bush, 1945).
24. Gibbons *et al.* (1994).
25. Martin and Etzkowitz (2000).
26. OECD (1996); see also Battelle (1996), Wagner (1997).
27. See ISNAR (2001) and www.isnar.cgiar.org
28. Kuhlmann *et al.* (1999).
29. Salo and Salmenkaita (2002).
30. Rutten (1997).
31. Sperling and Ashby (2001), Janssen *et al.* (2004).
32. Mintzberg (1983).
33. Van der Meulen *et al.* (2003).
34. Paarlberg (1999).
35. Hervieu (2001).
36. Von Braun (2004).

References

Battelle (1996) *Foresighting around the World: A review of seven best-in-kind programs,* Seattle: Battelle Research Centre.

Box, L., Ulmanen, J., Steinhauer, N. and Engelhard, R. (2003) *Review of Science and Technology Plans in ACP countries.* CTA and University of Maastricht.

Bush, V. (1945) *Science: The Endless Frontier.* Report to the President by Vannevar Bush, Director of the Office of Scientific Research and Development. Washington, DC: USGPO).

Cazes, B. (1986) *Histoire des futures. Les figures de l'avenir de Saint Augustin au XXème siècle.* Paris: Seghers.

Cornish, E. (2004) *Futuring: The exploration of the future.* Bethesda, MD: World Future Society.

De Jouvenel, H. (2004) *An Invitation to Foresight*. Futuribles Perspectives Series.

Diouf, M. (2003) Research for development: An historian comments, in: *Poverty and Governance*. RAWOO Lectures and 25th Anniversary Conference.

ESTO (2001) *Monitoring Technology Forecasting Activities in Europe*. Report for the European Commission (JRC–IPTS). VDI Future Technologies No 37, and European Science and Technology Observatory, Monitoring prospective S&T activities project (http://esto.jrc.es/monitoring_list.html).

Gaillard, J., Hassan, M., Waast, R. and Schaffer, D. (2002) *UNESCO Science Report 2002: Africa*. Paris: UNESCO.

Gibbons, M., Limoges, C., Nowotny, H., Schwartzman, S., Scott, P. and Trow, M. (1994) *The New Production of Knowledge: The Dynamics of Science and Research in Contemporary societies*. London: Sage.

Godet, M. (1977) *Crise de la prévision: Essor de la prospective*. Paris: PUF.

Gonod, P. and Gurtler, J.-L. (2002) Evolution de la prospective. *Oléagineux Corps gras Lipides*, 9(5): 317.

Griffon, M. (2004) Modèles et prospectives: pourquoi tant de divergences entre les prévisions des années 1990 et la réalité des années 2000. *DEMETER 2005, Economie et stratégies agricoles*.

Hatem, F. (1993) *La prospective: Practiques et methods*. Paris: Economica.

Hervieu, B. (2001) Agriculture et recherche agronomique. Une histoire et des enjeux partagés. Entretien avec Bertrand Hervieu. *INRA mensuel*, No.111.

Irvine, J. and Martin, B.R. (1984) *Foresight in Science: Picking the Winners*, London: Pinter.

Irvine, J. and Martin, B.R. (1989) *Research Foresight: Priority Setting in Science*. London: Pinter.

ISNAR (2001) *Planning Agricultural Research: A Sourcebook*. The Hague: ISNAR.

Janssen, W., Kassam, A. and de Janvry, A. (2004) *A Regional Approach to Setting Research Priorities and Implementation: Towards Satisfying National, Regional and Global Concerns*. Binghamton, NY: Haworth Press.

Johnston, R. (2001) Foresight: Refining the process. *Int. J. Technology Management*, 21(7/8): 711–725.

Kuhlmann, S. *et al.* (1999) *Improving Distributed Intelligence in Complex Innovation Systems*. Final report of the Advanced Science and Technology Policy Planning Network (ASTPP).

Latour, B. (1995) *Le métier de chercheur, regard d'un anthropologue*. INRA éditions.

McCalla, A. and Revodero, C. (2001) *Prospects for Global Food Security: A Critical Appraisal of Past Projections and Predictions*. 2020 Brief No. 71. Washington, DC: IFPRI.

Martin, B.R. (1995) Foresight in science and technology. *Technology Analysis and Strategic Management*, 7(2): 139–168.

Martin, B.R. and Etzkowitz, H. (2000) The origin and evolution of the university species. *Journal for Science and Technology Studies*, VEST, 13(3-4) 2000, 9–34.

Martin, B.R. and Johnston, R. (1999) Technology foresight for wiring up the national innovation system: Experience in Britain, Australia and New Zealand. *Technological Forecasting and Social Change*, 60: 37–54.

Mintzberg H. (1983) *Power in and around Organizations*. Englewood Cliffs, NJ: Prentice Hall.

OECD (1996) *Special Issue on Government Technology Foresight Exercises, STI Review* No.17. Paris: OECD.

Paarlberg, R.L. (1999) *External Impact Assessment of IFPRI's 2020 Vision for Food, Agriculture, and the Environment Initiative.* Discussion paper 10. Washington, DC: IFPRI.

Rutten, H. (1997) *Coping with Turbulence: Strategies for Agricultural Research Institutes.* NRLO Report 97/27. The Hague: Council for Agricultural Research.

Salo, A. and Salmenkaita, J.K. (2002) Embedded foresight in RTD programs. *Int. J. Technology, Policy and Management*, 2(2): 167–193.

Sperling, L. and Ashby, J. (2001) Participation in agricultural research planning, in *Planning Agricultural Research: A Sourcebook.* Wallingford, UK: CAB International.

Van der Meulen, B., de Wilt, J. and Rutten, H. (2003) Developing futures for agriculture in the Netherlands: A systematic exploration of the strategic value of foresight. *Journal of Forecasting*, 22, 219–233.

Von Braun, J. (2004) *Assuring Food and Nutrition Security in Africa by 2020.* Opening remarks to the conference 'Assuring Food and Nutrition Security in Africa by 2020: Prioritizing action, strengthening actors, and facilitating partnerships', Kampala, Uganda.

Wagner, C.S. (1997) *Critical Technologies in a Global Context: A Review of National Reports.* Technology Foresight, Asia-Pacific Economic Forum: Bangkok, Thailand.

Wagner, C.S. and Popper, S.W. (2003) Identifying critical technologies in the United States: A review of the federal effort. *Journal of Forecasting*, 22: 113–128.

Useful websites related to foresight and agriculture (in English and French)

European Commission, DG Research: www.cordis.lu/foresight/home.html

European Commission, Institute for Prospective Technological Studies: www.jrc.es/welcome.html

European Science and Technology Observatory (ESTO): http://esto.jrc.es/

Futures Research Centre, Finland: www.tukkk.fi/tutu/default_eng.asp

Futuris: www.operation-futuris.org/dyn_menu.asp

Global Business Network (GBN): www.gbn.org

Groupe Futuribles: www.futuribles.com

Groupe prospective du Sénat, France: www.prospective.org/

Institut National de la Recherche Agronomique (INRA): www.inra.fr/sed/prospective/index.html

Institute for Alternative Futures: www.altfutures.com

International Assessment of Agricultural Science and Technology for Development (IAASTD): www.agassessment.org/

International Food Policy Research Institute (IFPRI): www.ifpri.org

Millennium Ecosystem Assessment: www.millenniumassessment.org/en/index.aspx

National Council for Agricultural Research (NRLO), the Netherlands: www.agro.nl/nrlo/english/nrint2pg.shtml

OECD International Futures Programme: www.oecd.org/department/0,2688,en_2649 _33707_1_1_1_1_1,00.html

Policy Research in Engineering, Science and Technology (PREST), University of Manchester: www.les1.man.ac.uk/PREST

Rand Corporation: www.rand.org

Technology Foresight (2002 collection), UK: www.foresight.gov.uk

World Future Society: www.wfs.org

DEVELOPMENT OF SUSTAINABLE CONTROL OF DIAMONDBACK MOTH IN CABBAGE AND CAULIFLOWER BY PUBLIC–PRIVATE PARTNERSHIP

BERT UIJTEWAAL[1]

Most biotechnology research and development focuses on major agricultural crops. There is an urgent need for improvements in vegetable production, especially in developing countries where the economic, health and environmental benefits of bioengineered vegetables could be great. This chapter outlines a strategy to realize this potential, involving initiating an innovative public–private sector project for developing and releasing an integrated solution to an immense insect problem in cabbage and cauliflower. It describes the basic aspects of the concept, as well as the challenges experienced in its deployment.

1. Introduction

Cabbage and cauliflower are important cash crops for farmers throughout tropical and subtropical areas of Asia, Africa, Latin America and the Caribbean. They are also important staple foods, rich in vitamin C and other micronutrients. The production of these crucifers (a family that also includes broccoli, radish, kale and mustard) is severely affected by the diamondback moth, *Plutella xylostella*, especially in resource-poor regions.[2] Diamondback moth now occurs wherever crucifers are grown, and control of the pest worldwide is estimated to cost US$1 billion each year. Losses of cabbage and cauliflower due to the moth can reach 90% without the use of insecticides. Even when insecticides are used, the losses can be substantial. In tropical areas where pest pressure is high, it is not uncommon for insecticides to be applied every other day, posing hazards to farmers, consumers and the environment.

This paper provides an insight into the efforts of and challenges experienced by a public–private partnership to deploy a new strategy to develop and release a sustainable solution to an immense insect problem in cabbage and cauliflower cultures in developing countries.

Natural enemies are essential in any integrated pest management programme to control the diamondback moth. Although considerable research has gone into enhancing the role of the moth's natural enemies, they are rarely sufficiently effective, and so must be supplemented with other control tactics. Once established in newly planted areas, moth populations grow too fast for naturally occurring control agents to be effective. In tropical climates, where host plants are available year round, more than 20 generations of diamondback moth may be produced. The intensive use of broad-spectrum insecticides exacerbates this situation, as they also destroy the moth's natural enemies. The high reproductive rate, coupled with intensive insecticide use, has led to the creation of biotypes of the moth that are resistant to many common insecticides. Such resistance must be taken into account when planning new control strategies.

2. A technical solution

Diamondback moth caterpillars feed on above-ground portions of crucifers, frequently in parts that are inaccessible to crop protection sprays. The development of varieties with built-in resistance would have a number of benefits, including reducing yield losses and the incidence of diseases that enter the plant following insect damage. Resistant varieties would also reduce the need for frequent insecticide applications and the reliance on broad-spectrum insecticides, thus allowing an increased role for the moth's natural predators. Despite considerable research, however, plant breeders have not been able, by conventional breeding, to develop crucifer germplasm with sufficiently high levels of resistance to the diamondback moth to be considered useful for commercial programmes.

The approach proposed here is to develop cabbage and cauliflower varieties with built-in, consistent and sustainable protection from the diamondback moth through the insertion of two genes from the soil bacterium *Bacillus thuringiensis* (Bt). Over the past eight years various genes for Bt toxins have been deployed in corn and cotton, with great success. In 2003 the total area planted with Bt crops worldwide was 18 million ha, without significant environmental or health problems emerging.[3] Nonetheless, plant materials developed via this approach would be rigorously tested for their biological, social and economic impacts on small-scale farming systems before any move to commercialization is pursued.

The approach recognizes the potential benefits of using Bt crucifers as a safe and effective control strategy, but also acknowledges the concern that diamondback moth populations have the capacity to develop resistance to Bt proteins, as has already occurred in some areas due to Bt foliar sprays. However, theoretical models show that if two Bt genes producing different proteins that target different binding sites in the insect are used simultaneously in the plant, the evolution of resistance can be dramatically delayed relative to single gene plants used sequentially or simultaneously. Recent greenhouse tests with diamondback moth produced results that are consistent with this theory.[4]

3. A delivery solution

The diversity of vegetable markets, the short life time of particular varieties of the crops in question, and the regulatory costs of bringing such novel plant material to market make the process of developing, testing, assessing and gaining regulatory approval for (stacked-gene) Bt brassica prohibitive for even the largest commercial vegetable seed company. Today the costs involved in collecting the necessary data to prove the human and environmental safety of transgenic plant material, including the preparation of the regulatory dossier required for international registration, can exceed the development costs by more than four times.

For fresh produce like cabbage and cauliflower, the situation with respect to consumer acceptance and public commitment to transgenic varieties remains unclear. Due to this uncertainty, together with the high costs and relatively low acreages planted with vegetable crops compared with those devoted to the main commodity crops, biotech companies have focused their attention on corn, cotton and soy, and not on vegetables.

Sharing the responsibility for ensuring that developed plant material meets the highest regulatory standards would reduce the costs to each participant. Including strong public participation, as well as funding, would give the 'public' the opportunity to lever private investments in the direction of products that would benefit farmers and consumers in developing countries, and ensure the fair availability of plant material to all stakeholders. The combination of private and public expertise, addressing technical as well as socio-economic aspects, would help to guarantee the best outcome of the work, increase public confidence in the developed material and, therefore, acceptance of the strategy.

The magnitude of potential benefits to producers and consumers worldwide makes the development of such material of considerable public interest. For this reason a public–private initiative has been launched to develop Bt cabbage and cauliflower varieties resistant to diamondback moth. The use of public funding would help to ensure the appropriateness of the developed material for small-scale farmers and consumers in developing countries, and that the developed germplasm is accessible to vegetable breeders in developing countries.

The developed material will be deployed within a comprehensive integrated pest management (IPM) framework designed by expert entomologists. The distribution of the plant material will be accompanied by an extensive farmer training programme aimed at ensuring the appropriate and sustainable use of the technology, and maximum yields for farmers.

Project history

The history of this specific cabbage and cauliflower case dates back to 2000, when the Natural Resources Institute (NRI) in the UK was looking for a private partner to join in the development of a sustainable solution to the alarming increase in the use of insecticides to control pests in vegetables in India and Southeast Asia. The NRI had been involved in the development and deployment of Bt cotton and was aware of the serious situation in vegetable growing. What they were looking for was an experienced partner that could deliver locally adapted Bt varieties that could be used as the basis for improving the sustainability of vegetable cultivation.

At a first technical meeting in late 2001, participants from all over the world discussed the problems in cabbage and cauliflower and the possibilities for changing the situation. The outcome was a definition of a 'best approach', detailing minimum requirements to deal with the specific case of the diamondback moth.

A number of potential sponsors, most of them European development agencies, expressed their interest in the initiative, which appeared to be technically and environmentally sound, but they were nervous about joining a project involving the development and release of transgenic material. Another major drawback may have been the likely duration of the project – it is expected to take at least eight years from the start of technical work to the release of the developed plant material. It is difficult for ministries to commit to (aid) projects that will continue far beyond their electoral period.

The private company was an invited partner and agreed to work 'behind the scenes' as a material supplier only. It was appreciated that the plant material would take time to develop. Thus, at the end of 2003, the company started the preparatory development work, following the advice of international scientific opinion on the technical approach. In the interim, NRI and the company continued to develop their public–private partnership (PPP) concept and encouraged leading international organizations to support the initiative.

Project concept

The concept of the project was based on the following. The public sector had seen the need for the considerable regulatory and testing hurdles in the development and registration of transgenic plant material. It was therefore appropriate that the public sector should share the costs of bringing the benefits to poor farmers and consumers who would otherwise be excluded from the market due to the high cost of development and registration. However, if public funds were to be used, significant public benefits had to be ensured.

Rather than simply sharing the intellectual property – with all the accompanying problems in terms of regulatory constraints – the intention was to offer the technology in the form of locally adapted varieties that would perform well under local conditions to breeders and seed producers free of technology fees. This development programme would not stop with the development and selection of the physical material, but would continue to full registration of the material in the target countries.

The private company would carry the cost of 'making the product', which would include the introduction of the resistance genes in the cabbage and cauliflower varieties, testing and selecting their performance under local conditions, and performing the basic characterization studies to confirm stability and ensure full traceability. For their part, the public sector partners would bear the costs of 'releasing' the product. This would involve extensive field testing of the new varieties for effects on target and non-target insects, studies of human and environmental safety issues, and evaluations of the socio-economic impacts of the solution and the supporting integrated pest management (IPM) programme. This IPM programme would be based on an optimal mix of plant-based insect resistance in order to reduce insect pressure, and well planned agricultural practices, including natural predators and the selective use of insecticides if needed.

Both the insect-resistant plant material and the regulatory dossier would be transferred to a public organization that would make it available to local farmers and breeders. However, based on the same resistant plant material the company would be entitled to develop its own hybrids that may be released in parallel with the public varieties.

By making these concept principles clear from the beginning, the consortium believed that the work would lead to a clear and acceptable win–win situation for both the public and private partners, as well as for farmers and consumers in developing countries.

Project milestones

Based on the project concept outlined above, a number of project milestones were set. First, it was recognized that for such an extensive project it was essential to have the commitment of scientific experts who would make it clear that the best approach was being taken to create a sustainable solution to the insect problem. A group of scientists was asked to prepare a statement detailing the scientific rationale for the concept and to submit it to international experts for comment. The statement, which was modified slightly to take into account the comments received, not only established the scientific support for the concept, but also identified further environmental and other studies that would need to be undertaken in order to ensure the sustainability of the end product.

Second, it was necessary to make sure that the economic assumptions justifying the project were not based on personal perceptions. Independent institutions were therefore requested to undertake studies of the socio-economic impacts of the insect pest on cabbage and cauliflower production, the actual pest management systems currently in use, and the potential impact of the concept under development. Along with the scientific statement, these socio-economic studies provided the technical justification for starting the work.

Third, a clear condition set by the private company and the financial sponsors approached was that a clearly formulated request was received from stakeholders in developing countries. This project was not meant as a technology looking for a problem to address, but rather as a well prepared solution to the problem of managing a serious insect pest. Thus the clear commitment of local stakeholders would provide to all participants the best guarantee of an acceptable and accepted product.

Finally, once the international experts had defined the 'best approach', it would be up to the scientists to demonstrate its technical feasibility. This technical 'proof of concept' is a prerequisite for finalizing the project time-line and budget. As a major part of the work will be done by local public sector partners, it will be essential to identify which local institutions would be involved in what part of the project, to ensure that optimal use is made of available resources, and to bring together international and local expertise for their mutual benefit. Having an agreement on the concept and the com-mitment of stakeholders, potential financial sponsors are now being asked to indicate their interest in joining the consortium as financial partners.

Project timeline

The total time span of the project will be about eight years. It will take five years to introduce the resistance genes into the cabbage and cauliflower and to test and select the material in the field. The performance and stability of the trait, as well as the developed varieties, will need to be field tested in the target region over several seasons under different environmental conditions and genetic backgrounds.

Partly overlapping this development phase will be a three-year period of research, tests and analyses of human safety, including toxicity and aller-genicity testing, studies of the environmental effects of the material on tar-get and non-target insects, and assessments of the potential impacts on local ecosystems. This will lead into a series of official field trials, conducted jointly with local authorities, to confirm the quality and safety of the mate-rial.

All the results will be compiled in a regulatory dossier that will be sub-mitted to the authorities responsible for granting approval, which should lead to the release of the product. In anticipation of movements of the mate-rial across national borders, similar procedures will have to be followed in all countries for which the developed material is relevant.

4. The challenges ahead

It is now recognized that public-private partnerships are probably the only way to ensure that technologies and intellectual property developed in both private and public sectors can be brought together for the benefit of devel-oping countries. In the case of this project, however, it has proved to be difficult to finalize the preparation phase and get started with the technical work. This is a classic case of 'not being allowed into the water until you can swim'. Partners and funders would prefer to see answers to questions before committing themselves, yet these answers can only come from the work that needs to be undertaken and for which their support is required. Individual donors and sponsors are now coming forward to 'put a toe in the water', and this has bolstered the confidence of others in being a part of the partnership.

From the perspective of potential private partners, there are several major challenges.

Ownership of the material and of the regulatory dossier

What kind of organization can or will accept ownership of the genetically modified material on a licensing in/licensing out basis under conditions that are acceptable to both public and private partners? Transfer of ownership should also mean transfer of liability, so that what is captured with 'the material' needs to be carefully defined. An essential aspect of genetically modified material is its safety assessment and regulatory approval. It does not make sense to develop a product without taking care of this necessary hurdle to ensure its practical use. The regulatory dossier and its approval should be seen as part of the material and therefore transferred to the new owner.

Financial support

Even if the private partner covers a significant part of the costs, it is necessary that the major part of the costs be sponsored by the public partners in the project. This financial support can be sought for the overall project concept or for individual aspects that may be performed by different (sub)contracting partners. This would have the advantage that not every sponsor needs to commit itself to the eventual release of transgenic material. Initial support may be sought for parts of the process of determining the technical and social acceptability of the concept. By adopting such a phased approach, potential sponsors can be reassured that there will be 'stop or go' points en route to commercialization, and that they will be part of this decision-making process.

Project management and consortium hosting

Managing many international consortium partners and international sponsors will need special skills that may not necessarily be available to the (technical) partners. It may therefore be worthwhile to look for special expertise in both international project management and financial management and reporting.

Stewardship

Making material freely available introduces additional challenges with respect to stewardship, in order to ensure the safe and sustainable use of the material. A balance needs to be found between 'free access for all' and 'responsible stewardship', which should support farmers while ensuring that environmental and health risks are minimized.

Choice of material to be released

Linked to the issue of stewardship is the question of the form of material that will be made available to farmers and breeders. Environmentalists may request the use of male sterile material that can be biologically confined, whereas other groups may emphasize the importance of ensuring that farmers have free access to the plant material by releasing freely pollinating material. In the case of cabbage and cauliflower, farmers do not normally save their own seeds, as the plants are harvested before they seed. A final decision on the relative merits of these cases must be made by the consortium rather than just the private partner, in order to avoid accusations of a double agenda should the material be released in a form that limits its free propagation.

Local project but global registration of plant material

Even though the project will commence as a local project to develop material for a specific region, it should be recognized that the material can 'travel' as seed and as end products. To avoid export problems or local concerns if farmers in neighbouring countries start growing material that is not registered in their country, a registration system at the global level must be anticipated. For countries with similar environmental conditions (for growing the material), and/or concerns about exports of fresh or processed products, a global registration strategy must be developed and a timeline and cost overview prepared.

Manage 'contest' of material flow versus registration

Farmers and distributors, convinced of the quality of the varieties, may try to obtain the material in their own countries, even before registration is completed in these countries. It will be a challenge to restrict the movement of material to countries where the regulatory registration has been completed. To avoid unnecessary delays in approved countries, timely interactions with the different governments will be necessary.

Proactive communication strategy

Although it is recognized that all participants in this project, including the private partner, have the best intentions for all stakeholders, it will be a challenge to define a strategy to communicate this to organizations that are likely to see only the negative aspects. A careful selection of trustworthy advocates who can disseminate clear and honest information in developing countries, and in parts of the world where activists have their roots, should help to maintain the balance in an open and fair discussion of the pros and cons of the concept.

Notes

1. Bert Uijtewaal (bert.uijtewaal@bayercropscience.com) is Global Regulatory Affairs Manager at Bayer CropScience. Any opinions expressed in this paper are those of the author and do not necessarily reflect those of the company.
2. Talekar and Shelton (1993).
3. James (2003).
4. Zhao *et al.* (2003).

References

James, C. (2003) *Global Status of Commercialized Transgenic Crops*. ISAAA Brief No. 30. Ithaca, NY: International Service for the Acquisition of Agri-biotech Applications.

Talekar, N.T. and Shelton, A.M. (1993) Biology, ecology and management of the diamondback moth. *Ann. Rev. Entomol.* 38: 275–301.

Zhao, J., Cao, J., Li, Y., Collins, H.L., Roush, R.T., Earle, E.D. and Shelton, A.M. (2003) Plants expressing two *Bacillus thuringiensis* toxins delay insect resistance compared to single toxins used sequentially or in a mosaic. *Nature Biotech*, 21: 1493–7.

CODA

THE EMERGING CONTEXTUAL SPACE FOR PRIORITY SETTING IN DEVELOPMENT RESEARCH

PAUL DUFOUR[1]

This chapter examines the changing role of knowledge for development, and the issues that developing countries need to address. It argues that learning and experimentation are a necessary condition for development in the pursuit of S&T and knowledge strategies. It examines the cases of four countries to situate this context, noting the growing renaissance centred on new donor approaches to investing in knowledge for development, and suggesting that more 'joined up' decision-making processes are required for these strategies to be effective. The chapter underscores the need for attention to critical areas such as science advice, science communication and public engagement, and the emergence of participatory science processes. It flags the evolution of South–South partnerships, but also constraints on knowledge for development from trade to security, and from ethical concerns to human resources. It also makes the case for using tools such as foresight to anticipate outcomes and foreign policy and diplomacy to make best use of political memberships in clubs. Developing economies must also be more attentive to their own needs when interacting with donors. In the end, the South will require strong leadership, long-term commitment from society and global partnerships if knowledge is to be fully embraced as a currency for social and economic development.

1. Introduction

In order to grasp the new dynamics of so-called development-oriented research it is critical to understand both history and culture. The stage can be set by two quotes from authors working in very different fields and times. In

1963 Steven Dedijer, who was influential in the invention of modern-day business intelligence, contended that underdeveloped countries 'cannot avoid being aware that they are essentially pre-research cultures. All kinds of forces, domestic and foreign, political and economic, moral and historical, are acting on the governments of these countries with the inexorability of a law of nature to take some sort of action to promote the development of science in their own countries'.[2] Some 40 years later the economic historian Joel Mokyr argued that 'What matters clearly is culture and institutions. Culture determines preferences and priorities. All societies have to eat, but cultural factors determine whether the best and the brightest in each society will tinker with machines or chemicals, or whether they will perfect their swordplay or study the Talmud. Institutions set the incentive and penalty structure for people who suggest new techniques'.[3]

There are legitimate reasons for paying attention to knowledge capacity and research-based efforts in the South. In today's knowledge-based society, it has become a challenge for any government to construct its own innovations and knowledge assets. From the perspective of putting in place the required structures and institutions, this chapter explores how the required investments are made, under what institutional settings, with what objectives in mind, and for whose benefit.

2. Learning from others

How states organize themselves to strengthen or improve their knowledge-producing, transfer and research capacities is often a bit of a hit-and-miss exercise. There are different methodologies one can use – the OECD, for example, has made an industry of adopting national innovation systems as a technique for assessing the complementarities among research and innovation actors in any given country or region.[4]

This may be fine and good for the developed world, but what of the developing countries? How can they learn, innovate and shape skills? How can they develop effective mechanisms, policies and tools to encourage science and technology (S&T) – conventional and indigenous – and manage the impacts on their respective societies? How can they ensure that they participate in the global pool of knowledge production and take advantage of knowledge to improve their standards of living, eradicate poverty, and strengthen their capacities for decision making?

In April 2003 IDRC and UNESCO organized a joint workshop in Paris to address many of these issues. Both organizations have a track record in assessments of national knowledge and innovation systems. The IDRC has produced such assessment reports in partnership with Chile, China, Jordan, South Africa and Vietnam, while UNESCO has conducted country reviews involving Albania, Bahrain and Lebanon.[5] The participants learned that the impacts of such reviews may vary. For some of them timing was critical. IDRC's presence in South Africa at the time of the transition to the ANC government was a key factor in ensuring the successful impact of its S&T reviews. Politics almost always plays a role. How Vietnam has implemented the results of the reviews of its knowledge systems is in part tied to the changing nature of the political regime in that country. Champions are required. It makes no sense for outside experts to push recommendations for change unless they mirror the views of those in charge. Funding is also required. Unless states are willing and committed to change by investing in new support for knowledge production or institutional change, little will happen. And luck can be important.

The participants also learned that donors continue to play an important role. They are in a position to identify the frontiers of scientific and technological change in their own countries and to share them with developing countries. They can also open up channels of dialogue between North and South and among countries and institutions in the South. Donors also provide access to resources and programmes that can help strengthen the absorptive capacity of local actors and enhance the areas of expertise resident in various centres of excellence, and they can facilitate efforts to link this capacity to local policy-making processes.

Ultimately, an institutional capacity to absorb the recommendations for change is a must. However, as many in the Paris workshop recognized, unless there are sound frameworks for decision making, data collecting, communications and governance of innovation and knowledge infrastructure, little will come of recommendations designed to improve research and knowledge capacity. This was spelled out in the case of Jamaica, which flagged the need for regulatory and other requirements in order to put in place sound ICT infrastructures. Training is critical. This requires not just a well-developed education system, but also some institutionalized critical thinking on future directions for knowledge and its production. South Africa has put in place a variety of new training and development organizations for innovation since 1994. Ongoing assessments, benchmarking and evaluation are also crucial, as has been the case in Vietnam, where the government has attempted to respond to and update its activities related to the 1999 review conducted with IDRC.[6]

Responsibility for such implementation is not a one-sided issue, but requires the commitment and engagement of all levels of society. Stakeholder activities designed to involve these elements are critical to a successful course of action or policy direction. As the Paris workshop pointed out, learning from good practice is a healthy thing. Enhanced coordination and communication among donor groups on their respective approaches to partnerships for knowledge production needs to be reassessed. As a recent UNDP book has argued, the new network age has permitted alternative tools for capacity development and there is an understanding that local knowledge, combined with knowledge acquired from other countries and institutions in both the South and North, can contribute to a successful paradigm for growth and social development. 'The notion that the only ideas for development that are worth trying are those that derive from the North looks less and less plausible'.[7]

The same holds true for knowledge production. As developing states engage in advancing their knowledge and research systems, a learning process is taking place. Such processes soon lead to a better appreciation of the requirements for a stronger knowledge base and programme initiatives. But one should be wary of which models are examined. It is important to try to look at other models that are similar, rather than those that are vastly different from your own in order to affect change. The next section therefore examines four states that have undertaken such a transformation: India, the Maldives, South Africa and Vietnam.

3. Four states in search of knowledge

There are huge differences between developed and developing countries in terms of their capacity to generate and utilize knowledge.[8] In fact, there are huge differences *within* countries and *among* regions, which is why one has to be careful when using comparative data to make sweeping generalizations. The following examples of four very different economies show that clear attempts are being made by developing counties to manage and engineer knowledge.

In *South Africa*, the government, in its 2002 statement on research and development, made a point of noting that investments in science, technology and innovation would be designed to improve the quality of life with a focus on poverty reduction and improving national competitiveness in the international environment. The three pillars of the strategy are (1) to develop human resources in science, engineering and technology, focusing in key fields such as astronomy,[9] human palaeontology and indigenous knowledge; (2) to foster innovation centred around various technology sectors; and (3) to create an effective government S&T system. Among the areas of technology to be developed are those related to S&T for poverty reduction (health, energy and indigenous knowledge), new technology platforms in IT and biotechnology (South Africa has already launched a programme to improve the public understanding of biotechnology), and technology for manufacturing and resource-based industries. In the next generation of its national R&D strategy, South Africa has recently committed itself to focus on its human resources and on knowledge production.

In *India*, the government has embarked on the implementation of its 2003 S&T policy, which aims to improve the quality of life of all Indians, particularly of the disadvantaged; to make India globally competitive while utilizing natural resources in a sustainable manner; and to protect the environment and national security. The Indian Department of Science and Technology hopes to ensure greater integration of R&D activities into socioeconomic sectors and to adapt indigenous resources and knowledge, particularly traditional systems of medicine. It is also working to enhance the country's basic research strengths in cooperation with the international science community, and to popularize science and disseminate information to society. With the efforts to move away from being a donor-assisted country, India hopes to become be an important contributor to the global knowledge pool.

In *Vietnam*, the gradual transformation from a socialist to a more open economy has required an assessment of how knowledge and research can contribute to this process. In 1997 the Vietnamese government asked IDRC to undertake a review of its S&T strategy. Vietnam places high priority on accessing technology from overseas and then applying and adapting it to the needs of the nation. While there was a focus towards a demand-driven S&T framework with the private sector playing a strong role, there is still a tendency among individuals and institutions towards supply-side S&T activities. Vietnam has decided to assess its international S&T cooperation as a key element of its knowledge strategy. This review, in 2004, examined issues such as human resources; mobilizing and using financial resources; promoting enterprises to improve their linkages via foreign direct investment and international trade; and the question of whether to make or buy technology.[10] More recently it has focused on how to promote core areas of strength in Vietnam, notably in the life sciences.

Finally, in contrast to these emerging players is a small island state, *the Maldives*. An archipelago of 200 islands, the Maldives economy has grown considerably over the past few years with heavy reliance on tourism and fisheries-based industries. While the December 2004 tsunami has clearly had an impact, concern for the long-term sustainability of these industries has pushed the government to consider how S&T can be deployed to address new opportunities. Its S&T Master Plan (drafted in 2001) emphasizes the need to use and adapt external technologies to national needs, rather than on specific areas of national innovation and research. The plan includes establishing a new institution, a National Research Foundation, to coordinate research funding in selected areas. The plan recognizes the importance of information and communications technologies (indeed, the responsible Ministry is called Communication, Science and Technology), since such technology is useless without information to be conveyed.

One could go on to map the knowledge strategies of the other 192 nations on this planet, but the point is this: good governance, strong economic development and well developed social and environmental practices are all dependent to some extent on a sound knowledge strategy. A strong, integrated approach to link the objectives of the various functions of governance is critical; otherwise, the right hand will not know what the left hand is doing, or worse, well-intentioned policies could cancel each other out.

Given this, it should come as no surprise that India's objectives are tied, for example, to national security and global competitiveness; that South Africa and the Maldives emphasize indigenous knowledge; and that Vietnam's approach seeks to link to the global trade system. It should also come as no surprise given the nature of knowledge transfer that these countries pay particular attention to learning from elsewhere. In South Africa, for example, the R&D strategy is premised with a look at the innovation strategies of Australia, Malaysia and South Korea. As an observer to the OECD's Committee for S&T Policy, and (along with India) a member of the Commonwealth Science Council, South Africa can take advantage of these strategic linkages. For the Maldives, its small size requires international linkages and connections, and for Vietnam, its membership of the Asia Pacific Economic Cooperation (APEC) forum provides it with an opportunity to examine the use of knowledge through the APEC Industrial S&T Working Group in addition to the ASEAN group. In short, membership of such groupings can have its privileges if it can be used strategically and linked to domestic policies. And South–South partnerships are also emerging around innovation and S&T approaches.

4. Towards a global knowledge contract: does science advice matter?

The use of knowledge to advance society will need to be embedded in decision-making structures that are both independent of states, but also linked to some form of accountability. Society will expect nothing else, and with good reason. Turning knowledge into policy and then into outcomes requires a fair measure of integrity and trust. Look at any public opinion polls that measure civil society's assessment of trust in professional groups, for example, and you will invariably find that politicians are at the bottom of the ladder and health professionals and scientists near the top.[11] Dig a little deeper and you will see that public sector scientists are ranked higher than private sector researchers. That is why where a government places its knowledge assets is just as important as with whom.

In Zambia, for example, soon after the government had spent some considerable political capital rejecting genetically modified foods, in 2003 it adopted a \$40 million National Biosafety and Biotechnology Strategy Plan to support human resource and infrastructure development. The Nigerian government, in a flashy, expensive insert in the *New York Times* on 14 July 2003, labelled its new approach – 'Towards a knowledge-based society' – as being dependent in large part on plans to make Nigeria a key player in IT by 2005. This approach is currently under review, with a science reform process sponsored by the Nigerian government and UNESCO. Argentina has announced the notion of a 'debt for knowledge' scheme, whereby 1% of the interest it pays to foreign creditors would be reinvested in the country's S&T institutional infrastructure, and has just launched a national nanotechnology strategy with US partners and funding. These examples imply a new, creative engagement with society and, of course, with global partners.

Public demand has dramatically altered the knowledge landscape. Specialized institutions and elites no longer have a monopoly on wisdom. The spread of knowledge (not just Western science) has led to the opening up of more global and national debates on issues surrounding risk, choice, culture, the environment and the quality of life. This demand, manifested through new groups, advocacy organizations and NGOs (all of whom have ironically mastered the new information technologies), is a driver of change – sometimes to positive effect, but not always for the better or to the good of society.[12] There are signs that research or knowledge producers are also changing their ways. No longer insular, protective or arrogant about the implications of the implementation of new knowledge, they have gradually come to adopt new strategies to work with the public at large, and eventually have become more adept at communicating and consulting on the results of research and the implications for the future human condition.

Advocacy groups such as the Action Group on Erosion, Technology and Concentration (ETC) and Greenpeace have both engaged in the debate on the introduction of nanotechnology, and have argued that lessons need to be learned from the public controversies that have surrounded biotechnology and its social and environmental impacts.[13] South Africa's Public Understanding of Biotechnology programme argues for the public to inform itself with the best knowledge available and then decide for itself ('Biotechnology and you: read about it, talk about it, think about it ... and decide for yourself').[14] Taking a page from this, the IDRC has mounted an exercise to assess the landscape for changing receptivity to genetically modified organisms (GMOs) and biotechnology issues in the South, and is looking carefully at how to engage a multi-stakeholder dialogue on this controversial subject. The World Bank has been the leader in urging a global assessment of agricultural science, knowledge and technology that can improve rural livelihoods and address poverty in low-income countries. Similarly, the UK government launched elaborate public engagement processes for the future development of both the research and the policy associated with biotechnology and nanotechnology.[15]

But it will take more than a change of strategy from knowledge producers to have an impact on policy outcomes. After all, as Yankelovich has argued, 'most public policy decisions must rely on ways of knowing – including judgement, insight, experience, history, scholarship, and analogies – that do not meet the gold standard of scientific verification'.[16] Decision makers will have to be more creative in integrating and learning from various sources of advice. Multiple networks of knowledge are growing in complexity (not just those associated with government), making it difficult to isolate the causes and effects of policy outcomes. Governance and risk management here take on a much more meaningful public policy function. One of the key forms that this advice takes place is through science advice. Increasingly, attention is being paid to this dimension of knowledge production within most states. The reason is that decision making increasingly has taken on a social and public value function, along with the usual examination of economic investment framework. Indeed, the debate in many societies has shifted from a narrow focus of competitiveness and prosperity to more complex, yet socially inclusive innovation and knowledge trends.[17]

As a result of the growing nexus between science, citizen and state, many countries and organizations are reshaping their formal (and informal) science advisory mechanisms, while keeping an eye on how others do it. This latter point is critical since much of what is being discussed as 'changes in knowledge' and its 'impact on society' is not limited to domestic sources, but has become globalized.[18] The SARS epidemics, mad cow disease, HIV/AIDS, disaster mitigation and food safety scares are but some examples of issues that require transboundary advisory structures and channels. But science advice must go hand in hand with other forms of governance – it needs to be embedded in the full machinery of government. As Tony Blair bluntly put it: 'Bad science didn't cause the spread of BSE; it was bad agriculture and poor government'.[19]

The attempt by the UN to re-examine its own structures of science advice is a good example of recent recognition of the importance of this issue. In the 2002 report of the National Academy of Sciences, *Knowledge and Diplomacy*, the authors argue for a series of changes. First they recommend that the governing bodies of the UN that have substantial responsibilities for implementing sustainable development programmes should each create an Office of the Science Adviser or equivalent facility.[20] They further advise that each such facility should adopt an appropriate set of general procedures based on best practice and procedures of science advice, that the UN should help member states to strengthen their own scientific advisory capabilities,[21] and that assemblies and other deliberative bodies should make greater use of scientific assessment mechanisms that have transparency and credibility. Some of this advice was further elaborated for the UN World Summit in September 2005.

One should be circumspect about science advice – it is after all, only advice. It can be acted on but may also be (and often is) ignored. It is only one part of the policy equation. If science advisers are not used (or studies requested), their relevance quickly becomes an issue. In Canada, for example, the Advisory Council on Science and Technology, which (on paper) advises the Prime Minister on issues of national importance affecting S&T, was largely ignored by the past two ministers responsible for its work. Today, it has undergone a transformation and has been given a new remit to better address urgent questions. In April 2004 the Canadian Prime Minister appointed a National Science Adviser to his office for the very first time. In a similar vein, in the UK, the Council for Science and Technology (CST) has just undergone a quinquennial review, to which the government responded by stating that it will ask the CST to organize its work on five broad themes: sustaining and developing science, engineering and technology (SET) in the UK and promoting international cooperation, SET and society, SET education, SET in government, and SET and innovation.

Given its very nature, science advice needs to address global as well as domestic issues. For this reason, science advice is increasingly seen as an integral part of foreign policy, international finance, trade, global ethics and sustainable development issues. A more global science advisory capacity is required. While there are clubs that meet periodically to discuss such questions in the European context and the G8,[22] quite often the developing world has little say in such structures, nor does it have a major presence. Groups like the InterAcademy Panel established by the National Academy of Sciences on international issues have established a creative structure – the InterAcademy Council (IAC) – to provide these links. The IAC brings together the advisory expertise and experience of a worldwide group of national academies, including those in Brazil, China, Mexico, South Africa, and the Third World Academy of Sciences. In 2004 the IAC issued a major report, *Inventing a Better Future,* on ways to promote worldwide science and technology capacities for the 21st century. In 2005 the UN Commission on Science and Technology for Development published a report on the application of S&T to meet the Millennium Development Goals, which includes suggestions for enhanced science advisory bodies.[23] Leading up the G8 Summit in July 2005, the science academies of the G8 and some developing economies produced two public statements on science and technology for African development and on climate change.

Thus, science advice has undergone a much-needed renaissance, one that will look to using the knowledge assets and expertise of many states to resolve issues affecting sustainable development.

5. A failure to communicate

Knowledge networks of the future, especially those affecting the South, will be challenged by at least three key facts – that knowledge does not substitute for ethics, that new technologies require social and institutional innovation, and that geopolitical developments may hamper rather than strengthen international knowledge networks.

The first issue was succinctly raised by Prime Minister Tony Blair in 2002, when he stated that 'Science is just knowledge. And knowledge can be used by evil people for evil ends. Science doesn't replace moral judgement. It just extends the context of knowledge within which moral judgements are made. It allows us to do more, but it doesn't tell us whether doing more is right or wrong'.[24] For the advisory apparatus to be effective and politically attuned, it will need to pay attention to issues at the margins of (but not marginal to) knowledge development. A key concern surrounds ethical and legal issues affecting the introduction of new and emerging technologies in both developed and developing states alike. Most organizations, from the UN system through to Greenpeace, are taking up this challenge. Before September 11, 2001, the biggest debate facing the Bush Administration was in fact the ethical issues surrounding the use of embryonic stem cells for reproductive purposes. Other countries have followed suit and are now debating human cloning, xeno-transplantation and other medical issues associated with the revolutionary developments in the health sciences. A similar debate will emerge on nanotechnologies as countries like China, India, Korea, the Philippines, South Africa and Argentina adopt strategies for these new technologies. These issues are ripe not just for ethicists, religious leaders, philosophers and lawyers, but for concerned citizens as well. The mere mention of the need for biotechnology and GM crops is enough today to generate a raft of spins on the good, the bad and the ugly of this issue.

The media (including various Internet applications) will need to be engaged in such future debates. They play a strong role in shaping debates, and can influence public policy in significant ways. The adage that politicians are scientifically illiterate and scientists are politically clueless is not far off the mark. Add to this the often made observation that scientific communities tend to be insular or even arrogant, and combine this with the notion that governments are prone to spinning information to suit their needs, and you have a deadly fuel that can ignite quickly. Linking science journalists, communicators and practitioners of research and knowledge is a key element of a successful knowledge strategy. In the UK and Canada, efforts have been made to strengthen the communication of science to the general public, and guidelines have been produced to assist this process. In Canada, for example, these guidelines are intended to help shape communications as an integral part of the government's S&T policy. A recent report argues that federal science departments should embrace the concept of participatory communication, whereby audiences engage in dialogue, deliberation and decision making; adopt communications by integrating this element in the early planning phases of S&T programming; develop comprehensive communications strategies to complement and support the conduct of S&T; and invest in S&T communications planning, training and delivery.[25] Governments everywhere are realizing that in order for the public to both understand, become active in, and be informed of decisions that will affect public policy, they need to be part of the process, not separate, or worse, separated from it.[26]

If the research and knowledge communities are to build more powerful alliances with states and other sectors they will need to consider building on the changing dynamics of the science–society interface and develop newer tools that are more representative of the issues involving global civil society itself. Educating people is not the answer, as this implies a one-way flow of knowledge from the expert to the layperson. Rather, the issue is about involving the key stakeholders in all societies in the decision-making process, not just meting out information (which almost always has some spin on it).[27]

The second issue that will challenge knowledge networks, especially those in the South, relates to the fact that new technologies also require social and institutional innovation. Anticipating change will be one of the most important dimensions of this challenge. New technologies will never achieve their full potential unless they are accompanied by social and political innovation that alters the framework within which economic choices are made.[28]

So how can societies anticipate change and scan the horizon, and how do they put into place new mechanisms to do this? This will be a major challenge for societies bent on using reliable knowledge to make choices. Here, the issue is how to engage in a dialogue that will potentially alter visions of the future. Private sector firms engage in this type of exercise, Shell International being probably the most well known. But increasingly, governments are now experimenting with different forms of foresight exercises. UNIDO has recently produced a summary of these national exercises to highlight some of the common themes that are emerging with respect to economic and social change.[29]

Of course, this all sounds well and good, but as the adage goes, if you can't forecast well, forecast often. The UK, Germany and Japan have years of experience in this type of methodology, producing biennial versions, but gradually the list has expanded.[30] Foresight activities also require sound data collection and analysis. The data issue is problematic in many respects as several countries do not have the institutional capacity to collect the necessary data and analyze it in a way that can be helpful for decision makers. The UNESCO Institute for Statistics has launched a strategy that will elaborate requirements for S&T data and indicators in developing countries.[31] Creating demand for such information and linking data needs will be a challenge in this area. But this is one of a complex series of questions that needs to be addressed if communication of knowledge processes is to be adequately addressed. There are some bigger issues on the horizon though.

Are there brakes to local innovation and global knowledge production? As the public debate becomes more heated and engaged in the coming years over the development of knowledge, there will be more calls for ensuring a sound social function to this knowledge. To borrow from Auguste Comte's dictum: 'savoir pour prévoir, prévoir pour agir' ('knowing to foresee, foreseeing to act'). Those societies that have invested heavily in knowledge over the past 40 years are beginning to understand the hidden costs of such investments. True, knowledge has provided many gifts, but there are limits: limits in terms of costs, limits regarding choices and priorities, limits with respect to technical tolerance and risk, limits to ethical standards, etc. Above all, there are society's transactions costs. The bar has been raised. More will be expected of investments in this knowledge – more accounting, more transparency, more translation of the benefits and costs – some of which will fall on the shoulders of the research communities, some on the public, and some on the state.

The third issue that will challenge knowledge networks in the South relates to geopolitical developments. Ironically, at the very time the West has called for greater investment in knowledge (10 countries are responsible for over 80% of the world's total expenditures on S&T) in the developing world, and at the very moment that technologies have increasingly become more 'open-sourced' and freely available, geopolitical and security issues threaten to stall the potential for a new knowledge renaissance. Trade issues are blocking the ability of the South to develop intellectual property regimes that are relevant to their respective economies, including concerns over bioprospecting, and access to generic drugs for health care. Subsidy regimes for agriculture in the West are hampering the development of export markets for the South, not to mention their research infrastructure for agriculture. The development of global research organizations to address social and economic gaps has been short-circuited as funds are slow in coming. National policies designed to address a strengthened innovation and research effort are poorly integrated into national policies designed to assist developing countries; quite often, these policies conflict. Also, the knowledge community will be challenged to address its responsibilities as the landscape shifts with many more players than before. The media will play an increasing role in this; the public will become a more diverse stakeholder in these debates.

The geopolitics of security and the moral compunction of aid will have counteracting effects on the potential for a truly open knowledge system. The debates over whether the research community should refrain from publishing certain reports because of concerns about national security or the international spread of 'dangerous' technologies, will grow. The restrictions on movements of skilled personnel in certain fields, and from certain states, will clearly impact on creativity and entrepreneurship. Paradoxically, the knowledge community will be drawn into the security and defence fields as the demands in these areas grow, and the higher education community will feel the impact of this on enrolments and faculties. Already, visa restrictions are limiting movements of researchers, and foreign students are being watched. Certain key technologies in IT, biotechnology and nanotechnology will be contained because of security concerns. At the very time that the university community is becoming internationalized – with more and more players having a role in knowledge production – there is public pressure for them to be more responsive to a risk environment. New structures for knowledge production will emerge that respond to such limits.[32]

6. Linking up and linking out

Constructing knowledge networks around such impediments will be tricky. But a key will be continuous learning and investment in training and education. Paying attention to grey matter will be a major issue for developing societies. It is not for nothing that the number one Millennium Development Goal is universal primary education, or that the World Bank has focused on tertiary education systems, or that the G8 research councils have examined science education as a key element of development. All societies have their own rich pools of talent – entrepreneurs, skilled crafts persons and knowledge producers. Providing the right incentives and institutional capacity to attract such development is what often distinguishes the richer societies from the poorer ones. A healthy mix of investing in national educational policies for growth, and establishing strong linkages with the diaspora abroad will be critical investments to consider.[33] The development of national or regional centres of excellence will help keep talent at home, along of course with strong professional recognition of the knowledge producers and adequate support through wages and infrastructure.[34] Investing in teachers and rewarding them is also essential. Some countries have tried to develop teachers' awards to provide incentives in this direction. Encouraging diplomatic corps to use their networks for increased linkages to the diaspora and to new opportunities for investment in ideas and innovation from their respective host countries is another strategy in the knowledge toolkit. Countries like Argentina, China, Colombia, Eritrea and South Africa have all introduced strong incentives and mechanisms to tap into their talent pool living abroad.

In the end, specific attention must be devoted to a suite of measures that will maintain a healthy national knowledge system linked to the global environment. The rhetoric of investing in knowledge has to be followed up with the reality of long-term (not on and off) support for skills and people. Institutions and integrated policies that complement, rather than contradict each other need to be viewed as assets, along with attention to the specific cultural, economic and social fabric of the society one is trying to improve. Capacity to learn has to be built in – not just to blindly copy other models, but to study and analyze carefully the good practices that can be gleaned from such exercises (including examining the right countries for comparison). Also, an advisory and communications capability is needed that is able to interact appropriately with various stakeholders in society to ensure adequate and effective decision making about future knowledge strategies. Finally, the careful monitoring and analysis of global developments will be a *sine qua non* for positioning the society and economy in a well-rounded approach to development.

In this last context, more attention needs to be paid to the strategic use of and learning from regional and global clubs. All countries belong to clubs of one form or another (some belong to too many, making it difficult to provide adequate funding or inputs).[35] The use of such forums, whether the UN system, APEC, the Commonwealth, the African Union, the Organization of American States (OAS), la Francophonie, or NATO, etc., offers countries rare opportunities to leverage funding and talent. It is rare that states pay much attention to evaluating the benefits or impacts of their membership in these clubs. In fact, most states often join clubs because they see a political advantage to such adherence, not necessarily because the membership offers substantial intellectual rewards. Canada, for example, as a member of the G8, takes it as a given that it will have to continue to belong to many clubs simply because of the cachet such membership brings. Nevertheless, because of their limited resources, developing countries in particular should be paying more attention to how they can benefit from selected knowledge forums. The recent case of the government of Tanzania requesting its ambassadors in 14 countries to monitor and report on the GMO debate perhaps offers an example of how developing countries could deploy their trade and foreign policy assets to monitor S&T issues.

An assessment of existing and potentially new memberships should be developed in such instances. In addition, regular, careful examinations of bilateral and multilateral S&T and related agreements should be introduced into decision-making systems in order to ensure that national and international objectives can be met.

7. Renaissance of development research

There is another side to this equation. International organizations must themselves become more attuned to their clientele. It is axiomatic that international organizations are experimental and learning institutions. Nevertheless, they must be attuned to changes in the landscape. The Canadian action group ETC has radically transformed itself over the past few years to focus its efforts on emerging technologies that may have significant impacts on society. As part of its new long-range plan, the Swedish International Foundation for Science has substantially increased its work in support of young scholars from low- and lower middle-income countries. USAID is exploring a new approach to supporting science and technology in specific regions of the world.[36] of the world.[37] The Global Research Alliance of technology organizations has been established to create a network designed to build on opportunities for technology exchange and joint ventures – in short, to fill a perceived gap. NEPAD has established a new African Forum on Science and Technology for Development. The UNDP Human Development Report 2003 argued for a series of international forums to help establish research priorities required to meet the technological needs of the developing world. The list goes on.

What is behind this renaissance of institutional experimentation in development research for knowledge and capacity building? The World Bank, the Rockefeller Foundation and IDRC are positing that there is a renewed attention within the donor community to the important role played by knowledge, and research for development. Why has there been a sudden resurgence of the role of knowledge for development? Donor agencies are retooling as they address the new challenges of knowledge production in the South. But what is being done to integrate knowledge into the mainstream of public policy decision making and governance issues? The ability of governments to join up policy streams from various areas will become critical over the next decades as the advance of knowledge outpaces the ability to respond and be proactive. To some extent this is already happening in the development and aid policies of some countries. For instance, the International Assessment of Agricultural Science and Technology for Development, led by the World Bank, is intended to bring together a range of stakeholders involved in the agricultural sector to share their views and reach a common understanding and vision for the future. This effort to develop partnerships and provide robust information to policy makers represents a new generation of such research for action models. On another front, Canada is experimenting with a new approach to development assistance, one that will devote no less than 5% of its total domestic R&D to a knowledge-based approach to help address the most pressing problems of developing countries. It may also be time to consider some form of 'grand challenge' among like-minded donor agencies that can provide larger-scale institutional and governance capacities in the South devoted to the intersection of research and public policy.

Knowledge will continue to expand. Institutions designed to advance this knowledge will also increase. Donor agencies have a significant role to play in coordinating their efforts across the spectrum of knowledge issues that have emerged. The developing countries have an opportunity to position themselves well in this new arena if they pay attention to the lessons of the past, and help shape and dictate the direction of this new frontier of knowledge.

Notes

1. Paul Dufour (pdufour@idrc.ca) is senior programme specialist at IDRC seconded to the Office of the National Science Advisor in the Government of Canada, Ottawa. This chapter is based on a presentation to the DPAD/UNDESA Ad Hoc Group of Experts Meeting on Knowledge Systems for Development, United Nations, New York, November 2003.
2. Dedijer (1963: 61).
3. Mokyr (2002).
4. See Mullin (2003).
5. Other institutions that have also used this tool include the World Bank and its S&T assessments in China and Korea (see Dickson, 2003); USAID with its report on S&T and capacity development in cases such as India; Sida with its programming on universities and research in developing economies; UNCTAD with assessments of Colombia, Ethiopia and Jamaica; and the OECD with reviews of China, Korea and Mexico.
6. See Ca (2003).
7. Fukuda-Parr *et al.* (2002).
8. Sagasti (2005).
9. South Africa is well positioned to become a leading global player in astronomy due to its geographical location; see Mokhele (2003).
10. Few countries have actually tried to link their domestic S&T agenda with international knowledge and trade policies in a systematic way. Some recent examples include the Swiss attempts to establish a scientific foreign policy (using foreign policy to link with science issues), and Finland (see Science and Technology Policy Council of Finland, 2003). For further information, see the special issue of Science and Public Policy, 29(6), December 2002.
11. See the National Science Board (2004).
12. Ausubel (1999), for example, argues that the greatest threat to future well-being is the rejection of science.
13. ETC (2003).

14. Visit www.pub.ac.za/. There are signs that these knowledge producers are taking heed of the hard lessons learned from the GMO debacle in the emerging technology arena, nanotechnology (see Willis and Wilsdon, 2003).
15. See www.ost.gov.uk
16. Yankelovich (2003).
17. See Bozeman and Sarewitz (2002).
18. See Fukuyama and Wagner (2002).
19. Tony Blair, 'Science matters', speech to the Royal Society, London, 10 April 2002.
20. Similarly, the UK government through its Office of Science and Technology, has suggested that each ministry or science-based department should have their own chief scientific advisers (UK Department of Trade and Industry, 2003), who would meet on a regular basis.
21. On a related note, the National Academies have been working with both the African Academy of Sciences and the Arab states to introduce effective science academies that could serve as advisers on significant science-based issues of public policy for those regions. In February 2004 the NAS announced an initiative, with funding of US$20 million from the Gates Foundation, to stimulate the emergence of effective national science academies in selected African countries. http://www4.nationalacademies.org/news.nsf/isbn/02092005?OpenDocument.
22. The Carnegie Group of Science Ministers for the G8 meets twice a year to discuss (off the record) issues of mutual concern amongst the G8 membership (see Bromley, 1996).
23. A good deal of this has been stimulated by the work of the Task Force on Science, Technology and Innovation; see UN Millennium Project (2005).
24. Tony Blair, 'Science matters', ibid.
25. CSTA (2003).
26. At the global level, similar challenges are being addressed. For instance, the SciDev website www.scidev.net provides reliable information on issues related to science and science-based technology that impact on social and economic development. The service, funded in part by donor agencies and supported by the journals Science and Nature, is a valuable tool in assisting decision makers from the developing world and other professionals interested in the interaction between science and development. The site offers news and dossiers on issues such as the brain drain, GM crops, biodiversity, climate change, ethics of research, and most recently on R&D. Its geographic spread is increasing, with regional networks in sub-Saharan Africa, Latin America, Asia and China. As of May 2004, 54% of the site's 10,000 registrants were from developing countries, the top five being India, Brazil, China, Argentina, South Africa and Mexico.
27. For an interesting comparison of how the private sector and NGOs communicate complex S&T issues, see Einsiedel (2003).
28. Willis and Wilsdon (2003).
29. Among these common themes are: technological development will be the key agent of change; life cycles of products will be shorter; demands on education will increase; in developing countries, ICTs and biotechnology will dramatically influence the possibilities of growth; globalization will become even more accentuated with free flows of information, investment capital, ideas, products and services between countries; the proportion of women in the workforce will increase and a series of new systems and models for childcare and housing services will emerge (see UNIDO, 2003).

30. The International Council for Science (ICSU), for example, recently published a review of these reports and suggested areas that have an international or global scope for further assessment (Teixeira *et al.*, 2002).
31. UNESCO Institute for Statistics (2003).
32. The US Department of Homeland Security has an entire budget and sub-structure devoted to technology that subsumes the research activities of several existing agencies. As a consequence, it has become the biggest single recipient of funding for research in the US government. In Canada, a new programme for research and technology production in defence-related areas is now the biggest single recipient of new funding for a government laboratory.
33. See Gaillard (2003).
34. Of course, such investments are not limited to the South. In Canada, one of the principal reasons for the creation of 2000 well-paid chairs in research centres and universities was the need to address the brain drain of talent to the US.
35. It stands to reason that as more countries are created, more clubs will emerge, and that as knowledge becomes more specialized, the number of forums to discuss specific issues will also increase.
36. USAID has been the subject of a review by the NAS to examine its science and technology to support health care, sustainability and other aspects of development assistance. DfID has also been the subject of testimony before the UK House of Commons Science and Technology Committee.
37. USAID has been the subject of a review by the NAS to examine its science and technology to support health care, sustainability and other aspects of development assistance. DfID has also been the subject of testimony before the UK House of Commons Science and Technology Committee.

References

Ausubel, J. (1999) Reasons to worry about the human environment, *Technology in Society*, 21: 217-231.

Bozeman, B. and Sarewitz, D. (2002) *Public Failures in U.S. Science Policy*, Washington, DC: Centre for Science Policy and Outcomes.

Bromley, D.A. (1996) *Science Advisers to Presidents and Prime Ministers: A Brief History of the Carnegie Group's First Three Years, 1990-1992. New York: Carnegie Commission on Science, Technology* and Government.

Ca, T.N. (2003) *Donor Funded Reviews on Science, Technology and Innovation in Vietnam: The impact, the change and some thoughts for the future*, prepared for the IDRC/UNESCO workshop, Paris, April 2003.

CSTA (2003) *Science Communications and Opportunities for Public Engagement (SCOPE)*. Report to the Government of Canada. Ottawa: Council of Science and Technology Advisers.

Dedijer, S. (1963) Underdeveloped science in underdeveloped countries. *Minerva*, 2: 61-81.

Dickson, D. (2003) *Does the World Bank Really Care about Science?*, SciDev.Net, 4 July.

Einsiedel, E. (2003) *A Snapshot of Private Sector and Non-Government Organizations' Science and Technology Communications Tactics and Related Best Practices*. Ottawa: Council of Science and Technology Advisers.

ETC (2003) *The Big Down: Atomtech: Technologies Converging at the Nano-scale*. Ottawa: Action Group on Erosion, Technology and Concentration.

Fukuda-Parr, S. *et al.* (Eds) (2002) Overview: Institutional innovations for capacity development, in *Capacity for Development: New Solutions to Old Problems*, New York: Earthscan.

Fukuyama, F. and Wagner, C. (2002) Governance challenges of technological revolutions, in J. de la Mothe (Ed.), *Science, Technology and Governance*. London: Continuum, pp.188-209.

Gaillard, J. (2003) Overcoming the scientific generation gap in Africa: An urgent priority, *Interdisciplinary Science Reviews*, 28(1): 15-25.

InterAcademy Council (2004) *Inventing a Better Future: A Strategy for Building Worldwide Capacities in Science and Technology*. Amsterdam: IAC.

National Academy of Sciences (2002) *Knowledge and Diplomacy: Science Advice in the United Nations System*. Washington, DC: National Academies Press.

National Science Board (2004) Science and technology: Public attitudes and understanding, *Science and Engineering Indicators*. New York: Sage, ch.4.

Mokhele, K. (2003) *South African Large Telescope, Model for International Scientific Collaboration between Developed and Developing Countries*, paper presented at MEXT/OECD Global Science Forum Workshop on Best Practices in International Scientific Cooperation, Tokyo, February 2003.

Mokyr, J. (2002) *The Gifts of Athena: Historical Origins of the Knowledge Economy*. Princeton: Princeton University Press.

Mullin, J. (2003) *Reflections on the Review Process of National S&T and Innovation Policies*, paper prepared for IDRC-UNESCO workshop on Future Directions for National S&T and Innovation Policies in Developing Countries, Paris, March 2003.

Sagasti, F. (2005) *Knowledge and Innovation for Development: The Sisyphus Challenge of the 21st Century*. Aldershot, UK: Edward Elgar.

Science and Technology Policy Council of Finland (2003) *Knowledge, Innovation and Internationalisation*. Helsinki.

Teixeira, A., Martin, B. and von Tunzelmann, N. (2002) *Identification of Key Emerging Issues in Science and Society: an International Perspective on National Foresight Studies*. Paris: International Council for Science (ISCU).

UK Department of Trade and Industry (2003) *The Forward Look 2003*. London: HMSO.

UN Millennium Project (2005) *Innovation: Applying Knowledge in Development*. Final report of the Task Force on Science, Technology and Innovation. New York: Earthscan.

UNDP (2003) *Human Development Report, Millennium Development Goals: A compact among nations to end human poverty*. New York: Oxford University Press.

UNESCO Institute for Statistics (2003) *International Review of Science and Technology Statistics and Indicators*. Montreal: UIS.

UNIDO (2003) *Technology Foresight Initiative for Latin America: An Overview of the Programme*.

Willis, R. and Wilsdon, J. (2003) *Technology, Risk and Environment*, Working Paper No.7, for the Progressive Governance Summit, London, July 2003.

Yankelovich, D. (2003) Winning greater influence from science, *Issues in Science and Technology*, summer 2003.

WORKSHOP PARTICIPANTS

Cynthia Bautista
University of the Philippines
Quezon City, 1101 Diliman, The Philippines
dekano@kssp.upd.edu.ph

Louk de la Rive Box
Institute of Social Studies (ISS)
PO Box 29776, 2502 LT The Hague, the Netherlands
box@iss.nl

Wiebe Bijker
Faculty of Arts & Culture, University of Maastricht
Postbus 616, 6200 MD Maastricht, the Netherlands
w.bijker@tss.unimaas.nl

Moussa Cisse†
Environnement et Développement du Tiers Monde (Enda-TM)
PB 3370, Dakar, Senegal

Julius Court
Overseas Development Institute (ODI)
111 Westminster Bridge Rd, London SE1 7JD, UK
j.court@odi.uk

Paul Dufour
International Development Research Center (IDRC)
Albert St, Ottawa, Ontario 250 3H9, Canada
pdufour@idrc.ca

Sara Farley
Rockefeller Foundation
420 Fifth Avenue, New York, NY10018, USA
Sfarley@rockfound.org

Judith Ann Francis
Technical Centre for Agricultural and Rural Cooperation (CTA)
Postbus 380, 6700 AJ Wageningen, the Netherlands
francis@cta.int

Jacques Gaillard
International Atomic Energy Agency (IAEA)
PO Box 100, A-1400 Vienna, Austria
j.gaillard@iaea.org

Marie de Lattre-Gasquet
Centre de coopération internationale en recherche agronomique pour le développement (Cirad)
rue Scheffer 42, 75116 Paris, France
marie.de_lattre-gasquet@cirad.fr

Gerti Hesseling
Africa Studies Centre, Leiden University
Postbus 9555, 2300 RB Leiden, the Netherlands
Hesseling@fsw.leidenuniv.nl

Sunil Mani
Centre for Development Studies (CDS)
Prasantha Nagar Road, Ulloor
Trivandrum-695011, Kerala, India
mani@cds.ac.in

Henk Molenaar
Netherlands Ministry of Foreign Affairs DCO/CO
Postbus 20061, 2500 EB Den Haag, the Netherlands
henk.molenaar@minbuza.nl

Johann Mouton
Centre for Research on Science and Technology (CREST)
University of Stellenbosch

Private Bag X1, 7602 Matieland, South Africa
jm6@sun.ac.za

John Mugabe
NEPAD
PO Box 395, Pretoria, South Africa
john@nepadst.org

Osita Ogbu
African Technology Policy Studies Network (ATPS)
PO Box 10081-00100, Nairobi, Kenya
oogbu@atpsnet.org

Theo van de Sande
Netherlands Ministry of Foreign Affairs DCO/CO
Postbus 20061, 2500 EB Den Haag, the Netherlands
theo.sande@minbuza.nl

Arunarachalam Subbiah
M.S. Swaminathan Research Foundation
Third Cross Street, Taramani Industrial Area
600113 Chennai, Tamil Nadu, India
arun@mssrf.res.in

Bert Uijtewaal
Bayer CropScience
Postbus 4005, 6080 AA Haelen, the Netherlands
bert.uijtewaal@bayercropscience.com

Léa Velho
Department of Science and Technology Policy
University of Campinas, Brazil
velho@ige.unicamp.br

Caroline S. Wagner
Center for International Science and Technology Policy
George Washington University
1957 E Street NW, Washington, DC 20052, USA
cswagner@gwu.edu

Workshop support team

Rutger Engelhard
Contactivity bv
Stationsweg 28, 2312 NL Leiden, the Netherlands
rutger@contactivity.com

Willie Pronk
Contactivity bv
Stationsweg 28, 2312 NL Leiden, the Netherlands

Valerie Jones
Contactivity bv
Stationsweg 28, 2312 NL Leiden, the Netherlands

Hanne Johnsrud
Faculty of Arts & Culture, University of Maastricht
Postbus 616, 6200 MD Maastricht, the Netherlands

Irene Olaussen
Faculty of Arts & Culture, University of Maastricht
Postbus 616, 6200 MD Maastricht, the Netherlands